THE MARKING ENTERPRISE

THE MARKING ENTERPRISE

Business success and societal embedding

Jean-Claude Thoenig
Charles Waldman

INSEAD

Business Press

First published 2007 by
PALGRAVE MACMILLAN
Houndmills, Basingstoke, Hampshire RG21 6XS and
175 Fifth Avenue, New York, N.Y. 10010
Companies and representatives throughout the world

PALGRAVE MACMILLAN is the global academic imprint of the Palgrave Macmillan division of St. Martin's Press, LLC and of Palgrave Macmillan Ltd. Macmillan® is a registered trademark in the United States, United Kingdom and other countries. Palgrave is a registered trademark in the European Union and other countries.

ISBN-13: 978– 0–230–00187–9
ISBN-10: 0–230–00187–4

This book is printed on paper suitable for recycling and made from fully managed and sustained forest sources.

A catalogue record for this book is available from the British Library.

A catalog record for this book is available from the Library of Congress.

10 9 8 7 6 5 4 3 2 1
16 15 14 13 12 11 10 09 08 07

Printed and bound in Great Britain by
Creative Print & Design (Wales), Ebbw Vale

CONTENTS

CONTENTS

LIST OF FIGURES AND TABLES

Figures

Tables

ACKNOWLEDGEMENTS

This book honors the practitioners who, often without even realizing it, reinvent the art and skills of management.

Observing business practices is the great laboratory in which new knowledge is generated. One of the responsibilities entrusted to management science is to make more than just common sense interpretations of the advances and innovations observed in the field. This book is the fruit of long, painstaking research conducted by the two authors over four years.

Nine medium- to large-scale European companies, most of them with an international presence, were studied first-hand through in-depth interviews of their executives and observation of their actual operations. Their attitude toward this detailed and often intimate investigation exemplified transparency and cooperation.

Additionally, documentation was collected from six European and North American companies, from case studies and from the trade press. This information was supplemented by firsthand observations made during consulting assignments and from executive education programs in certain companies, as noted in the text.

Catherine Paradeise and Brigitte Waldman accepted with grace and intelligence their husbands' spending three years appeasing their passion to write. Pascale Gadroy and Caroline Jamart provided secretarial assistance. Samantha Wauchope's diligence and attentiveness in translating and editing the text were highly appreciated. Philippe Affif was an outstanding intellectual and editorial sparring partner. Stephen Rutt encouraged the publication of this text with discreet tenacity and a sense of professionalism. Professors Catherine Paradeise (University of Marne la Vallée), Yves Doz (INSEAD), Raymond-Alain Thiétart (Université Paris Dauphine), and David Wilson (Warwick University) gave welcomed advice at various stages of the project.

This book is a substantially revised adaptation of a work that originally appeared in French under the title *De l'entreprise marchande à l'entreprise marquante* (Paris: Éditions d'Organisation, 2005).

JEAN-CLAUDE THOENIG AND CHARLES WALDMAN

A MARKING SELF-EVALUATION GRID: IS MY COMPANY A GOOD MARKER?

Even before starting to read the book, it could be useful to know where you and your company stand. Are you more on the marker side, or are you in fact non-markers, perhaps without even being aware of it?

The following grid will allow you to benchmark your company's current business postures according to two major issues:

- How far has your company engaged in effective marking? (Items 1–3)
- If the company has engaged in marking, what kind of marker is it? (Items 4–16)

Once the grid has been addressed, you may check your profile (see below).

And then, and only then, start reading the book and, hopefully, learn something out of it!

1. How far has your company engaged in effective marking?

	A	B
Item 1	Our mission is to sell and deliver goods and services to customers.	Our mission vis-à-vis the market is to respect a promise organized around well-spelled out values.
Item 2	The market is a temporary expression of society at large, and we can contribute to shaping it through our propositions.	The market is an established world that guides our action plans.
Item 3	We think of and handle customers as buyers.	We consider our customers as active participants in the value-building process.

2. What kind of "marker" is your company ?

	A	B
Item 4	Our strategic ambition is largely inspired by our knowledge of market needs and by our willingness to exploit competitors' deficiencies in serving those needs.	Our strategic ambition is geared at filling societal gaps. We are not into satisfying needs but into building new cognitions.
Item 5	Marketing and marketers play the leading role in our understanding of the market.	Everybody in our company, whatever his/her function and hierarchical status, is involved daily in the construction of a new cognitive world.
Item 6	Top management defines our strategy and makes sure that it is properly implemented from a technical standpoint.	Top management's roles are to continuously reinforce and re-inspire shared values and to make sure that actions are constantly aligned with them and our promises.
Item 7	We view our relationships with our customers as a string of successful selling–buying encounters.	Our customers' satisfaction is built up over time, through their accumulated experience as users.
Item 8	The producer–distributor dyad is the vital mechanism for channeling products to customers.	Multiple stakeholders are involved in delivering the promised values to the users.
Item 9	Our performance benchmarking is mostly focused on direct competition. Our competitive advantages are often built around incremental progress on current practices.	We do not have direct competition of any significance. We do not construct our territory as a slice of the pre-established battlefield.
Item 10	We view as a competitive advantage the ability to stretch the "symbolic territory" around our product offerings. Communication is therefore largely into image building.	Our offerings strongly emphasize the tangible benefits for users. Communication is largely informational and educational.
Item 11	Services are considered as key differentiators, in addition to our products. Sometimes we only create services when we think that competition on our products is becoming too tough.	Services are, from the start, integrated in the value proposition. This results from viewing our relationships with customers as mutually reinforcing social interactions and not mere commercial acts.

continued on next page

	A	B
Item 12	We are very concerned about getting the selling price right. When sales are sluggish, we have a tendency to blame it on "excessive" price.	We are educating our customers to judge us on "cost-in-use" rather than sale price. When sales are sluggish, we know that we have to rework or redefine the value proposition.
Item 13	We only start to collaborate with our suppliers (or distributors) when confronting them becomes detrimental to our business efficacy.	We share with our suppliers (or distributors) the same vision and passion to build an enhanced future for our end customers and users.
Item 14	Our major sources of information to inspire our strategic and action plans are market research and competitive benchmarking.	We are more sensitive to qualitative and weak market signals than to quantifiable data. Our sources of information go far beyond traditional business boundaries.
Item 15	Our organizational functioning is structured around planning, processes, job descriptions, and clearly delineated areas of expertise.	Our team functioning is guided by a shared ambition/project and shared values. Polyvalence and empowerment are key ingredients. Specialization and bureaucracy are enemies we fight.
Item 16	Faith in our strategic choices creates a lot of confidence across our company.	Our progress catalyst is permanent dissatisfaction with the status quo. We continuously want to refine our propositions to users, regardless of our current success.

3. Analyze your answers and your profile

■ *How far has your company engaged in effective marking?* (Items 1 to 3)

    * *Not at all*   **A** on item 1

                          B on item 2

                          A on item 3

    * *Quite far*   **B** on item 1

                          A on item 2

                          B on item 3

■ *What kind of "marker" is your company?* (Items 4 to 16)

    * A reactive marker   **A** on all items

    * A proactive marker   **B** on all items

INTRODUCTION: BACK TO BASICS

Consider a fruit and vegetable seller in a street market. His products are always fresh, tasty, and inviting. Moreover, he knows his customers personally and always treats them with courtesy. He sometimes engages them in small conversations. In return, his customers demonstrate true loyalty to him, even if his prices are occasionally higher than neighboring stands. This retailer has no banner, no logo, no brand, no packaging that would differentiate him. Nevertheless, he is practicing a very powerful form of local marking. In addition to buying his fruit and vegetables, his customers chat among themselves, sharing the pleasure of spontaneous conversation. Ultimately, they appreciate the social experience. The fruit and vegetable stand is the pivot of a network of one-to-one relationships going far beyond the bilateral transaction of buying and selling fruit and vegetables.

This example suggests that, despite the fact that the seller does not explicitly use a brand, he is shaping a certain form of societal embedding that goes beyond mere mercantile exchange relationships. In a way he acts as a marker and builds a territory for himself.

The purpose of this book is to inventory specific forms that marking and territory take. For each one, it lists the most appropriate kinds of know-how or knack called for.

MARKING, TERRITORY, EMBEDDING

The use by a management book of terms such as marking, territory building and societal embedding is a deliberate choice.

Practitioners, more than academics, may feel that once again authors play the usual game of differentiation: complicated words to describe self-evident business and management accomplishments. Why not use familiar words such as marketing, branding, market or even customer need?

The problem lies in the fact that the latter are often imprecise, and that in practice they do not mean much these days. Anything is called marketing, from intuition to applied mathematics. Brands are sometimes considered as the magic formula whose capacity to generate financial performance is never in question. The terms client, stakeholder and market become catchwords that bias the identification of relevant empirical facts for business more than they simplify strategic as well as daily management.

What do Starbucks, the Toyota Prius and the iPod share in common? Outstanding marking management, lasting societal embedding, specific territories crowded with loyal stakeholders. Why do companies like Walt Disney, Sony and Viacom look quite similar? They have marked a new societal status for entertainment. Walter E. Disney in the 1930's, and Akio Morita and Sumner Redstone in the 1990's had elaborated a business model that was radically different from the way radio and cinema majors were operating – advertisers rather than viewers being major payers (Epstein 2005). Their companies have also acted as societal change engineers. Our ways of living today are no longer identical to how we entertained and communicated in the 1970's. They had the intuition that some revolutionary trend might be emerging – access of kids to mass consumption, family homes as physical sites integrating in a massive way electronic communication and sound and image entertainment, and so on. Their bet and their success were to define business conditions so that such trends would become economically viable and socially acceptable. They pushed them further and extended them to most parts of society.

A number of the marking ventures studied in this book – from Royal Canin and Wal-Mart to Club Med and Benetton – are headed or were founded by individuals who, in one way or another, were and still are dissatisfied with the status quo in society and the economy. Some had been in their youth political and social activists. Most were not born into elitist social milieus. Marking companies and their managers openly flaunt their *drive for societal reform*. As one CEO puts it: "You and I do not go along with many things in our world, or in my country. We find them intolerable. Now, I never had much chance to change the world by myself, not through politics. Can you really contribute to evolutions and reforms? Well, business makes it possible quite often. The advantages and the pride it gives to all the stakeholders – customers, partners, employees – make it worthwhile. And on top of that, usually with stunning economic results!"

Marking enterprises are economic actors who induce major societal changes when building a territory of their own. All these components distinguish theses businesses from ordinary markets and protect them from direct competition

This book deals with marking businesses that stand out because of their fame, their weight, and their results. Starting from a few outstanding model companies, we try to spot the management fundamentals they employ, and that underlie their performance. What these companies do follows from deliberate choice. They mark the market and society, in the sense that they construct a specific territory where they leave their imprint as a testimonial. Controlling their own territory is a basic requirement for their impressive business success. Managing the space and guarding the borders are its engines.

The marking business combines two talents. It sniffs out or carves out a promising societal territory. It spells out its control of it in the actions taken by management. In other words, neither nice products nor beating people over the head with advertising will save an ill conceived or badly managed territory.

Like territory, marking is a pragmatic or managerial concept. It defines the art and skills that a business adopts to put its management methods and its ways of operating at the service of its positioning and of its actions in a given societal environment. The term "marking" describes a process and a mindset enabling a business to find its own marks or traces, to affirm its identity in a heterogeneous and fragmented world. Therefore marking does not mean branding. While the roots of the two terms are similar, they do not mean the same thing in management.

The term "brand" refers to branding cattle with hot irons. This technique is used when the grazing land is not fenced in, as was the case on the American Great Plains to distinguish and assert respective ownerships. Indeed, the logo or the name of the owner creates a property right on behalf of someone who applies the hot iron to the animal's hide after first wrestling it to the ground.

Modern marketing as it developed in the United States borrowed the metaphor of branding. Companies signaled products offered to the consumer to differentiate them from competitors. The sign or the symbol is just one facet of a brand; a product stops being anonymous for the customer. The signature on the packaging also commits the producer, inducing a moral duty or contract with consumers.

In many respects raising cattle and occupying market segments derive from the same art. Branding does not stop with marking a single animal. It is generally thereafter that trouble begins and that vigilance and management know-how start to matter. The customer is no more disciplined than a steer. Their loyalty is fragile. Just using force is not enough. Borders are permeable. Ranchers may not agree about respective limits and jurisdictions. Other inhabitants than ranchers may live on the territory.

While branding deals mainly with symbolic facets of the products, marking deals with much more. The marker's path requires the business to identify with its economic success and find legitimacy in serving, even transforming, society's needs and lifestyles. Its task is to civilize wants, behavior, and values. The management disciplines, from strategy to marketing, have all been built around this plain fact. The economic and societal space in which a company's policies are embedded form a complex and evolving reality, one not easily tamed. For economic rent is only justified when in compensation for something else. Worse, territories can implode, even collapse, since their inhabitants are free to migrate elsewhere, insofar as multiple alternatives crop up. The problems, in this respect, with monopolies and trusts – the scarecrow waved around by regulatory authorities in terms of fair trade – do not have much to do with those of territories. Territories are fragile, for the stakeholders are not captives. If they stick with it, it is because they get something out of it; there is for them some added value.

The term territory may be considered as identical to the term market. Why not adopt the latter one?

One aspect to further consider with the term market is that the world in which enterprises are operating is not a passive, static, cold universe. Customers are mobile. They may leave from one day to the next. They are not prone to accept just any promise from any company, even if it holds a dominating position, offers a stunning innovation, or the business floods them with advertising messages. The canonical axioms of consumer need and price remain of limited help in anticipating opportunities or leaping obstacles.

Obviously, every business acts upon and within an environment where it is embedded. A territory is not merely a place or location, as the accepted term suggests. It is also something more than a space – that is, an unknown, wild, uncivilized patch. A business conquers and even establishes it. It is in fact the product of collective activity, in this case of a business and outside stakeholders who mean to chart it, organize it, and civilize it and who may end up destroying it. Also, territory evokes a concrete image that cannot be reduced just to economic forces like competition, price-setting, and customer preferences. Its character is broader, more to do with society, mores, identity, and thought. The territory, whose center is the business, is embedded in a given society and trying to change its face.

The business keeps up relationships of interdependence and exchange with numerous third parties upstream of, within, and downstream of its own activities. It appoints certain suppliers, users, opinion-makers, and dealers over others. It even happens that it actively contributes to changes in government regulations or codes of ethics. It brings out alternative values and lifestyles. It helps stakeholders emerge and gives them a platform to speak from. A territory includes, therefore, relatively tangible elements (such as, for example, transactions and affinity groupings), as well as less tangible ones, like identities or cultural norms. The business and its products recognize them all, legitimize them, and help them transform.

This societal capital – using it and growing it – enables the business to construct and perpetuate its governance and its legitimacy over a distinctive space. Assuring that the space develops durably becomes one of the major goals of the business's performance.

STYLE AND CONTENTS

This book is an essay. It does not intend to adopt the conventions of scientific colloquia.

It is addressed to practitioners. Regardless of industry, discipline, job title, or organizational rank, marking concerns everyone. Indeed, this skill is in no way reserved just for the elites of business management. The book will blend management principles with many references to a large set of actual enterprises (see the index).

To practitioners it articulates three main propositions:

- The success of a business flows from its ability to conquer, mark, and develop a societal territory. While branding is about product, marking is about relationships, values and product. Societal embedding adds more values than do ordinary market transactions.
- A company's territory is constituted of many stakeholders (customers, suppliers, staff, civic organizations, experts, innovators, groups

having a prescriptive influence on customer behaviors and beliefs, and so on.) The marking business unites them around its work through identical values, joint identities, and durable partnerships.

■ The marking enterprise implements a specific managerial mindset and practice: making a meticulous, detailed definition of the goods or services offered; obsessively following events that might affect this definition; putting up protections against intrusions and threats; and using a communitarian organizational model.

The book is also addressed to colleagues in the academic world and, more broadly, to any mind curious about the dynamics of business, the economy, and society.

To them it holds a brief against a social science of consumption that would isolate it from other, upstream activities – organized retailing, for example – and downstream ones – for example, government regulation. It aims to upset the division of work and of management education into narrow, rigid disciplines walled off from each other: Strategic marketing, operational marketing, communications, quality control, brand defense, human resources and so on. It questions the heroic tales of innovation that favor explanation in terms of one man's genius. Its principal argument is to demonstrate the existence – alongside the market, the company, and the network – of a fourth form of organized economic reality: territorial marking.

Five major blocks build the outline of the book.

A first one highlights the importance and relevance of marking as a specific way to relate a business to the market.

Chapter 1 gives a brief preliminary definition of what marking is and is not. It also indicates why marking may be needed more than ever in the economies and societies of the 21st century. To the reader who may still feel somewhat doubtful, the conclusion of the book is worth reading immediately. It lists a set of outcomes marking is associated with such as shareholder value, to mention but one.

A second block aims at explaining marking approaches pragmatically and in detail. To avoid too much abstraction without empirical flesh, an inductive process is suggested.

While referring to a grid located at the end of Chapter 1, the reader will benefit from examining two cases of marking as developed by a mid-size production company, Royal Canin (Chapter 2), and a distribution giant, Wal-Mart (Chapter 3). Chapter 4, one of the key parts of this book, will explore marking approaches in detail and illustrate them with lessons derived from the two cases.

The third building block is operationally focused. It examines managerial prerequisites needed for effective marking. They rely heavily on explicit and short examples based on a set of six widely known companies.

Chapter 5 underlines the fact that marking implies a right mindset. Managers should better stick to it, and enforce it in daily acts and across their whole organization. Chapter 6 lists errors, mistakes and violations of the mindset that should never be made, and that may destroy the best marking intentions.

A fourth block, also a key part of the book, goes much deeper into the issue of territory building.

Chapter 7 deals with the difference between a market approach and societal embedding of an enterprise. Chapter 8 handles the way an enterprise builds and governs a territory. Some benchmarking is done using a 6 Cs model of territoriality and which is applied to three industries (retail banking, pet food, distribution).

A fifth block covers another prerequisite for effective marking: organizational and people management inside an enterprise.

Chapter 9 will argue that marking implies a special model of organizational development and leadership style called the moral community model.

An executive summary is available at the end of the book. The authors recommend readers to look at it after their initial reading of the book, or at least part of it.

1

MARKING: A FIRST CUT

The objective of this chapter is to give a first rough definition of what marking really means, and to distinguish it from other approaches in management.

Marking is a policy that expresses managerial will to relate a business to the market and society in a specific manner. It is made out of four fundamental components:

- Perfect fit with the wants of target markets and societal values addressed,
- Steady commitment to the promises made to customers and other stakeholders,
- Durable (not volatile) signals sent out to the market,
- Endorsement of a leading part in societal change (going beyond pure consumerism).

Marking as a policy is aimed at creating and governing a territory. A territory can be roughly defined as a world, as an economic space or market that is structured as a moral and social community (Becker 1982). While the market involves quite few actors, links them together via intermediaries and brokers, and governs their interdependence relations with a hegemonic and competitive pattern, the territory involves more participants, it links production to consumption via a much wider array of roles , and it is governed by a governance pattern that favors cooperation and coalition between parties involved. In many ways a territory is a pattern that is socially dense and morally integrated, as compared with a market in which selfish agents act in an opportunistic manner.

Holiday packages offer an interesting comparison. One important part of this business sector is quite poorly marked and functions like a mass market where operators sell rather standardized packages. Figure 1.1 presents a synthesis of the main actors of this market.

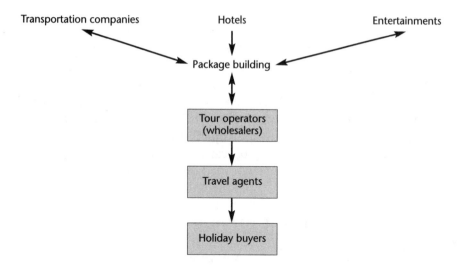

FIGURE 1.1 **The market of standardized holiday packages**

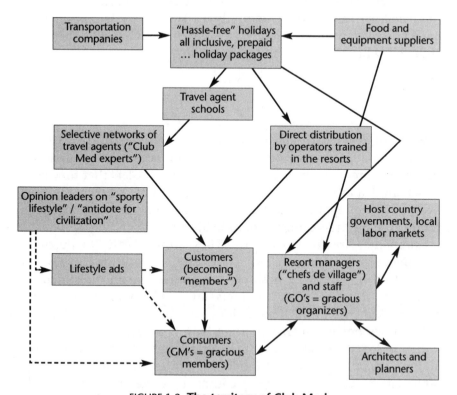

FIGURE 1.2 **The territory of Club Med**

Figure 1.2 shows an example of a marking and territorial building approach. Club Med has been a pioneer in marking holiday packages. It has elaborated a new concept of vacations during which social encounters carry much more weight than traditional hotel criteria such as comfort or room service.[1] The specific territory built by the marker has not much in common with the market Figure 1.1 synthesizes.

Marking and territory allow a company to avoid the arduous tasks of periodically negotiating or bargaining with customers, and to escape a strategic business logic whittled down to price alone.

RELATING THE ENTERPRISE TO THE MARKET

Marking deals with the way an enterprise approaches customers and markets. The fact is there are many other ways that management may use. Marking is just one among many.

To understand better the essence of the marking approach, it will be compared with two other commonly used ways to relate business to the economy and society: trading and branding. Comparing them will underline what marking is and what it is not.

Trading

The trading relationship to the market is a non-marking approach of business. Manufacturers provide commonplace, functional, inter-changeable products through a network of wholesalers that they keep under the thumb and that hold on to the retailers down the line. Except for monopolies, the market is understood as a fact of life, a context the business cannot intentionally alter.

Companies are free to choose. They either decide to pursue a marking objective or they accept a non-marking position. However, in accepting a non-marking position, companies remain indistinguishable from others – their products are purely commodities and consumers choose through price alone.

This does not mean that non-marking is a dead-end or a lower-status choice. It can lend itself to a profitable business structure. For example, manufacturers that produce goods exclusively for retailers' house labels accept a purely sub-contractor status. However, a non-marking strategic position exposes a company to specific business situations that marking, while not avoiding them entirely, at least significantly mitigates.

Non-marking often implies accepting a high level of dependence on the market, in which resellers can, to a great extent, dictate their terms to the company. Manufacturers of items packaged under a store's own label have no access to their end-market consumers.

By keeping its products as commodities, the company does not benefit from any visible identity of its own with which it could differentiate itself from competitors. In other words, its products carry no added value. To be successful in this situation, to construct a durable economic advantage, depends on other exogenous factors – such as a geographical monopoly, privileged access to natural resources or cheap labor, or some sort of regulatory protection.

The ramifications of a non-marking policy may ultimately be difficult to gauge. The company might have to accept a strategic logic reduced to price alone. Because its relationships will be characterized by uncertainty and will rely on repeated negotiations, it also means, at best, working within a confrontational environment or, at worst, navigating through open conflict with distributors or customers.

Branding

The 20th century has given pride of place to another form of relationship to the economy and society.

The effectiveness of branding has been historically flawed because it was the main way of relating to the consumer. Its power lay in its capacity to gather consumers under its banner, with advertising being an essential tool to this effect. It drew clear borders, for example in terms of the price spread between branded and non-branded products. The customers found themselves guaranteed only a few rights or basic promises such as risk-free innovative offerings and dependable quality. The brand conveyed synthetic and static information intended for a fairly undifferentiated mass. This information proved to be more decisive the less consumers had in the way of alternative sources of detailed information and supply.

The origin of branding, it should be remembered, was tied to packaging. The American company Quaker Oats played a pioneering role in this respect. While it was trying not to face competition from products that were less good and less costly to produce than their own, it did not wish to see its prices dictated by wholesalers. So Quaker decided to package its rolled oats and write its name on the package. By this means it based competition no longer on price alone but also on product quality and the responsibility of the brand (Cochoy 2004).

Practicing marketers have articulated a new action principle. The market can be molded by the business (Strasser 1989). The connection to the market constructed by practitioners and theoreticians segments the market and differentiates the products accordingly. And the enterprise's accomplishment is signed up with a brand. Two variants however coexist in this construction.

The first one assumes that the market is confinable and confined by a demand that pre-dates the organization of production and sales. Business success derives from the fact that the market is an entity, a given, something real, tangible, definite, countable, and therefore manageable. The task of management here is to examine, with the help of quantitative studies, the social and economic characteristics that affect product consumption. From them, a profile of the average customer can be drawn. Customers are assumed to be looking at the objective qualities of the product. Advertising is seen to inform and educate them in relation to objective product qualities. The theoretical buyer is thus presumed to act as a rational decision-maker, and viewed as the main, if not the only, resident of the business's territory. On its side, distribution is treated as an independent, exogenous activity. Because consumers are seen as showing a willingness and consciously expressing a need, the business can never lose sight of them. It has to adjust its production and circulation to the nature and distribution of a previously revealed demand.

The second variant sees products as imposed on the market. Compared with the first approach, this one aims at profoundly altering existing images and constructions of the market. The consumer is thought of as evolving in his or her patterns of consuming or using products. However, it is the job of the business to reveal, model and bring out this evolution potential. Management's talent is to anticipate demand and create products that respond to consumers' not-yet-formulated expectations. Customers are considered to be incapable of prompting tomorrow's great innovations. It is the business's role to be on the alert for anything that might happen or be said anywhere, to be sensitive to the weakest signals in every field, from marketing to technology, to sort them out and in the end to give its employees the chance to bloom and free their potential in the execution of these ideas.

This second variant of branding is closer to the marking discipline than the first one. However, the enterprise is still dictating its interpretation of the market to the customers rather than sharing societal values with them as well as with a larger community of stakeholders.

Marking

Marking is not at all the same as branding. Marking sublimates branding to such a point that marking can even exist in the absence of explicit brands, as suggested in the Introduction with the example of the fruit and vegetable seller in a street market.

Many economic players can make a difference without having an explicit brand. Their marking impact results in part from the quality of their products and services, but other relational practices are built up too. Proximity retailing is familiar with such practices; particularly hairdressers, barbers, booksellers, neighborhood Superettes, and bakeries. Even an industrial company such as a cement producer can mark its territory while delivering cement in bulk to construction sites, although liquid cement cannot carry any brand or logo. Which dimensions of marking are, then, activated and managed in this case?

Insuring regularity in the quality of the delivered product and eliminating all variability in its components are very strong promises for a cement manufacturer. Guaranteeing timely deliveries and carefully managing supplier inventories, proactively delivering cement to job sites to eliminate all risk of stock-outs, are great levers for marking one's territory. Here, marking becomes synonymous with trustworthiness. The "contractual" agreement has taken, in this instance, the form of additional services that instil the cement user with peace of mind. Incidentally, through this type of approach, the cement manufacturer can distance itself from the concept of commodity that generally characterizes unmarked products, a concept that negates the history and relationships a company builds while interacting with the market.

Another area in which marking can impose itself without explicit branding is the service industries. This sector lends itself to a better understanding of what relational links mean. In essence, service is relational and experiential. It includes a large dose of intangibility. For Club Med as for Disneyland, marking results, first and foremost, from an ability on the part of the service provider to create for its customers (and for its employees) the magic of an individual experience within a collective setting. If this magic fades away, pasting the Club Med name or the Disneyland logo on T-shirts, key rings or sun-protection creams will not rekindle it. You cannot fool the market. No gadget invented by an advertising agency will make up for, or hide, the fact that promises are not being fulfilled. Advertising that is devoid of real meaning is very costly and leads to no return. It is an intellectual fraud, not a placebo.

Marking can also accommodate the coexistence of multiple brands within one company. While brands can obviously contribute to marking, the link between them requires a number of conditions to be met.

The first imperative is that the brand must not be a mere artefact. More precisely, brands must be true responses to actual market needs. An undifferentiated product or a product that doesn't answer any real need will impoverish brands and not contribute to marking. The majority of brands do not match responses to the market, delivering a plus or added value (Kapferer and Thoenig 1989). Moreover, product offerings require associated, appropriate services. It is only when these requirements are fulfilled that synergy can take shape. Marking then becomes meaningful and the brand may become a powerful lever in the marking process.

The second condition relates to how appropriate the brand is to a clearly linked socioeconomic space. Let us assume that a company is marketing several product ranges under several brands. Each brand must be inscribed in a rigorously defined space, both in terms of values and assumed market behavior. With such requirements satisfied, the relationship between marking and branding can be more perennial, notwithstanding the different signatures the company is using. The success of Sam's Clubs at Wal-Mart bears witness to this. Sam's Clubs are built around a very specific territory: member customers buying products for professional use or for resale. Wal-Mart has demonstrated that two different brands can coexist within one marking project – pared-back selling of lowest-price merchandise.

Whether semantic links should be made between the different brands sold by a company, such as Nestlé using the Nes prefix for a great number of its products, is a purely tactical issue. The bond that marking creates between the company's diverse brands – whether or not they are connected semantically – has nothing to do with the concept of umbrella brands or store brands, which can incorporate host brands and sub-brands that are not inspired by the same marking philosophy. Store brands and the umbrella brands of suppliers can in this case become nothing more than rudimentary commercial tricks.

WHEN TRADING AND BRANDING DO NOT SUFFICE

Marking as a specific type of connection to the market is not in itself a recent invention. In 1888, coca, traditionally used as a headache remedy, was sold by an Atlanta pharmacist as a health drink. Asa Candler took this and created a new territory, soft drink, that is more than just a beverage market in modern societies. Similarly, Kodak deliberately built a demand, a world structured around moral ties and societal values that had not existed by introducing the concept of amateur photography. There are many strong signals suggesting that the 21st century will coincide with an even wider diffusion of the marking approach.

Major transformations are shaping the environment in which competition and economic action occur today. Most of them, such as globalization and sustainable development, are so obvious that they may not need much attention here. Nevertheless three of them may require a closer look.

An evolving relation to the market

Concentration of distribution power in the hands of a few enterprises is touching every industry, products as well as services, business-to-consumer as well as business-to-business. It has also become widely international. Across countries and in most business sectors, it is common for two or three retail companies to control more than half the sales.

Concentration re-deals the cards. The point of sale has triumphed over the manufacturer's brand (Kapferer and Thoenig 1989). The game is much less symmetrical, with the reseller setting the rules between the upstream and downstream economic flows. Retailer organization upsets the suppliers' branding game by giving value to the store's banner as a promise that associates shopping in a particular store with a type of consuming, an atmosphere, a level of service or friendliness. The market's codebook is harder for the supplier to come by and seems only to get more confusing. Retailers/resellers equip themselves to pick up on their customers' behavior and needs, in detail and non-stop (Solomon 2003). Market intelligence is today a major weapon on the economic battlefield, and will continue to be.

Another massive and obvious transformation derives from the decline of mass-market approaches. The notion of an undifferentiated market postulates two basic conditions: undifferentiated needs and a passive market. Marketing was justifiably based on its capacity to persuade human beings that their needs were such-and-such and that such-and-such product was necessary to satisfy them. The business looked like an absolute monarch. It built the market as a perfect hegemony. The territories it carved out were simple because defined in the image of the product alone (Laufer and Paradeise 1990).

Differentiated markets render this approach distinctly less relevant. End users have more resources such as information and direct transaction access to producers, via e-Business for instance. They also more actively create their individuality, for instance by customizing their demand. And the consumer's voice is also being heard in a more public and civic way. The number of stakeholders is growing, and is not limited to purely consumer associations and consumerist issues. Social demands and public opinion are awakening simultaneously.

A third transformation with lasting and heavy impact is the fact that innovation becomes an ordinary strategy for success and competition. One key lesson should be kept in mind about business approaches linked to innovation. The technological factor, as such, hardly constitutes a decisive motivation for economic innovation. A scientific breakthrough or a good performance by R&D does not in itself guarantee a decisive advantage. Innovation is happening on another level than the technological: that of value.

Furthermore, value is often uncoupled from technology. That does not mean value pioneers make no use of technologies. But the technologies they mobilize to this end are already used elsewhere, whether in their industry or another. Innovation through value creates a market space characterized by one major fact: no one contests it. Innovation erases competitive forces. It creates and attracts new demand. It is accessible at once to new entrants and to companies already in place. It is in play and equally profitable in industries seen as frivolous, like the circus; industries considered prestigious and serious, like automobiles; industries that have been around and considered mature, like steel, and industries that used not to exist, like computing (Kim and Mauborgne 2005).

Are established management solutions still so valuable?

Such massive transformations of the relationships between business and society induce relevant consequences for daily management. Some tools that had been successful in the past seem less effective in a new business and societal environment. Some professional know-how that provided widely recognized solutions in the recent past seems today to reach a limit in delivering its success promises. This is quite obvious when looking at branding and marketing.

For instance, do strong brands and branding approaches still guarantee by themselves 70% or even 90% success? Some doubts are expressed here and there about traditional management wisdom. It might well occur that a brand, if it gets too strong, overshadows the company's view of the market and actually damages its relationship with consumers. Is the good will of a company proportional to advertising spending, as many branding consultants claim; the more money being spent for media exposure, the more value being created for the shareholders? Is in fact the brand name still a most precious asset, financially and otherwise?

Evidence from the marketplace is ambiguous. Many leading brands are facing some form of economic stagnation. In a few countries and sectors some leading brands even face decline and suspicion. In food, brands are undergoing attack from unmarked, no-name products sold by hard discounters. In mass-market electronics, their share is declining by about 10% a year. Furthermore, the decline of the brand is also moral and cultural. In ceasing to buy brands, the customer is silently rebelling (Pons 2004).

Though the very foundations of manufacturer's brands seem long-standing and durable, they are threatened by a conjunction of five factors. Pro-consumer movements have become active and influential. Private labeling is rapidly growing more powerful. Brand names and packaging are becoming commonplace, with the near disappearance of bulk items. Some large-scale retailers have in one way or another internalized production. And regulations and government controls on makers and the traceability of products have become both more effective and more widespread.

A global food giant like Kraft Foods, though the owner of tens of famous brands, totally changed its plans in the early 2000's. Kraft's market approach turned its back on brand names. Its goal became to be differentiated. One of its favorite tools has been a free quarterly magazine, sent by mail and called *Food and Family* – Kraft sends out 11 million copies of this magazine, which places it about third among U.S. magazines. Besides advertising, it contains recipes, articles on food, and features. The magazine is highly personalized. Thanks to detailed information furnished by the reader when requesting it, each issue directs the consumer, calling him or her by name, to the sections containing things appropriate to his or her interests. The magazine is rounded out by a range of other consumer relation vehicles, from call centers to cooking schools set up and run by the company.

Serious doubt even arises about basic concepts such as the need of the customer.

The common vocabulary of marketing makes such frequent use of "need" that one could end up believing need is self-evident, that it actually exists and above all that it sufficiently encompasses reality.[2] In fact experience shows that needs are not by nature artificial, totally fashioned by marketing, advertising and the social environment. Beyond a certain limit their contents cannot be manipulated to make the consumer buy into a market concept marketers have dreamed up. Needs of consumers are in no way completely malleable and contingent.[3]

A serious miscarriage occurs when the brand becomes nothing more than a mere advertising tool. It then contains the basis for its perversion and probably its eventual decline. For to really be differentiated it will increasingly have to be exciting (or at a minimum, become more esoteric) and so remove itself from the clarity of the contract, from the legibility of the terms of the exchange.

It is not surprising that marketing people make up a professional group that feels under pressure in a number of countries (Peters 2004). In surveys they express a mood that suggests their function is in crisis. Their disillusionment is fed in various ways. Investments are made for the very short, in fact much too short, term. Innovations give advantages whose lifecycle is too short, and are not really new. Furthermore, top management keeps marketing people out of the strategy-setting process, to the marketers' regret. Finally, marketing people feel that consumers are really just too fickle and unreliable in the way they respond.

Violating basic marketing rules of thumb even becomes recognized as a rational managerial approach. Magnificent successes are attained by businesses breaking in a deliberate manner professional conventions. They reject methods considered orthodox and know-hows perceived as respectable. Not marketing – doing *non-marketing* – can sometimes be the best kind of marketing.

Hermès does just the opposite of what a number of its competitors do. This giant in luxury goods never commissions a market study of any kind. Hermès never runs ads featuring celebrities. What the company deems appropriate is what is good for the market. They take the line that their products speak for themselves, and have to.

Royal Canin, a leader in pet food, has no marketing department as such, hires no certified marketers, and relies neither on market studies nor on consumer panels. Such heterodoxy has apparently not kept it from becoming the worldwide leader in cat and dog nutrition. Even better is that, by rejecting marketing, a group of workers and managers, none of whom has an MBA, invented a marketing approach that has revolutionized the pet food industry.

Good marketing and good strategy may often ignore all the recipes hot off the press. They dispense with the classic marketers and licensed strategists. The exceptions one finds are numerous; this book will in the next chapters suggest that we cannot simply attribute their success to sheer luck or the intuitive genius of their founders. These curious companies have one thing in common: they mark territories.

Marking as a managerial concept

Branding and advertising are only two aspects, though the most visible, of the difficulty in relating business changes to new market and society conditions. Wrong answers abound such as lowering the price when price is not a buying motive. And yet, misgivings about management icons do not justify trying to demolish everything. This is why current limits about the effectiveness of marketing tools do not in any way mean marketing will die. Products will continue to be dressed up. Believing that the creation of non-brands will help consumers to make choices or will develop their loyalty, even lead them to consume, is a pious wish. Packaging and naming the product remain important elements in the customer relationship. But this relationship will be built on a different foundation: marking territories.

The breakdown calls for a radical revision of the way businesses construct their approach to the market.

In other terms, they opt, with deliberate contrariness, for an anticipatory management of their offering. They play on true differentiation, sometimes inducing an actual breach. They create values. They conquer and establish new territories. These values reflect a vision they carry around with them.

An old saying should never be forgotten. A customer is loyal to your brand so long as he or she has not found something better on the market. "Better" means they have looked into at least two aspects:

- the tangible value expressed by the price–quality relationship,
- the intangible value, defined in terms of recognition, a sense of belonging, or the proximity and good governance of the business.

For a brand's territory is a space on which anyone can intrude. Thus only a regular, deep marking lets the business create and maintain a desire to belong to this brand's community. To achieve marking, two major mental and managerial modifications are required.

The first is to give up on the concept of market and adopt the concept of territory.

Because the pace of social change has accelerated in a spectacular manner, companies have to get away from their simplistic fixation on the satisfaction of needs and adopt a diametrically opposite approach. They must research the tangible gaps in the selling proposition made to consumers. They must look for good-sized, multidimensional, sociological gaps. The company constructs an economic and social space in which it will fit, lastingly. This space, or this territory, is not the same thing as a market already presumed to be there, overarching and overshadowing the company. The company's exchanges with the society in which it is embedded operate on another level than just that of market price. It is not content to be a trader. It wants to be a pioneering force, creating new territories.

The second required modification drops a narrow, technocratic and a societal view of what marketing is.

The status of marking is more political, because it is automatically part of a network of vested interests. The company gives customers their roles as users, who in turn give the product a value they measure by its usefulness. The company relies on in-depth research of these users. In this way, even in a so-called mass market, it learns to think with a niche mentality – like a customer. It bestows its pedigree upon an offering when it is tangible to the consumer. It relativizes the importance of advertising. It assumes a model of close, rigorous, multiform interaction with interested parties, internal to and external to the construction of the marking. The connection to the market is woven through a series of confrontations between heterogeneous logics – it is a permanent interaction between multiple social milieus. In an everyday and metaphorical sense, the company enters into a dialogue with the market, and the brand is just one instrumental element of this dialogue.

This construction considers that the consumer is neither modern (that is, rational and disciplined) nor post-modern (that is, un-centered and conditioned). Consumers mutate, incorporating and foiling the markings and the territories one tries to pin them to. More-over, an economy more geared to quality and to respect for civic, ethical and moral values – to mention just these factors – implies that companies will try to give a richer, more societal meaning to the consumption of their goods and services (Laszlo 2003). This is where they will gain their legitimacy. Unless they are content to have no control over their environment, companies have to reinsert them-selves as actors in the new consumption game. If they want to become central in the territories they invest in or invent, they must mark them with their imprint and impose their centrality.

To give flesh and blood to marking and its operational manage-ment, two real company cases will be provided in Chapters 2 and 3. Each in its own way may be considered as a quasi-perfect example of marking.

While Chapter 4 will analyze both cases in a more comparative and systematic manner, the reader could benefit from a list of seven key dimensions to apply in understanding general lessons to be derived from each case (see Table 1.1). They define more pragmatically the main facets of what marking means.

While these seven facets build the core of the marking process, they do not include other management aspects that are of primary impor-tance too and that are more related to matters internal to the enter-prise such as human resources, organizational development, codes of conduct, manufacturing, logistics, and so on. While reading the two cases, please keep them in mind too. They will be addressed later on (see also Chapters 5 and 6).

TABLE 1.1 A reader's guideline for case analyses

1. What is the strategic ambition pursued by the enterprise?

2. What are its actual market intelligence and the way it shapes its offer?

3. To what extent does its marking induce societal upheaval or consolidate social order?

4. What is the delivered value? Is it linked to product in use or is it linked to some perceptual value?

5. What features of the offering does the marking approach enhance? Are they tangible or symbolic?

6. What communication approach does the marker use? What are its objectives? What is the status of the customer?

7. How is the relationship with the manufacturer (for the retailer) or with the retailer (for the manufacturer) managed?

But, and this is another of the book's messages, marking is not just about marketing and strategy, or about relating to the market and society. It covers also another challenge, internal to the enterprise, and not the easiest one to address in daily life: marking enterprises, or enterprises able to construct and govern a territory, are also organizations that are able, inside their own walls, to develop cooperation and coalition patterns, vertically between the top and the bottom of their hierarchy of authority, and horizontally between their various functions. They function like highly integrated moral communities (see Chapter 9).

2

PROACTIVE MARKING: THE ROYAL CANIN WAY

Our first case tells the story of an inventive type of marking and of the building of a new territory by a mid-size enterprise. The enterprise is called Royal Canin. Its territory deals with dogs, cats and their nutrition.

One may consider pet food as a sort of exotic business, from which nothing much serious and relevant could be learned or applicable to other sectors. Reading the story will definitely convince the reader that, on the contrary, Royal Canin should be considered a master case. It fits all the criteria of perfect marking, whatever the business sector.

In the space of only a few years, Royal Canin has become a trendsetter and a world leader in its industry. How and why did a small French company succeed in a sector dominated by powerful multinationals and a marketplace that seemed to be already mature, if not saturated? (Thoenig and Waldman 2003) It has built up new market segments and framed a new societal status for the pet.

Royal Canin does nothing the way its competitors do. Actually, the company could be considered a maverick, the black sheep of the industry, or an unsolved mystery. Its management style is vehemently opposed to so-called effective and logical practices. Put into a marketing or management class, this pedagogical case would score poorly. The company adopts unconventional practices that go against what the industry considers common sense.

When it comes to pet food, current branding and marketing practices perfectly fit, at first glance, fundamental principles of mass consumption; such as "create instant brand awareness," "gain the loyalty of customers browsing through the aisles of superstores," "add value to convenience goods for which the formulation remains largely unknown." Almost all pets are expected to consume this type of food during their lifetime. Effective practices specific to mass consumption products are all valid in this industry. In addition, they play largely on emotions. Ads praise the benefits of a wet diet by playing upon the affection pet owners feel for their dog or cat. "All you need to do is add love!" Whatever makes the owner happy is presumed ipso facto to be good for the pet.

And yet Royal Canin keeps focusing on the pet, its physiology and morphology as well as its real biological and nutritional needs. "Knowledge and Respect" is its leitmotif. The emotional needs of the master are no longer criteria to address and to satisfy. The company consciously rejects any subjective criterion or anthropomorphism of any kind. Its philosophy is simple and rather blunt. Owners who respect their cat or dog are owners who take their pet's biological needs into account, who do not project human needs and desires on their pets. Its products are not sold by superstores. Its sales come 100% from specialized stores and distribution outlets such as veterinary clinics, breeders, pet shops, farm stores, and garden centers. Last but not least, its products have become all the more specialized and are the direct result of applied innovative scientific research. In other words, there is one specific product targeting almost every single pet, based on its age, activity level, breed, and overall health.

Royal Canin is often referred to as the "L'Oreal of pets." Between 1993 and 2005, the company's global sales tripled, with health nutrition sales increasing 19-fold. These numbers represent an average annual growth of 13.2% in terms of global sales and more than 31% annually in health nutrition. In 2005, more than 80% of the company's sales took place outside France, its home market. Its operational results have risen 17-fold.[1] It has become an international leader in health nutrition in Western and Eastern Europe, in Russia, and in Latin America.

THE LEGACY OF THE FOUNDERS

For the worst or for the best, past events mold the culture of an enterprise. They shape path dependencies. Dry food, dogs and breeders have been key legacies of Royal Canin's early days.

There are two approaches to feeding domestic dogs and cats. The first way – the most traditional – consists of recycling leftovers from the family table or cooking a separate meal for the pet. The second, and more modern, method is to feed it commercial pet food. There are three types of manufactured pet food: wet food (in cans), semi-moist food, and dry food, or kibble. This last category is expanding rapidly the world over.

Commercial pet food goes back as far as the 1920's. It first made its appearance in the United States, where farmers used to feed their livestock dry food and looked for similar products for their dogs. Back then, seed farm stores and cooperatives were selling corn flakes, and from the beginning of the 1930's, kibble, a complete food based on a combination of proteins, cereals and lipids. In contrast with the country, grocers in urban areas tended to favor and market wet food. Its packaging resembled, at least from the outside, canned food for human consumption. Big enterprises specializing in livestock food, such as Ralston Purina, or in human food, such as Quaker Oats and General Foods, expanded their core business activity to include new lines of pet food products.

Royal Canin took off on a hunch: feed the pet well. Jean Cathary, a veterinarian living in a village in the south of France, started manufacturing dry flakes and kibble for dogs. Convinced that various disorders, such as obesity, eczema, and hepatitis, were directly linked to poor nutrition (family's leftovers, canned pet food), he created a more digestive soup in which he used flaked corn as well as a more balanced formulation of minerals, vitamins, and trace elements. These ingredients were mixed with cornstarch, then cooked and dehydrated. In 1968 he registered a trademark under the name of Royal Canin. He was the first pet food manufacturer in Europe to use an extruder.

Royal Canin began selling products for puppies and for breeders' dogs. Its products were distributed through proximity channels: to reach breeders and associations of German Shepherd owners. Unlike his competitors, Cathary launched a series of television ads to promote his trademark.

Cathary was the first manufacturer in France to produce and market dry food for pets at a time when canned wet products were storming the market. There were two reasons for the success of wet food: its "human aspect" – it closely resembles human food – and its palatability – these products are rich in lipids, proteins and moisture (75% to 80%). Dry food has two main advantages: nutritional quality (ingredients can be more carefully formulated and specifically balanced) and cost. Although the market price per kilo is slightly higher for dry food compared with wet food, dry food contains only 8% to 11% moisture, which translates into a concentration of nutritional ingredients three to four times higher. A daily serving can cost a third as much as wet food.

In 1972, Royal Canin set up shop in Aimargues in the south of France, employed some 40 staff and was producing 5,500 tons of food a year. The target market was mainly the south of France with some limited exports to Germany and Sweden. This growth led to an irreversible financial deadlock. In March 1972, Royal Canin was acquired by Guyomarc'h. This sizable family business produced among other things food for poultry, pigs and livestock.

The new owner was a firm believer in decentralization. With the exception of R&D, he treated the pet food industry separately and independently from animal nutrition. He also positioned Royal Canin as a technical and scientific trademark. He highlighted the rural and local roots that gave the company its unique identity, while expanding the company on the international scale by increasing exports.

Two more plants were added in France. The company's exclusive distribution network was considerably expanded to cover France from one end to the other. Subsidiaries were established all over the European Union and Brazil. In 1987 and 1989, two small pet food companies were acquired in the U.S., including a plant in Rolla, Missouri. These historic brands, Wayne and Kasco, had not been able to upgrade their products from basic nutrition, also known as premium food, to health nutrition or super-premium.

Meanwhile, in Europe, facing the considerable growth of supermarkets and megastores, Royal Canin launched in 1982 a specific brand designed for them while keeping its presence in the channel of professional breeders.

Royal Canin's corporate culture was based on its specialization in dry food for dogs. This was a unique choice since at that time the competition mainly targeted cats through wet food. But when it came to dry food for cats, Royal Canin doubted the financial sustainability of this market segment. In addition, it did not feel technically equipped to address the impenetrable world of cat professionals and lovers. To further complicate matters, cat food was traditionally wet food, with the market dominated by canned food, which meant food sold by hypermarkets. Royal Canin stuck to its guns. Its brand would remain technical and favor knowledge of the dog. It decided to develop two main areas: science and service.

Cooperation agreements were signed between the company and university laboratories. Believing that R&D was a key element for success in the industry, Royal Canin established a research center that would soon become its backbone. It created partnerships that offered a variety of services to breeders and retailers, including training and 24-hour delivery even for small orders. It even invented a whole new profession, cynotechnician. These technical salespeople offer service and advice to breeders with regard to dogs. They demonstrate dedication and passion for dogs. They are also known to the world of dog lovers. Most of them had been dog show judges, international renowned breeders, or dog officers for fire departments, the army or the police.

The driving force behind the crusade to attract breeders was the emphasis placed on digestibility and nutritional performance. Large breed dogs, for instance, are known to have a sensitive digestive tract and fragile joints. To a large extent, the issue was linked to the growth of dogs. From the time they are born to the time they reach adulthood, their weight may increase by between 80 and 100 times their birth weight. Conversely, the weight of small breed puppies, like human beings, increases only 20 times. A specific food to address puppies' needs was launched in 1980. Ten years later, Royal Canin had become a specialist in large breed dogs.

In 1993, the company was thirty times the size it had been in 1972 – 811 employees, 180,000 tonnes of food produced per year and sales worth some 200 million euros. Nevertheless there were still three black marks on its record.

Royal Canin succumbed to the pressure of "strategic dispersion," trying to swim both upstream and downstream. As a result, it opened too many fronts by trying to enter any distribution channel it could.

It did not place enough faith in its own capacities. Consequently, its sales in nutritional food were barely 13%, because the company was struggling to compete with "me-too products" of mediocre or poor quality.

Although Royal Canin as a brand was widely known, it held a marginal position on the European and international food market for pets. Its five major competitors accounted for half of all international sales. They belonged to powerful multinationals for which pet food was an activity alongside many others. They had a reputation for adopting strong marketing techniques. They knew everything about large-scale distribution. They had conquered strong markets positions in Europe and in the United States.[2]

In 1990, a French bank, Paribas, bought out the whole Guyomarc'h Group. The bankers wanted to see a return on their investment, and they wanted it quickly. At the beginning of 1994, the head of Guyomarc'h and of its subsidiary Royal Canin retired. Paribas looked for someone who did not necessarily have a background in pet nutrition or in pet food and would not be limited by historical ties with Guyomarc'h or with Royal Canin. Henri Lagarde was appointed.[3]

SETTING UP A BRIGHTER FUTURE

In 1994, the Guyomarc'h Group was split into four legally independent companies, one of them being Royal Canin. Royal Canin had lost money the year before, due mainly to its management hesitating on what strategy to follow. Henri Lagarde's predecessor thought that pet food had entered difficult times and had become a commodity, its price being the only differentiating factor. The new president did not share this point of view. He recognized the know-how of the team in place. He established two main priorities: to redirect the company toward specialized distribution, to favor quality and send the company's products to the top of the charts. Quality should never be subordinated to savings, was Lagarde's open statement.[4]

In September 1996, Lagarde became Royal Canin's chairman and CEO. To convince Paribas not to sell the company just then, but instead to list it on the Paris stock exchange, which happened in 1997, he told the shareholders that he would "write one of the most beautiful and elegant stories of European industry." All he needed was 10 years. Additionally, he appointed in 1999 a new COO, Alain Guillemin.[5]

Lagarde listed problems resulting from selling Royal Canin in grocery stores, even under different brand names. Having managed ranking electrical appliance brands, and having dealt with giant distribution companies, he had experienced the ruthless tug of war between modern distributors and leading brands (Dupuy and Thoenig, 1996). Discounts, brand imitation, and side payments manufacturers were forced to make, and did not benefit the end customers, threatened well-known brands that invested in their trademark and adopted a product innovation strategy. Selling Royal Canin via food supermarkets was weakening its position. Its image was becoming fuzzy for customers as well as for specialized distribution channels. Its products were losing their "technical" and "specific" aura because they could be found on hypermarket shelves, just like any other run-of-the-mill product.

This argument was substantiated by facts. An overwhelming majority of Royal Canin's competitors had chosen the grocery channel to make the most of their sales and generate the biggest part of their profits. In contrast with other companies, Royal Canin's total sales stemming from groceries were barely 36%, which meant that the company was ranked in the lowest bracket of this market segment. In compliance with so-called best practice, it should have sought to improve its position and to further penetrate it. Lagarde was persuaded that though Royal Canin's sales in grocery stores were limited, they still represented a real threat: to margins, to corporate culture and strategy, and, above all, to the essence of the brand. The key strategic target to protect and achieve, namely dogs' health, meant authentic nutrition based on science, and not on anthropomorphic concepts.

All efforts had to concentrate on specialized channels, namely breeders, pet shops, and multispecialized shops such as garden centers and farm stores catering to suburban and rural consumers. Royal Canin was strongly present in these channels, which accounted for two-thirds of its sales. They still provided the stronghold for the brand, even if in the 1990's supermarkets and mass-marketers dominated pet food distribution. Royal Canin could never hope to measure up to its competitors in grocery store channels.

The shareholders were doubtful of Lagarde's recommendations. However, as an act of faith, they decided to stay on side. The reaction was more hostile within Royal Canin itself. Some marketing managers deliberately ignored the new instructions. For instance, they continued to prominently display Royal Canin's logo on the grocery channel packaging. Even well-established international consultants considered its new strategy as suicidal. They compared its CEO to an old-fashioned stubborn Stalinist. Opponents had evidence to back up their objections. Selling in supermarkets and other superstores would be crucial to cover fixed costs. And selling in supermarkets would encourage consumers to convert from wet to dry food and allow them to subsequently look for Royal Canin products in specialized stores and other venues.

Despite such resistance, the management team kept stressing the vital importance of breaking free from grocery channels. At the end of 1996, and in a rather authoritative move, Royal Canin withdrew all its products from superstores and mass merchandisers in most countries. In a few remaining ones, any new product development targeting grocery store distribution was banned. Grocery sales ceased to be of interest for the company. From now on it would prohibit putting them as an item on any agenda or mentioning them in any meeting in which the CEO was present. Reports on sales and results would no longer include sales in grocery stores and sales of mainstream products that did not belong to the nutritional category. Salespeople operating in countries that still sold in grocery store channels, namely France, Belgium, and Spain, were given 24 months to increase operating results in these segments to the level they had in specialized distribution channels, which meant a jump from 4% to 18%. The CEO hoped that grocery chains would be discouraged from buying.[6]

INVENTING NEW MARKET SEGMENTS

Focusing exclusively on specialized distribution and health nutrition channels implies that new opportunities are discovered and exploited.

The working force assigned by Royal Canin to sales specialists tripled. In 1994 Lagarde eradicated the word "traditional" from any computer, report, status report, document, and official company discourse whenever it was used to designate retailers, big or small, who did not fall into the grocery store category. The word was from then on to be substituted by the term "specialist." This meant that the figure of the specialist would become Royal Canin's key partner. New wording paved the way for a radical change in how to make sense of pet food: to help all stakeholders, from the pet owner to the food producer, to imagine a different pet world.

As CEO, Lagarde was obsessed by the idea of putting the pet at the center of the business.[7] This goal was to be reached in daily management through three methods.

The first evolved around the need to further improve on knowledge about pets relating to physiology, biology, and psychology. This would imply a major investment. Such knowledge would create new market opportunities that would meet new needs. Winning the knowledge race would allow the company to get a leg up on the competition.

The second method was that any product developed would have to respond to clearly specified physiological needs. The head of R&D imposed a rule that no veterinarian or university should be able to refute any of Royal Canin's nutritional arguments.

Last but not least, the company banned any human parallelisms. A pet has biological, physiological, and psychological needs that are different from those of human beings. To really love a pet means to recognize these specificities. The company's historical slogan, Knowledge and Respect, was displayed and drummed out in every form possible in any company activity or occasion. It would also be embraced by distributors, including retailers, and by any stakeholders in the canine and feline world: veterinarians, breeders, and so on.

Although Royal Canin had started mainly by feeding dogs, it expressed a growing interest in cats. Lagarde believed that the cat market would soon become as large as the dog market. His statement caused some skepticism among his associates. However he pointed out that cats were not given enough exposure – the ratio of cats' and dogs' veterinary visits was one to three – and that the notion of healthy food was hardly ever considered, mainly because anthropomorphism was stronger with cats than with dogs. In 1996, there were 42 million cats in Europe as opposed to 36 million dogs. In 1994, dry food for dogs in Europe represented 50% of manufactured food (as opposed to 80% in the United States); dry food for cats was barely 18% in Europe (as opposed to 55% in the United States). Compared with the United States, Europe had great growth potential in terms of volume and value of cat food. An average cat consumes 60 to 70 grams (17 to 20 ounces) of food per day. For that reason, Lagarde argued, cat owners would be willing to pay more per pound for products of superior quality that provide palatability and nutrition.

The company had real know-how in feline nutrition without being aware of it. In September 1994, a comparative test published in a leading French consumerist journal had tested 39 different kinds of cat food. All 28 moist foods on the list fell under the category of "non-nutritional," whereas 8 out of 11 dry foods were rated as "good." Three of the latter were Royal Canin's products. They were ranked second, third, and fourth.

Royal Canin would from now on offer more and more technical and targeted products to meet the needs of cats as well as dogs and to provide them with added value, not only with respect to palatability, but first and foremost in terms of the pet's well-being and health. At the same time, it would progressively abandon any approach that favored basic food in order to concentrate its efforts on health nutrition, to feed and prevent illness or, as the veterinarians would say, feed and cure the pet. In the case of dogs, for instance, Royal Canin would identify five different segments.

■ The first segment deals with basic or cheap food. It translates into a single product for mass consumption. The pet would eat the same food, regardless of its age, breed, or health status. This type of food is to be found in supermarkets, mainly under the retailer's private label. The food looks cheap and is easy to manufacture. However, other factors, such as palatability, digestibility, nutritional performance, in other words everything that relates to a pet's specific physiological needs, greatly vary from product to product.

■ A second segment, called "mainstream brands," refers to dry pet food that offers a more complete and balanced diet. Mainstream products are similar to basic products in that they have been on the market for a very long time and are not specifically targeted. Instead they cater to the needs of the average dog and cat. Products in this category offer better palatability and are more digestible than basic products.

- The third segment is a rather new segment. Called "premium" in the 1980's, it makes the critical distinction between feeding and nutrition. It addresses the pet's needs based on criteria such as age and activity levels. The products belonging to this category are balanced in nutrients, namely proteins, carbohydrates, lipids, vitamins, trace elements, minerals, and so on. They are made from high-quality raw materials. Highly technical processes are needed to manufacture them. They offer good digestibility and palatability, as well as quite good nutritional performance.
- The fourth segment, known as "Super-Premium," but called Health Nutrition by Royal Canin, refers to food that meets the very specific needs of each pet in relation to its age and its activity level, as well as its breed and health status. Its digestibility, palatability and nutrition levels are excellent.
- A fifth segment is dietetic. Prescribed and sold by veterinary clinics, these products meet pets' medical needs, tackling problems such as obesity, diabetes, kidney failure, or diarrhea. They offer excellent digestibility and stronger palatability. The formulation of these products is highly specific.

Each of these segments may include wet food (canned) and dry food (kibble). However, to the extent that buyers of wet food favor a humanizing approach when feeding their pet, wet canned food only exists in the first segments or in high-quality human-like products, mainly for cats. The exception to the rule is found in a few nutritional canned foods targeting veterinarians, who prescribe them for very old pets, with fragile teeth or no appetite.

Royal Canin expects that sooner or later dry food will dominate all five segments. The fact is that, in Europe at least, veterinary clinics and other specialized points of sale are already prescribing dry food at a rate of 95%. It offers nutritional quality, is easy to use and handle, and weights a quarter as much as wet food.

If one considers the industry in general, this segmentation remains fluid if not volatile. Consumers may vary their purchases during the year by going from one segment to the other, so much so that the main market remains for the most part the dry food market. This is particularly true for the dog market. With the exception of veterinary clinics and the hard discount area, products from the different market segments can be seen side by side on the shelves of the same stores.

CHANGING HOW SOCIETY LOOKS AT PET AND MASTER

Royal Canin's core business model, which spans three nutritional market segments, is unique to the pet food industry. As the 1990's drew to a close, these competitors, especially American companies, looked on, not without some irony and a fair deal of skepticism, as Royal Canin announced that its product philosophy such as size and breed diets, would soon set the trend for the world pet food market. Subsequently, albeit with quite a bit of catching-up to do, the world's leading pet food companies would change course and adopt classifications set up by a small regional European company: for example a weight typology for dogs going from Mini breeds (2–10 kg, or 4–20 lbs) to Giant breeds (above 55 kg; or 120 lbs). This is all the more ironic when one considers that the idea for this nutritional revolution came from an American, Stan Howton, formerly chairman of Royal Canin USA.

Just as Toyota had transformed complexity into opportunity, the Royal Canin brand expanded formulations and targeted diets in a remarkable industrial and logistical symphony based on Lean Production and Make to Order practices none of its competitors has yet been able to duplicate. It allows specialized distribution to fully differentiate from supermarkets and mass merchandisers.

In 1997, two brand new lines for cats and dogs were launched within the framework of the size concept. In 1998, the company introduced the first program for spayed and neutered cats. That same year, a new product for cats incorporated five technological breakthroughs: anti-aging complex (fighting free radicals), immunity boosters, tailor-made cat kibble shapes, variations in kibble hardness depending on the cat's age, and nutrients to regenerate skin and hair. In 1999, a food line for Persian cats was the first worldwide product to take a breed's physiological specifics into account.[8] In 1999, product lines for dogs and cats targeting veterinary clinics were still created with three objectives: to feed and cure sick pets, to feed and protect at-risk pets – such as the very young or old – and to feed and care for healthy pets and purebreds. In 2000, a nutritional product for dogs even addressed, for the first time, giant breeds of 45 to 100 kg, as well as considering their allergy risks and digestion problems. Specific innovative products have continued to be launched, such as special kibble for indoor cats, which reduce stool odors or risks of hairball vomiting or weight gain. The development of specifically targeted pet food is on the rise.[9]

Targeting also looks to change owners' attitudes. The majority of cats do not find a home as a result of careful planning by their master or as a result of a commercial transaction involving a breeder. More often than not, cats are acquired as gifts from a friend who happens to be moving or are picked from the litter of a neighbor's cat on a whim. However, Royal Canin encouraged the creation of true breeding markets for pedigree cats that certified purebreds. When buying a pet as the result of a rational decision, owners are more aware of its health and nutritional needs. They are also more likely to choose a specific breed in tune with their own temperament and expectations.[10]

American and European grocery stores do not have the capacity to customize and give advice on highly innovative and targeted products. The best they can do is to offer a few pre-sold and therefore pre-selected products. Royal Canin has a different marketing approach. It persuades key influencers, such as veterinarians and other experts, that the market segmentation demanded by consumers and the increasing complexity of the market provide product differentiation opportunities that only they are capable of introducing and explaining. That buyers, as the pets' owners, will be so thrilled to see that the specific needs of their cats or dogs are not only taken into account but embraced that they will be prepared and even happy to pay a much higher price for its very specific nutritional diets. Considering that a pet given balanced and nutritional food needs less food than a pet fed on traditional products, owners see that Royal Canin, by comparison, offers an affordable and quite reasonably priced product. It should be noted that a cat on a diet of healthy and nutritional products will live on average three years longer than a cat on a traditional diet.

From 1993 to 2005, Royal Canin's overall sales growth was on average 13.2% per year and its CAGR (cumulated annual growth rate) in nutritional products was 31.2%. This was by far a world record, and was achieved in spite of the transfer in July 2002 of 25.1% of its sales (and of its EBIT) to a Spanish company at the request of the European Commission in Brussels during the acquisition of Royal Canin by American company Mars. The company has produced a dizzying array of innovative products: during the six-year period from 1997 to 2003, more than 85% of its sales in nutritional products were consistently realized with products that had less than 24 months' presence on the market. This percentage did not start to diminish until 2004, as a result of the increasing importance of veterinarians who strongly desire stability in product lines. It should be noted that in 10 years (1993–2004), sales in veterinary clinics have gone from 0.9% to 31.5%

of all sales, while at the same time cat food sales went from 1.7% to 31%. All these products were 100% health nutrition diets. In addition to accelerated innovation, it is important to consider the make-up of the pet food field. To implement a prescriptive approach to nutrition implies a massive increase of technical skills, from cynotechnicians to technical sales representatives and veterinary delegates.

AN UNORTHODOX MARKETING STYLE

Royal Canin does its marketing without marketers, well almost. The department known as marketing only has six associates. According to the company's philosophy, no one group should have control of this function and marketing should certainly not be conferred solely to marketing experts. There is no specific product marketing position in the sales network nor in the factories. No particular executive manages the brand.

The client, or the pet, and the key influencer or the specialized distributor should be everyone's concern, from R&D to delivery people. The responsibility for marketing, whether strategic or in the field, should be shared by each associate and should be the collective business of the entire staff. Not one single person should have exclusive ownership of company information, opportunity identification, competitor monitoring, access to the client, or image and brand communication. Royal Canin's executives smile ironically whenever their competitors hire so-called marketing wizards. By rejecting pet food marketers and their jargon and procedures, the company reinforced its sense of identity.

Royal Canin does not perform any surveys of dog and cat owners' consumer habits. The company refuses to find out if going from wet to dry food or from traditional to nutritional food changes the owner's and the pet's image, or if the purchase of health products can be explained by consumers going to their veterinarian instead of to their pet shop. No statistical data is used to determine if the Royal Canin brand stands out among its competitors. To work on the basis of prescribing products that promote health and well-being, it is assumed that supermarket buying habits do not offer any useful insight on buyer purchasing habits in a specialized store.

Royal Canin does not conform to any of the communication principles that its competitors follow. For instance, it spends a negligible amount of its budget on mass media advertising campaigns. The only country in which the company funds televised advertising is France, and this is for admittedly historical and sentimental reasons.

Nevertheless, internal and external communication, combined with extensive training, is considered a priority. For instance, every Tuesday, associates receive on their laptops a weekly training quiz that allows them to update their knowledge about pets. The company also issues numerous books with the support of world-class academics from veterinary departments: thick and comprehensive encyclopedias on pets (4 million copies and published in 15 languages), guidebooks on canine and feline breeding, nutrient guides, academic and professional publications for veterinarians and breeders, deluxe technical brochures on each breed targeted by a specific diet. Publications also include *FOCUS*, a scientific quarterly that appears in 11 languages and reaches 70,000 veterinarians around the world, and 1,450 Waltham-Royal Canin veterinary publications (compared with the almost 400 publications from the company's closest competitor). Four million pages are visited every month on its website. The *Royal Canin Magazine* is distributed several times a year to buyers and specialized distributors.

Technical books and professional journals add to Royal Canin's quest for integrity and reputation. They create leadership in the business. They induce real proximity with pets and exceptional communication with key influencers. The chairman, chief operating officer, and management team are directly involved in handling this written communication policy. They dialogue with specialists and invest much time upgrading their level of knowledge about scientific matters dealing with pets.

Royal Canin has developed close relationships with many professional veterinary schools in France, Europe, the United States, Canada, and South America. It co-finances some of their research projects. Some of the scientists subsequently join the company. It also invests in technical functionalities. To work with leading pet experts is a matter of priority. Whenever a new breed-specific diet is to be introduced, a technical meeting is held with the breed's top international professionals. The first line of external communication is managed in the field by the technical sales force. Substantial budgets are invested around the world in the technical training of sales representatives and veterinary assistants. In each country veterinary delegate teams, which sometimes number over 70 people, are specifically dedicated to professionals. In Europe, Royal Canin sponsors or is active in 3,500 dog shows and 400 cat shows each year. In France for instance, 35 cynotechnicians work with 4,000 dog breeders and 400 clubs. A "Feline Club" is open to more than 2,000 breeders. Superstore employees get training from Royal Canin's staff.

The distribution center is a key concept in the company's business network. The idea is that vendors and delivery people should behave as entrepreneurs. Given that one of the competitive advantages of the nutrition industry is its capacity not only to educate but also to train breeders and specialized retailers, and to deliver products to them within 24 hours' notice, proximity to customers really matters. Retailers are served through distribution centers. In France, there are 15 such centers. Each one receives trucks loaded with pallets that are then split into smaller quantities to be delivered to the point of sale. The distribution center's role goes beyond simple logistics. Marketing products is considered as part of the normal job of each of its associates, whether trainers, commercial inspectors, pet technicians, merchandisers, or telemarketers.

MOBILIZING A MORAL COMMUNITY

Royal Canin numbers around 2,600 employees worldwide. Nevertheless it has no formal organization chart. It also makes a point of not creating job descriptions.

A non-bureaucracy

The company functions with an executive committee of a dozen people. Every member personally assumes operational tasks and spends the majority of his or her time in the field, in one of the 75 subsidiaries, 10 factories, and so on. Their seniority in the company and in their position is unusually high for this industry: often more than 10 years, if not 20.

Within the executive committee, the working language is French. However at the local level only the native language of the country is used. Supporting local languages is motivated by respect for associates and local cultures. Local meetings take place in Chinese in China, Portuguese in Brazil or Thai in Thailand. It is up to the executives who work abroad to learn the local language within six months of their arrival. One consequence is that the company boasts a cohort of associates in their thirties and forties who, having worked in several countries, speak three to seven languages fluently.

A campus built on the original Aimargues site houses the R&D department, dog and cat kennels, and the pilot factory. All formulations used in the company's factories are established and managed by central R&D, with the support of the laboratories hosted in the various production sites located around the world.

The central industrial team, consisting of only two managers, directly supervises the ten plant directors and oversees any new plant design: namely compact, on line, and very flexible factories. There is no engineering and design department. These two executives are also in charge of investment planning.

The strategic marketing team decides on product launches and coordination. It is headed by a manager with the support of five professionals who are experts in dog breeding, cat breeding, and veterinary studies.

Royal Canin scrupulously abides by the principle of a flat management structure. Even in the biggest factory, there are no more than three levels of management: a plant director, two team leaders, one HR manager, one "technologist," and the shop-floor associates.

Decentralizing execution to each market and allocating initiative to each operational unit are underlying action principles. Versatility and accountability are the order of the day. No central staff specialist is allowed to directly interfere with a factory's activities. Moreover, the company does not have any quality director or department, or any department responsible for new investments. And as for business subsidiaries, they constitute simple integrated units to the extent that they are given monthly information about their real industrial cost prices (raw materials, factory costs and logistics) and margins, which they incorporate into their respective vertical operating accounts. No transfer prices being negotiated, no conflict should occur between industry and marketing and sales. Profits are all-inclusive. They symbolically belong to everyone. Factories as well as marketing and sales are mere cost centers. Profits are known only in geographical terms.

Community integration takes on many forms. For example, the company does not call upon external consultants, with the exception of three people, who have been working with Royal Canin for 10–25 years and who intervene only on industrial matters such as investment, training, and employee relations. Elsewhere, elitist training such as an MBA is not considered a guarantee of competence as far as executives are concerned – quite the contrary. In this light, the CEO was able to reject many tempting external growth opportunities, despite their being profitable, because, as he stated, managing the acquired corporation would force him to step outside, albeit partially, the Royal Canin philosophy.

This explains why in an 11-year span, the four highly targeted external growth operations the company has realized only make up 3%, 1%, 2% and 7% of sales, thus allowing Royal Canin to rapidly and efficiently integrate its acquisitions. The merger of its British competitor, James Wellbeloved, with Royal Canin's British subsidiary in the UK in 2000 took less than two years and involved no personnel loss. The same for Lawler in Argentina, Vet's Choice in South Africa, Medi Cal in Canada, and IVD in the United States.

A common mission and vision

"A person who understands and shares Royal Canin's vision and philosophy is more valuable than the most brilliant of our executives." This statement may seem a little provocative but hardly an exaggeration when describing management styles and leadership practices. The company's ethics influences every employee.

Indicators measuring personnel morale are high. Staff members are loyal to the company and resignations are rare. The annual turnover rate is less than 1%. The integration of newcomers is carefully handled so that they become familiar with the culture of the company. Cooperation between departments is intense.

Senior managers spend much time imparting the vision to staff, transcending in a way the company mission, and a sense of urgency. Over an eight-year period, Henri Lagarde and Alain Guillemin have made 120 to 140 presentations a year on their vision and strategy – to associates, veterinarians, and other business or academic partners all around the world. The more the company structures itself on a federal model, the more it is vital that its associates and partners understand and share a common destiny blueprint. "The company has a vision and it is this vision that brings people together. Joining Royal Canin is like joining a religious congregation," states one of its senior executives. Passion is preached. Associates should be driven by moral virtues and behavioral duties such as strategic courage, solidarity, humility, local footholds, and collective values.

The figure of Epaminondas symbolizes courage. This general of Thebes headed a small army in 371 BC and routed the rival Spartans at the battle of Leuctres. The Spartan army, which was three times as big, was considered invincible. The general's unexpected success was due to the fact he had defined and shared his vision with his soldiers. He also had the courage to concentrate his thin manpower on a single front, his left flank, at the expense of the rest of his forces. His unwavering determination to breach the enemy's ranks was critical in leading his army to victory.

Solidarity means unfailing mutual support among associates. It also implies avoiding unnecessary paperwork and red tape. Long-term interpersonal relationships are encouraged while cliques and private turfs are discouraged. Senior managers make constant reference to a social psychologist, Moreno, who had studied American bomber pilots in 1943 and 1944. He wondered why there was a very high disparity in combat performance among fighter squadrons, the most successful in their missions enduring four times fewer losses than their counterparts. The reason was that these pilots were neither supermen nor exceptional fighters; they had simply been together in the same squadron for a longer time, they had always lived together, they needed only short briefings before their missions, they did not often use radio in the air to communicate with their comrades. In other words, well-knit communities perform miracles, even with ordinary people. Royal Canin associates label themselves the "Moreno Squadron."

Respect for individuals and their problems is another value promoted by management. Even modest employees deserve to be treated with consideration and as unique, the same as any company partner or end client who has a right to have his demands heard. Any incident or failure must be dealt with not as a potential conflict, but as an opportunity to improve the company. As far as directors are concerned, all problems, even the most insignificant ones, are to be handled, for they induce learning processes. The ability to publicly recognize its errors is considered legitimate, desirable and of great help.

In a global economy, a company draws its strengths and consistency from local roots. Such identity factors are carefully reinforced and legitimized. The fact that a factory located in a rural part of southern France has become international and calls the tune of the business is a challenge and a source of pride.

Quality as a shared value

True nutritional quality raises two issues. Some products are rather complicated to produce. For example, where a mainstream pet food contains 15 to 25 basic nutrients, a health nutrition diet contains at least 50 to 60 nutrients in very balanced doses, or even micro-doses. Diet differentiations require expensive raw materials. If the cost of a tonne of raw material to produce mainstream dry pet food is $100, a health nutrition diet costs $400 in raw materials, and a breed-specific diet from $500 to $900, even though prices of the latter are no more than 20% to 30% higher than normal health nutrition pet food. The cost ratio of ingredients goes from one to nine. That clearly suggests the tangibility of the offer.

Strong commitments have to be upheld. Senior managers do not tolerate any cheating on marketing, whatever the circumstances. Complexity is considered a unique opportunity for differentiation. Old management recipes such as Fordism and Taylorism just do not make sense, in manufacturing as well as in distribution.

Product quality and pet well-being must be every employee's permanent focus, regardless of his or her post. Lagarde set the tone. Whenever new products were designed, he dived into the specifications. Even though he is not an expert on nutrition, he personally took part in writing targeted technical brochures, in researching nutritional information, or in getting advice from veterinarians, technicians, distributors, delegates, and vendors he came across.

Quality insurance procedures designed to deal with incidents occurring in the field were suppressed when a dog died at a breeder's kennel.[11] The very same day, all procedural documents and examination guides on quality claims and incidents in which pets died were eliminated from the company. From that point onwards, any client claiming that a Royal Canin product caused illness or death of his animal, regardless of whether the client was right or wrong, had to be dealt with immediately and be treated with the utmost importance. A few months later, the CEO, his wife, and a felinotechnician had lunch at the breeder's home. This incident has gained myth-like status. Everyone in the company views it as a badge of belonging to a community that distinguishes itself from its rivals.

This organizational model helps Royal Canin reach a time to market for new products of less than seven months. And the more the company designs multiple and sophisticated products, the more it picks up the pace. Making sophistication, efficiency, and reactivity compatible facilitates the production of medium and small run products and the marketing of wide-ranging and specific product lines.

The company is skilled at managing lean production methods and at total quality control. In a matter of a few years, and despite the massive increase in product volume, the length of packaging lines in the main French factory has been reduced from 280 to 90 yards. All its factories around the world follow lean production principles. There are never more than four days of raw-material inventories and never more than one to two and a half days of finished-product inventories which are located in the factory premises. Royal Canin does not have any finished-product warehouse, except those in factory premises, it works only on a made-to-order basis. Manufacturing costs in Royal Canin's factories, outside of raw materials, are 30% to 50% lower than its competitors. Logistics, inventories, and reactiveness fit the requirements of an ideal Toyota-style approach.

THE NEXT STAGE

In July 2001, Paribas sold Royal Canin to Mars for more than 1.5 billion euros.[12] Obviously a good marking creates value. This figure of 1.5 billion euros, while the net asset value was only 109 million euros, meant that the goodwill paid by the purchaser, in other words, the value creation, represented 93% of the total value. Royal Canin was purchased by Mars at 22.3 times its EBITDA (earnings before interest, taxes and depreciation), a ratio to be compared with a multiple of 18.7 for Purina when it was bought by Nestlé at the end of 2000, and of 14.2 for Iams/Eukanuba when purchased by Procter & Gamble.[13]

Following recommendations by the Boston Consulting Group, Mars decided to keep its two pet food business divisions separate: its Masterfoods brands (Pedigree, Whiskas, Sheba and Canigou), which are sold mainly in grocery stores and mass-market retail stores, with some specialized points of sale; and Royal Canin, which targets key influencers (veterinarians and breeders) and specialized points of sale.

Lagarde remained in command on the condition that he could keep his management team and apply his policies. The Mars family endorsed them and gave him strategic and operational leeway. Only three executives from each corporation – Masterfoods and Royal Canin – were to have regular contact with each other. Any other information or comparative data exchanges had to receive their approval ahead of time. Marketing objectives became even more ambitious: 20% sales growth and 25% EBIT growth.

The American market was given top priority. Since 1989, Royal Canin had been part of a nutritional market dominated by brands such as Hill's (Colgate Palmolive) and Iams and Eukanuba (Procter & Gamble), and controlled by powerful pet superstore chains such as Petsmart and Petco. But it was not a major player. It had inherited an unclear marketing position with six different traditional brands and was suffering from me-too marketing products and strategy. In 2002, senior management convinced its American subsidiary to embrace its vision and to gradually focus only on health nutrition. Subsequently its development has become quite remarkable, propelled by the development of veterinary products, major specialized chains, and breed-specific diets. This new approach has gained the confidence of gatekeepers in the veterinary and breeding communities. It also allows specialized distribution to offer unique products that are highly differentiated from those sold by grocery stores and mass distributors. Such diets make a lot of sense to owners of particular breeds of dogs ("that's for my dog") and make a difference that is visible within two or three weeks (healthier coat, better digestion).

Because they attract clients with a high awareness of nutrition and who seek advice, veterinary clinics become main strategic targets. Up until 1996, Royal Canin had looked at veterinarians as just one profit center among many others. It sold them only three products. A new approach enlarged this product range, making it more targeted and efficient. Even though these new lines were not immediately profitable for Royal Canin, they included 10 to 15 different diets for cats and dogs.

The basic vision sponsored by Lagarde is that the 21st century will be the century of health, thus the century of doctors and veterinarians. By 2015, 90% of pets will be brought to a veterinary clinic at least once a year and 20% will feed on products purchased in this distribution channel. Therefore Royal Canin should from now on offer a veritable service to veterinarians and their patients, specifically pets.

Royal Canin refuses to use veterinarians as mouthpieces and key influencers to subsequently promote identical or equivalent products that "experts" endorse at points of sale. This practice, which is very popular with some leading competitors in the United States, causes veterinarians to fall into disrepute in the long term. From the client's point of view, they go from being "doctors" to simple salespeople "like any corner pet shop." Therefore, the company proposes a strong and enduring alliance based on specific diets and services, strengthening efficiency, image, and the veterinarian's special status.

Veterinary clinics should account for 30% to 40% of Royal Canin's total sales, up from 0.9% in 1993. The company is on the way to becoming the leader in Europe, where the area of dietetic pet food sold by veterinarians has traditionally been dominated by Hill's with over 60% of the market. In March 2004, it acquired Medi Cal, uncontested leader in services and diet sales to veterinary clinics in Canada, and IVD, a veterinary provider found in more than two-thirds of the 18,000 veterinary clinics in the United States.

As announced in early 2003, Lagarde resigned his position as chairman of the corporation at the end of June 2004. The COO, Alain Guillemin, took the job of chairman and CEO.

Royal Canin keeps outdoing initial forecasts. An annual sales volume of one billion dollars had been met by February 2005. Its internal growth is bordering on 20%, even in markets such as Europe where it already has leading shares. The pet market is increasing in value. Since the middle of the 1990's, dry nutritional pet food in Europe's main markets has enjoyed an average total growth of 8% to 15% per year. Royal Canin's expansion in this market from 1993 to the end of 2004 has equalled 31.2% per year. The time is not far off when nutritional dry pet food sold in specialized distribution circuits will overtake in value and volume sales in supermarkets and mass-market channels. Furthermore, cats, food for which requires less space in stores and less marketing attention, may well overtake dogs in popularity.

3

REACTIVE MARKING:
THE WAL-MART WAY

Despite the fact that the Wal-Mart saga has been extensively covered by the press, the media and management books, there is still much to learn from its business model and its approach of the market and society. Its marking approach is quite different from the Royal Canin posture. No major societal innovation, no invention in management techniques, no new territory building, but near perfection in embedding itself into already existing territories, and in assembling widely used marking tools and functions.

BORROWING MARKING CONCEPTS AND TOOLS FROM COMPETITORS

The first Wal-Mart store opened in July 1962 in Rogers, Arkansas. For the fiscal year ending January 31, 2006, Wal-Mart reported sales revenues of $312 billion and 1.7 million employees. Moving from the U.S. backwaters into the world's largest retailer is, by all standards, an amazing story. What is flabbergasting is, this was achieved by a company that was an imitator-follower in terms of retail concepts and was a late entrant in all the sub-sectors it now operates in – and frequently dominates: discount retail department stores; hypermarkets (which Wal-Mart calls Supercenters); warehouse clubs; and more recently, supermarkets (Neighborhood Markets to Wal-Mart). Borrowing ideas rather than being creative never bothered Sam Walton. He was not ashamed to admit that just about everything he'd done in his career he'd copied from somebody else (Slater 2004).

Companies and brands have their iconic tales – examples that have become indispensable references or benchmarks. They often reveal such obvious tactics that you wonder why nobody had thought of it before. They also illustrate substantial financial achievements. They suggest that innovation and niche-building strategies do not provide the only sources of lasting economic success. To be a follower and to act in a business crowded with competitors may also become winning strategies. They just require excellence in implementing existing marking approaches.

One such living legend is Wal-Mart. In less than 30 years it has become the world's No. 1 company and an American business icon. What is distinctive about Wal-Mart was, and remains, its ability to imitate established strategies. To exploit their gaps and deficiencies, but also to implement them more thoroughly, consistently, and originally than anyone else. Sam Walton used "excellence-in-execution" and "retail is detail" as key corporate competencies to beat the competition.[1]

After graduating from college he joined J.C. Penney as a trainee, at the age of 22. He was very impressed by a visit to the store from the company's owner, James Cash Penney, who taught him how to use the smallest amount of ribbon possible to tie a package that would still look attractive. Walton learned two major lessons from his apprenticeship years. Top management's involvement in the field is of crucial importance, which implies that headquarters should not be secluded in fancy executive suites. The other lesson relates to common sense, a notion that large and successful competitors often neglected to conform to: cost efficiency does not only matter, it makes the difference.

Walton served in World War II as a captain in the U.S. Army Intelligence Corps. This experience helped reinforce some personal values that would later become Wal-Mart corporate values: accurate and precise information is key for the success of any human or economic venture; rivals and competitors must be observed persistently, to understand their strengths and weaknesses and to guide your own behavior; leaders' involvement in the field is not a waste of time or merely a symbolic gesture occasionally made to rank-and-file personnel, it is a virtuous factor for efficient policy-making; clear, simple rules, backed by rituals that reinforce a sense of company identity, are key managerial mechanisms and employee incentives.

In the aftermath of World War II, when the consumer age was taking off, Walton decided to open his own store. He bought his first Ben Franklin franchise in Newport, Arkansas with $20,000 borrowed from his wife, Helen's, father. In four years he had turned it into the top Ben Franklin franchise in Arkansas.

Sam Walton had no predetermined ideas about retailing and he spent a lot of time observing rivals and working on the floor in his stores. Borrowing ideas from others never bothered him at all. But he also was quick to feel constrained by Ben Franklin's rather autocratic vision of franchising, in which franchisees were told what merchandise to sell and at what prices. In 1949, he lost the lease on the Newport store and was for a while tempted to move to a bigger city. But his wife insisted on living in a small town. So Walton bought another Ben Franklin franchise in Bentonville, Arkansas, a town that would become the cradle of the future Wal-Mart empire. Thirteen years later, Sam Walton was operating sixteen franchise stores. He had become one of the largest independent variety store operators in the U.S.

Ben Franklin franchises were five-and-dime stores. As a retailer selling general merchandise at moderate prices, Sam Walton became convinced that there was a future for merchandising in small towns. He also believed that people in small communities shouldn't have to pay more for merchandise than large city dwellers. But was the variety store approach really the right answer? He increasingly had doubts. He'd felt that the old variety store was missing the point with its 45% mark-ups, limited selection and limited opening hours (Walton 1992). He became convinced that the future for his business was in discounting, not in five-and-dimes (Slater 2004).

A major explanation for such a change in his beliefs was his observation of the growth of discounting. In fact, discount stores had emerged in the U.S. in the 1950's. They were selling general merchandise items with gross margins that were 10% to 15% lower than those conventional department stores were accustomed to. To compensate, discount stores cut costs to the bone, with the help of un-luxurious fixtures, self-service, and scarce ancillary services. By the 1960's, discount retailing was burgeoning. Its sales were growing at a compound annual rate of 25%.

Sam Walton was feeling threatened by discounters. He began to travel extensively around the country, checking out how they were doing. He concluded they were paving the way to the future. Walton's major concern was that, once the urban areas were under their control, discounters might set up business in rural areas. To survive as a businessman, he felt that he should react quickly.

A DEEPER AND BROADER DISCOUNT OFFER

Too small and too poor to take on discount retailing giants head-on, Sam Walton decided to maintain his focus first and foremost on rural areas. After his idea of opening discount stores in such locations was turned down by Ben Franklin, he and his brother Bud opened the first "Wal-Mart Discount City" on July 2, 1962 in Rogers, Arkansas. To set up this store, Sam Walton co-signed the lease with his wife, providing 95% of the investment. Though heavily in debt, he pursued his vision. For years, while he kept launching new Wal-Mart stores, Walton continued to run various Ben Franklin stores, gradually phasing them out by 1976.

Sam Walton structured his approach around one policy: to offer his customers low prices across a large spectrum of good-quality general merchandise. This was made possible by a marked reduction of gross margins. He generated profits by lowering operating costs dramatically. In this early stage, Sam Walton thus acted as his own distribution center. He traveled in his pickup, driving miles to suppliers and returning to his store with a loaded truck.

When it came to store merchandising, Sam Walton was truly experimental, what he called "fiddling and meddling." He defined his way of handling merchandising as that of a maverick who enjoys shaking things up and creating a little anarchy. This clearly meant that it was all right to be wrong at times, errors being used as opportunities or acceptable costs in trying to increase profit.

Another major engine of his merchandising strategy was to be distinctive from other retailers. If everybody else is doing it *this* way, why don't we try to do it *that* way? Walton was very much in favor of eschewing the well-trodden path in favor of the road not taken. Challenging the status quo was part of his usual way of doing things and he was constantly instilling that posture in Wal-Mart's operations and corporate culture. Sam Walton was once described as spending his every waking moment trying to outthink, outwork, and outperform his competition (Bergdahl 2004).

And luckily the competition let him develop discounting in small towns because they initially thought this focus was foolish and economically suicidal. If established retailers had followed Wal-Mart in those small communities, they probably would have pulverized his initiative, since he had so little experience and few resources. But they let him invade these "one-horse" towns at his own pace. They realized his success too late (Slater 2004).

However, Walton was concerned that other retailers would sooner or later wake up and identify small towns as a new frontier to conquer. He therefore decided to build up as many stores as he could. But he was not a pure expansionist. In his own words, Walton wanted just to be "the best, not the biggest." His basic motivation was to protect his turf from those who were stronger. By 1969, he was able to raise enough money to open 32 stores in north-western Arkansas, later expanding into Oklahoma, Missouri and Louisiana. But in spite of impressive growth, Wal-Mart was dissatisfied by the high costs of making its sales, a fact that Sam Walton attributed in part to distributors not being attracted to serve Wal-Mart, which was located in the "boondocks," as efficiently as competitors in larger towns. According to Sam, "the only alternative was to build our own warehouse so we could buy in volume at attractive prices and store the merchandise" (Rudnitsky 1982). Since warehouses, at $5 million or more a piece, were capital intensive, in October 1970 Walton took the company public, raising $3.3 million (Bradley 1994).

BE THE BEST IN IMPLEMENTATION

Wal-Mart's business model was powerful, right from the start, because it relentlessly pursued and combined three objectives: extreme cost efficiency, distinctive competitive positioning, and employee dedication to building outstanding customer value.

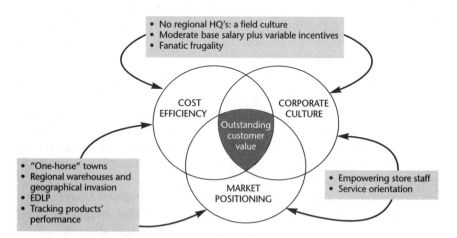

FIGURE 3.1 **The three disciplines of value-building at Wal-Mart**

The cornerstone: cost efficiency

Wal-Mart's ability to lower its costs is a result of multiple strategic and operational postures and choices.

The concentration on rural areas led, off the block, to lower real estate costs than competitors. For instance, in 1990, Wal-Mart's property rental costs equaled 0.8% of its sales, versus 2.5% for other discounters. Logistical efficiency was achieved from 1970 on through a "hub-and-spoke" system of store expansion, whereby stores were clustered around warehouses, one distribution center ideally serving 150 surrounding stores. Wal-Mart would not move to a new geographical area before saturating the previous one. The sheer number of stores in a given area led to market dominance in quantitative terms.

In addition to such a territorial density of stores and proximity to local infrastructure such as suppliers' warehouses and factories allow Wal-Mart to optimize transportation costs. Delivery trucks, for instance, are on average 60% full on backhaul trips. Frequent deliveries also reduce reliance on backroom inventory. Store space can be used productively – for selling, not for stocking.

Logistical excellence is helped along by Wal-Mart's emphasis on information availability and thoroughness. Scanning at point-of-sale allows for sophisticated tracking of product movement, enabling immediate corrective action to be taken whenever needed. The technological innovations that permit such fine-tuned merchandise management are welcome. It is interesting to note that Wal-Mart first used scanning soon after its stores took off, in the late 1970's. But when the company reintroduced the practice in 1983, it did it better, faster, and more intensely than others.

Information is also the grist for Wal-Mart's relationships with its suppliers. By the late 1980's it had installed vendor-managed inventory systems, whereby suppliers could replenish Wal-Mart stores and warehouses without formal reorders from Wal-Mart. Every evening, Wal-Mart would transmit store sales data to participating suppliers, along with data on its warehouse inventories. This system enables suppliers to produce to order rather than to inventory. It offers a win–win solution, decreasing the suppliers' as well as Wal-Mart's costs. Inbound materials often spent no time in inventory: through cross-docking, high rotation merchandise was delivered to warehouses, immediately repacked, and dispatched to stores.

In 1990, the sophistication of its information sharing with suppliers moved one step further. Wal-Mart introduced Retail Link, giving more than 2,000 suppliers direct computer access to its point-of-sale data. This also simplified administrative tasks, as about two-thirds of its suppliers began invoicing electronically, with many also introducing EFT (electronic funds transfer).

All of this information sharing does not imply, however, that Wal-Mart was not, or is not, a tough negotiator. Like all major retailers around the world, Wal-Mart's purchasing economies of scale are key to its overall cost efficiency and success. Yet Wal-Mart is unique in one way. Unlike its competitors, it does not rely purely on volume purchasing. The company has always made a point of carrying all of its suppliers' major brands, refusing to exclude brands with high consumer awareness just because their suppliers would not initially offer them at low enough prices. Wal-Mart prefers to pay a little more and continue selling such products. Besides the major advantage of creating store traffic, stocking popular brands also gives Wal-Mart more commercial leverage. This strategy also allows it to play leading brands off against each other, and sooner or later to get better purchasing prices.

Other strategies contribute to its cost efficiency. Labor costs are relatively low compared with competitors, because of the lower salaries paid in rural areas. Wal-Mart also has a policy of recruiting young people fresh out of college, reducing wages further, and makes very effective use of part-time staff.

Wal-Mart advertising expenses are much lower than those of other discounters. This is linked to its overall EDLP, or "everyday low prices," claim. In fact, most other retailers spend vast sums of money advertising their promotions. Promotions being by definition much less numerous with an EDLP positioning, this further reduces the advertising tab.

Last but not least, its control–costs ideology and company practices that some see as stingy naturally feed savings. Examples are numerous. Its Bentonville headquarters are rudimentary, and it does without regional headquarters. Traveling is no alibi for fancy expenses, to the point that managers often share hotel rooms. Overheads are stripped down to a minimum.

But no matter how essential it was as the basis of the Wal-Mart business model, that amazing cost efficiency alone would not have been enough to make it such a retail star, one that vacuumed up early discount retailers. In fact, not one of America's top 10 discounters operating in 1962 remained in 1993. Large companies like King's, Korvette's, Mammoth Mart, W.T. Grant, Two Guys, and Woolco either went under or were sold to more successful competitors.

The winning proposition: a distinctive positioning

Although saving money through low prices is a key driver in bringing shoppers to a discount store, Wal-Mart believes this must be part of a larger package of benefits – such as, among other things, product quality, variety, and availability or well-tuned customer service skills. These benefits are means to achieving an ultimate objective: satisfaction guaranteed. Truisms like "everything we've done since we started Wal-Mart has been devoted to the idea that the customer is our boss" and "we've never doubted that the customer comes ahead of everything" became dogmas at Wal-Mart.

Applying this objective in rural areas and small towns gave those local populations unprecedented easy access to consumption. This could be viewed as Wal-Mart's real societal and political input to America's economic fabric.

But how did Wal-Mart bring value to its target customers beyond just low prices?

It first boosted the quality of its merchandise assortment by always carrying major national brands and keeping its personal label, on average, at below 30% of total sales volume. This gave shoppers a variety and choice that was more appealing than competitors' offerings.

Inasmuch as is possible in a discounting environment, Wal-Mart also has a definite service orientation. An example is the greeters operating at the store entrance. Its extensive opening hours are also appreciated by the local community. A no-questions-asked return policy smoothes over problems and indicates how much the company trusts its clients. These benefits, provided at the lowest prices – EDLP – lead to outstanding value for money for targeted customers.

Those rock-bottom prices were, from the start, the results of cost efficiencies that allowed Wal-Mart to operate on much lower gross margins than other discounters and still be more profitable. For instance, Wal-Mart's gross margin amounted to about 22% of sales in 1990, whereas it amounted to more than 29% of sales in the rest of the discount retail industry. How did this ultimately translate into a price advantage over the competition? A study in the mid-1980's showed that, where Wal-Mart and Kmart were located next to each other, Wal-Mart's prices were roughly 1% lower. Where Wal-Mart, Kmart, and Target stores were separated from each other by around four miles, Wal-Mart's average prices were 10.4% lower. When they were distant by six miles, its prices were 7.6% cheaper. But in remote locations, where it had no direct competition from large discounters, its prices were 6% higher than if it were next to Kmart (Bradley 1994). But even then, Wal-Mart's prices were far lower than those of the mom-and-pop shops that were operating locally before its arrival.

Another element also boosts the stores' appeal. Store managers and store department managers are encouraged to adapt merchandise and prices to their local environment. This is micro-marketing at its best, beginning probably even before the word was invented. Embedding its stores in the specificities of local markets and communities was linked with what Walton called Q.M.I., or Quick Market Intelligence. To get valuable intelligence, he pushed his managers to constantly visit rival stores, as he did himself. When he found an item priced lower than at Wal-Mart, Walton phoned the nearest store manager and had him or her immediately undercut the price (Slater 2004).

The outstanding value proposition Wal-Mart offered its target shoppers had an extraordinary effect on store traffic. In the early 1990's, its stores' space productivity, measured by sales per square foot, was 2.5 times greater than Target's and 3.5 times greater than Kmart's. Space productivity in turn generated economies of scale at store level.

To sum up, Wal-Mart's original business model, still largely adhered to today, was not a conceptual revolution. It was much closer to a significant, imaginative, ambitious implementation of the discount retailing model invented by competitors. This incremental step toward excellence in implementation had quite a few relevant dimensions. Wal-Mart's assortments were made more appealing by including major national brands. Its stores introduced a service dimension to discount retailing. The price differential with traditional retailers was vastly increased. Communication was immensely simplified through the EDLP claim. Stores were empowered to fight their local battles in their local environments. While Wal-Mart did not invent any alternative approach, it showed unusual competence in two ways. It was particularly good in activating the virtual loop of discounting, and it constantly tried to broaden its core expertise and to apply it to other discounting battlefields. In this case, the road was paved with trial and error.

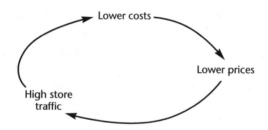

FIGURE 3.2 **The virtuous loop of discounting**

Widening the discounting spectrum

In fact, Wal-Mart has been testing several new formats since the early 1980's – very much in an experimental spirit, the company being clearly not willing to content itself with the status quo. It opened the first three Sam's Clubs in 1983 and soon after began opening Dot Deep Discount drugstores and Helen's Arts and Crafts stores. By 1990, those last two formats had been discontinued and sold off. In 1987, Wal-Mart opened its first Hypermart USA, a format borrowed from the French hypermarket concept of large, self-service, discount, combined grocery and variety stores. Wal-Mart later dropped the hypermarket concept in favor of smaller Supercenters.

In 1990, Wal-Mart acquired the Texan McLane Company, a grocery wholesale distributor, to service its Supercenters. It also bought Western Merchandisers, a wholesale distributor of music CDs, videos, and books. And on top of external growth, it developed a chain of closeout stores called Bud's. About 75% of Bud's merchandise was Wal-Mart surplus merchandise, the rest was closeout goods shipped directly from vendors.

But its major successes in terms of format diversification are its Sam's Clubs and Supercenters. Whereas Sam's Clubs peaked very rapidly, through a mix of organic growth and acquisitions, Supercenters would become the major vehicle of Wal-Mart's expansion after 1992.

Pioneered by a company and a brand called Price Club, warehouse clubs rely on high-volume, low-cost merchandising to leverage their buying power and minimize handling costs, and pass their savings on to their members. Since their inception by Wal-Mart, Sam's Clubs have offered a limited number of SKU's, or stock-keeping units, in bulk only – 3,200 SKU's versus 30,000 in a full-size discount store – and in a no-frills warehouse-type building. No-brand merchandise is sold at wholesale prices to members for use in their own operations or for resale to their customers. About 70% of the merchandise is received via direct shipment from suppliers, rather than from the company's distribution centers. Finally, faithful to Wal-Mart's overall strategy of invading selected geographical areas, Sam's chose to cannibalize its own sales by opening Clubs close to one another in many markets, rather than giving competitors any openings.

In 1992, the year Sam Walton died, Sam's Clubs sales amounted to $12.3 billion. In the fiscal year ending January 31, 2005, those sales amounted to $37.1 billion, with 551 Sam's Clubs throughout the U.S.

The associates' drive for success

As already mentioned, Wal-Mart's recruitment policy is largely directed to young people for whom Wal-Mart is their first job. Even today, three-quarters of its store managers began their careers in hourly positions. This approach gives Wal-Mart an opportunity to assimilate them culturally to the house's way of thinking and doing. One of the cornerstones of Wal-Mart's management know-how is its success in motivating its "associates," the company's name for employees, so they will continuously run the extra mile. Two often-quoted slogans catch the spirit of this policy: "we're a company of ordinary people overachieving," and "associates live for the glory of Wal-Mart."

Such an extraordinary level of commitment is built up in a sophisticated manner. Associates are given, very early in their careers, some actual area of responsibility and accountability. They are empowered to the point that each product department operates as a "store within a store."

Empowerment implies that relevant information is available. For instance associates have constant and open access to all data on their store's operational figures. They are also continuously informed about broader strategic evolutions. Wal-Mart was the first company in the world to own its own communication satellite, and management makes great use of it.

Associates are not only recognized and supported. They are also rewarded with management responsibility in their merchandise area.

Managers who have never been to college make it to the top. The stores offer opportunities for upward mobility to young people in rural communities. Various financial incentives and symbolic initiatives are worth mentioning. In 1991, the "Yes we can, Sam" program encouraging suggestions led to four hundred ideas that altogether generated $38 million in savings. Its "shrink incentive plan" gives associates bonuses for keeping shrinkage down. Profit sharing based on profit growth is available to associates after one year of employment, put into a plan that the associate, on leaving the company, can take either in cash or in stock.[2] Likewise, associates are encouraged to become stockholders. About half of them participate in its annual stock-purchase plan.

Another feature of Wal-Mart is its refusal to allow employee unions. Sam Walton viewed unions as devices that would ultimately increase costs, and would not permit anyone to unionize a store, claiming he would rather close the place.

The worst enemy of Wal-Mart's culture for excellence was, at least from Sam Walton's standpoint, bureaucracy. Walton saw the home office as a necessary evil that dealt with the company's inevitable paperwork. All in all, he wanted the company to be store-based and store-specific. At his ritual Saturday morning meetings in Bentonville, Walton would invite executives to discuss the previous week's sales figures, pending issues, future perspectives, and so on. One of the initial purposes in calling those meetings was that, as long as employees and store managers had to work in the stores on Saturdays, it was a matter of fairness that executives gathered for a few hours on Saturday mornings.

By many standards, Wal-Mart could be viewed as a total institution. The young employees it recruits generally have no experience of any other company. They are arguably brainwashed with its corporate philosophy. Multiple mechanisms of social control and acculturation ensure that the members of the tribe will maintain life-long loyalty. Even the executives' Saturdays are controlled by the company. At a time when business and management media were astonished if not frightened by ceremonies that took place in Japanese and Korean companies, Sam Walton introduced propaganda methods and indoctrination processes on American soil. The Wal-Mart cheer is a ritual that associates have to perform every morning in each and every store.

TABLE 3.1 **The Wal-Mart cheer**

Wal-Mart managers lead their employees (or "associates") in a cheer each day before opening the store. They can vary from store to store. Here is one from Store 3115 in Windsor, Ontario.

Here you go ...

Gimme a W	. . . . W!
Gimme an A	. . . . A!
Gimme an L	. . . . L!

Gimme a squiggly!
(Their term for a hyphen. At this point, instead of shouting out "squiggly" in response, the employees wiggle their hips while bending their knees, then spring back up again.)

Gimme an M	. . . . M!
Gimme an A	. . . . A!
Gimme an R	. . . . R!
Gimme a T	. . . . T!
What's that spell?	. . . . Wal-Mart!
Louder!	. . . . Wal-Mart!
Who's number one?	 3115

We're the best!

We're a team

NOW, who is really number one? . . . . The customers!

Cha-Ching! *(Sound of a cash register, accompanied by punching the air at waist level)*

Since staff empowerment and decentralizing decision-making processes could be conducive to a lack of strategic consistency, the name of the game is also, of course, control. But at Wal-Mart this control does not rely on bureaucratic tools. Not only did Sam Walton hate them, they are not needed. Information is readily available for everybody. Cultural control is in the hands of regional managers who, not having regional offices to supervise, spend their days touring the field. This MBWA, or managing by walking around, is aimed at making sure that whatever is done at the shop floor is done the Wal-Mart way. Total compliance with its corporate values and positioning is demanded. Regional managers essentially act as cultural envoys and socialization controllers.

Because so many of Wal-Mart's corporate values came from one man, "Mr. Sam," was the founder farsighted enough to set in place a transition framework that would guarantee Wal-Mart's functioning and generate future prosperity after his death?

REMAINING THE BEST AND BECOMING THE BIGGEST

Wal-Mart's sales increased from $44 billion in the 1992 fiscal year, the last one Sam Walton was at the helm, to $312 billion in the 2006 fiscal year. In the same period, net income jumped from $1.6 billion to $11.23 billion. The number of associates has grown from 370,000 in 1992 to 1.7 million in 2006. Sam Walton's heirs have become America's richest family. They control about 39% of the company's stocks, worth some $90 billion in 2004.

The major vehicle for such an astonishing growth has been the Supercenter. This discount store/supermarket hybrid, created in 1986, did not actually take off until 1992. As of January 31, 2005, Wal-Mart operated 1,713 Supercenters in the U.S. (compared with only 10 in 1992), and another 285 in international operations (compared with none in 1992). Because Supercenters include a grocery section, the company has also become, since 2001, the largest grocery retailer in the U.S., surpassing giant supermarket operators such as Albertson's and Kroger.

The two major architects of that growth were David Glass, who took over after Sam Walton's death and managed the company for eight years until January 2000, multiplying sales by four, and Lee Scott, Glass's successor as CEO. But neither of them was alone in driving growth. They were surrounded and supported at top management as well as at the grass-roots level by thousands of associates and managers who shared the same corporate values and fought the same discounting battles. The Wal-Mart business model was still feeding growth, even if some slight tweaking had to be made occasionally, to take the size of its operations into account.

Piloting explosive growth

With only a few exceptions, the post-1992 Wal-Mart management team consisted of executives in their forties and fifties who had started working for the company straight after leaving school and had risen through the ranks as the company grew.

David Glass was one of the few who started his career outside Wal-Mart. He joined Sam Walton in 1976 as an executive vice president of finance. He was known as an operationally oriented executive and made an important contribution to the sophisticated distribution process in place at Wal-Mart. He was even referred to as a logistics genius (Sellers 1996). Like his boss, David Glass emphasized frugality in his administrative style. He was on the road two or three days a week visiting stores, and constantly pushed managers to challenge the status quo, embracing change as a fond companion. For years, Sam Walton had been grooming Glass to step, when the time came, into his shoes.

At the same time, Walton wanted his family to remain involved, to guarantee that Wal-Mart's vision and values would be respected in the future. In appointing his son Rob – the only one of his children to play a serious operational role in the company – as chairman, but not asking him to be CEO, he made it crystal clear that the actual running of the company should be left to a non-family CEO. None of the members of the new management team tried to become a replica of Sam Walton. Indeed, the emphasis has always been on leadership as the role of the team. There was an unwritten agreement that power should be shared and divided among three senior figures: Rob Walton, David Glass, and Don Soderquist.

These team members had complementary skills and personalities. David Glass was the operations man par excellence, with highly developed organizational skills and a respected ability to tackle issues that arose on a day-to-day basis. Don Soderquist, with his great communication and people skills, became the key leader in articulating Sam Walton's values and culture.

One major nuance differentiated Sam Walton and David Glass, Glass experienced less fear when considering fast growth than did Walton. In the mindset of Wal-Mart's founder, growth potentially meant horrendous phenomena such as debt or bureaucracy. He also believed much more than his predecessor that technology and systems had to become more sophisticated as the company was growing. It was Glass who turned Wal-Mart into one of the greatest growth machines of all times, who took it from rural America and made it a global brand.

The risks in being Supercenter-driven

Once again, Wal-Mart did not invent the Supercenter concept that would boost its growth. It acted as a follower, but with more ambitious goals and better and faster implementation.[3] For Wal-Mart to diversify into Supercenters was a great idea in many respects.

There were in fact fewer and fewer local communities and regional markets in the U.S. that Wal-Mart could capture with its "distribution-centers-surrounded-by-150-discount-stores" concept. Further expansion was not obvious. Groceries had become a major traffic-builder. General merchandise too would benefit from the added traffic. Wal-Mart was determined to become the first grocery retailer in the U.S. with both a national presence and a national EDLP claim. In only a few years it had achieved this goal.

Its Supercenters benefit from Wal-Mart's reputation. Consumers have a growing appetite for time-saving convenience and so appreciate the one-stop shopping experience that this kind of combination store offers.

Another advantage is that most of Wal-Mart's stores built in the 1970's and 1980's were designed with future facility extension and logistics expansion in mind. Many existing Wal-Mart discount stores could easily and at a low cost be converted into new Supercenters.

While opening Supercenters looked a promising strategic opportunity, there were still a few major challenges to address.

Gross margins on groceries are smaller than on general merchandise. Grocery products – and even more so, fresh produce – need dedicated logistics. To be profitable and stay true to its EDLP policy in the food sector would require a high volume of sales. Food retailing also needs specific expertise, quite different from that of general merchandise. Its competitors in the early 1990's were large U.S. supermarket chains that knew what they were doing, and Wal-Mart did not have an obvious alternative for success.

Making Supercenters the core of Wal-Mart's future strategy meant that the transition phase was likely to erode margins and company profits for at least a few years. And this is what happened. Business media and the press started to wonder, doubt, and even openly express skepticism about its relevance – "CEO David Glass sees a bright future in food retailing. Wall Street has its doubts" (Sellers 1996). There was a major drop in the value of Wal-Mart stocks.

The issue was addressed internally. The CEO and the COO held a company-wide satellite broadcast to explain to associates, half of whom are also shareholders, why their company stock prices were down. They simply reassured them that the price of the stock would in time reflect the company performance

Making sure that associates wouldn't be worried about Wal-Mart sailing temporarily through troubled financial waters was just one issue. The other one to be addressed was organizational and mental. How was it to make sure that the company's gigantism would not imperil its sacred field culture? In fact, the sheer size of the company did not allow top managers to be as present and visible at the store level as they would have liked. To handle this dilemma, Rob Walton coined a solution: "institutionalization of the culture."

In the new Wal-Mart, its fifteen regional VPs, operating from Bentonville, fill the same social control role and socialization function that Sam Walton played in the former Wal-Mart. They visit the stores. They spend about two hundred days in the field each year. They spread the Wal-Mart gospel and identity. They are expected to gain that quick market intelligence that Sam Walton once captured on his yellow pad. Wal-Mart makes a sharp distinction between "management," which it downplays, and "leadership," which it promotes. Wal-Mart presents a paradox in being a company that has first-class procedural know-how and functional management but does not rely on it to manage its personnel and harmonize their acts.

Company managers, for instance, are referred to as "coaches," the idea being that hierarchical authority structures deter teamwork and individual commitment at all levels. Shifting power to more junior managers did not mean that top senior managers would stop transmitting, when not hammering, the company's cultural messages and slogans. They would just do it in front of larger Wal-Mart audiences. This new context has also impacted the Bentonville Saturday morning meeting rite. In addition to operational reviews, a lot of time is now spent rehashing the company's corporate values, to the point that these are sometimes referred to as "culture Saturdays."

Diving headlong into the twenty-first century

In January 2000, Lee Scott succeeded David Glass as CEO.[4] The new trio in command was composed of Rob Walton, Lee Scott, and a new member, Tom Coughlin.

Wal-Mart offers another paradox. The world's No. 1 company continues to build its domestic market. International expansion, although a major contributor to the company's overall growth, is not its top priority in terms of development. Scott believes that two-thirds of its sales should still come from its U.S. operations. The main vehicle used to achieve this objective is expanding the number of stores. With more than 1,700 Supercenters in January 2005, Wal-Mart sees potential for around 4,000 in its domestic market. This expansion would be fueled by converting 1,200 existing discount stores and creating around 950 new ones.

While these numbers look almost too good, Wal-Mart is facing a few challenges.

The first is the question of Wal-Mart's ability to penetrate big cities with the same success it has seen in small towns and medium-sized cities. In an analysis of the 250 biggest MSA's (Metropolitan Statistical Areas), the six largest – New York, Los Angeles, Chicago, Washington, Philadelphia and Boston – were among the bottom 10% in terms of Wal-Mart's penetration (Bell 2003). For the Arkansas-based company this reflects a complex set of difficulties it has to confront. Real estate costs are often prohibitive in large metropolitan areas. In addition to its own size, the Supercenter concept draws advantage from owning its surrounding shopping center, and this also allows it to control the competitive environment. But owning shopping centers would make the real estate bill in larger cities even more prohibitive. Large cities are also slightly more difficult and costly to serve from a logistical standpoint. For instance, moving big trucks around is not easy, to say the least. Last, but not least, large urban areas tend to be cultural melting pots, much more so than rural and small urban communities. The diversity of social, economic, ethnic, and lifestyle patterns requires assortments that are even more tailored and fine-tuned than in the rest of the country.

Another challenge, linked to the previous idea of finding new vehicles for market penetration, is further diversifying store formats. Although this process has already begun, progress remains slow.

One new concept designed as a potential further step in diversification is the Wal-Mart Neighborhood Market. Launched experimentally in 1998, it combines a supermarket and a drugstore. But its growth is still sluggish, at least according to Wal-Mart standards.[5] This is partly due to Wal-Mart's doing immensely well and its major expansion vector, the Supercenter, growing at full speed while still offering huge potential. There may also be some strategic hesitation in terms of positioning the new concept. One possibility could be to view the Neighborhood Market format as complementary to the Supercenter format. Neighborhood Markets could provide grocery coverage in areas too small for a Supercenter, or fill in coverage between Supercenters as a more convenient alternative to shoppers. Another positioning could be viewed as a "Supercenter-light" strategy, a somewhat homothetic reduction of the Supercenter. This would give Wal-Mart access to poorly penetrated large cities.

Another slowing-down factor is that current results, in sales per square foot or operating profits, are still lower in Neighborhood Markets than in Supercenters, although they are described as having so far fully justified the company's investment. But core management mechanisms and factors of excellence at Wal-Mart, such as regional profit and loss responsibility or logistics, are still common to the two formats. This may imply that the Supercenter concept remains the priority, marginalizing the Neighborhood Market concept, and that regional managers may not want to be distracted from the implicit priority signal linked to the Supercenter. The less positive performances of Neighborhood Markets as compared with Supercenters might therefore be a self-fulfilling prophecy.

At the same time, historic evidence suggests that Wal-Mart is always initially somewhat experimental, a slow starter in new format development before it speeds up in a spectacular manner. A typical example was the slow take-off of its Supercenters. Wal-Mart has been applying its cost-reduction managerial skills to its Neighborhood Markets quite well in recent years. For instance, bread is trucked in daily in partially baked form and finished off in a browning oven in the store, leading shoppers to believe there is an in-store bakery. The store's meats and deli sections also appear to offer store-prepared products, but again, these are shipped in daily. Six cash registers out of eight are self-checkout. Altogether, this means that a Neighborhood Market operates with 10% less staff than a competing supermarket (Duvall and Nash 2004). If Wal-Mart decides to speed up in this area, it could spell bad news for existing supermarket chains.

EMERGING MARKETING AND ORGANIZATIONAL CHALLENGES

In early 2005, two major marketing challenges appeared that may push Wal-Mart to fine-tune its strategic postures and actions. Needless to say, these marketing adaptations need to be accompanied by organizational changes.

One key potential challenge is the explosive growth of Google as a price comparison engine (Lohr 2005). In fact, by making price information available whenever and wherever the customer wants it, Google can tell Wal-Mart's shoppers whether better bargains are available. Wal-Mart needs to be more focused than ever on its EDLP claim and continue to improve its cost efficiency.

A more immediate danger is of a totally different nature. Wal-Mart does not do as well as one would expect from such a dominant market leader when it comes to the lucrative upmarket segment.

At its 2005 shareholders' meeting, Wal-Mart's top management recognized that, although performance was satisfactory in the U.S. with core value-conscious customers who appreciate EDLP, the group was missing a trick in failing to attract high-spending customers. Wal-Mart is under pressure from the growth of its rival, Target, which attracts wealthier customers through a more upmarket offer (*Retail News Letter* 2005). This shows in the figures. In the 2004–2005 fiscal year, Target posted a comparable-store sales growth of 6.3% whereas Wal-Mart posted only 3.3%.

More importantly, Wal-Mart seems to be modifying its marketing postures significantly to boost store sales. For instance, in 2005 it carried out wide-ranging customer research for the first time. Surprisingly, while the retail giant has collected terabytes of data on what its customers buy, it had traditionally left market research to its suppliers (Birchall October 2005). It had gradually become more customer-centric than it ever had been. In the same spirit, in October 2005 Wal-Mart launched a more upmarket fashion brand, Metro 7, while its advertising is switching its focus to lifestyle rather than prices. The challenges it is facing are seriously shaking Wal-Mart's historical marketing foundations. Wal-Mart does an outstanding job of marketing to the masses but it doesn't even attempt to get to know its customers on an individual basis (Duvall and Nash 2004).

Another underlying question more broadly linked with its reactive marking posture is: Should Wal-Mart try once again to imitate a competitor (in this case Target), or should it find a different way to revamp itself? Would adding more fashion-oriented merchandise please or antagonize its core customers? How will it also impact its relationships with its current suppliers? In fact, Wal-Mart's effort to upgrade merchandise and add more exclusive brands to improve sales may put increased pressure on its suppliers of more routine merchandise. Actually Wal-Mart announced in March 2006 that it has plans to reduce inventories in its 3,800 U.S. stores. And, although it asserts that these inventory adjustments will be done in a fully collaborative way with suppliers, based on tighter analyses of consumer needs, those suppliers are definitely feeling the pinch (Reed 2006). It looks like the so-called cooperative game is largely played on Wal-Mart's terms.

Alongside its new marketing strategy, Wal-Mart also seems to be reshaping its overall organization – and to be tweaking its management recruiting policies a bit.

Analyses of store performances triggered organizational changes. In the 2004–2005 fiscal year, the annual sales growth of its 800 best-performing stores was on average 10 times better than that of the worst performing stores, with a clear correlation to staff morale and customer satisfaction. By and large, underperforming stores were in clusters managed by given district managers. Consequently, Wal-Mart has now appointed fashion and food merchandisers to assist each of its district managers – now called "market managers," which can be viewed as more than a semantic evolution – who will advise them on the look and feel of their stores (Birchall November 2005).

Wal-Mart is also moving 9 of its 30 regional managers "into the field," initially in strategic markets such as New York or California, where it faces the toughest political, cultural, and competitive challenges. It is revealing that the company has recruited John Fleming, a former Target executive, as chief marketing officer. It is also trying to attract promising talent from major food companies such as PepsiCo's Frito-Lay division or McDonald's.

There is no doubt that Wal-Mart is and will remain a robust giant. It is strongly embedded in its core "historical" business model which has been appropriately adapted over time and across multiple discount formats. This situation is unfailingly delivering growth and profitability. However, Wal-Mart is also taking seriously – as it always did – signals that suggest some renewal of its proposition is needed. It also weighs very carefully how and to what extent those signals should be translated into Wal-Mart terms. In fact, finding the right click between imitating competition and respecting the discipline of one's own territory is a fundamental issue in reactive marking.

4

ESSENCE OF MARKINGS

What can be learned from the two cases, one in distribution and one in production, when reading them using Table 1.1 and the dimensions listed at the end of Chapter 1? A comparison enables us to define marking in a more precise manner.

Three key aspects of marking will be revisited: promises, clarity and durability, and territory. Two types of marking will be identified and detailed: proactive and reactive. The specific examples of Royal Canin and Wal-Mart will also enable management to derive more general implications at two levels: when and why marking becomes a necessity, and what are the contingencies linked to a marking approach.

THREE BUILDING BLOCKS

Marking is a promise made by an enterprise. It implies loyalty, continuity, and excellence. Such a moral contract and such a pragmatic commitment bind the enterprise and its management vis-à-vis a territory and the stakeholders who are part of it up to a level called societal embedding that goes beyond mere economic opportunism.

Promises

Marking makes promises as to how the company and the market will interact.

A key point is that these promises are not limited to communication and position statements. They, and the company's commitment to them, imply that the market will truly understand them, that it will test them and ultimately make these promises part of its inner life. Repeated experience fleshes out and magnifies their value and substance, as a "history" builds up, bit by bit, between the company and its market.

The contract that marking represents is explicit, clearly articulated, and unambiguously announced. It stems from an intent spelled out by top management that is formulated into a strategic policy. This is then translated into operational plans or projects that headquarters impose on each and every member of the company. A classic illustration of this contract was Sam Walton's decision to build his own Wal-Mart stores rather than trying to tweak Ben Franklin franchised stores to his personal philosophy.

At the same time, the magnitude of the breakthrough and the demigod-like power of the entrepreneur shouldn't be exaggerated. Marking is firmly rooted within a much wider context. It is nurtured by past events and often built up over a significant period of time.

Discount stores were successful in the United States well before Sam Walton decided to run his own show. Although he was convinced that discounting could be pushed further, mostly through tighter implementation, and to other target markets such as rural and small-town America, Walton was not denying the existing achievements of established discount stores. Even today, Wal-Mart remains culturally obsessed with copying whatever competitive approaches and stratagems seem to work. But Walton thought that his competitors did not take full advantage of what they were inventing. To make a long story short, Wal-Mart fully accepted and integrated prior discounting structures and Sam Walton's own pre-Wal-Mart retail experience to construct an even more successful model. The difference Walton made was total and perfect exploitation of innovations made by others.

Likewise, the marking exercise that Henri Lagarde formally initiated in 1996 did not turn its back on the history of Royal Canin. To a large extent, respect for pets, the strength of a well-established brand, and targeting influential opinion leaders (such as breeders and veterinarians) were already well established. In fact they were waiting only to be cultivated further.

Shared implicit values and contractual continuity

By definition, marking cannot be simplified to a marketing project spelled out into a formalized plan, described in a fully explicit and conscious manner, once and forever. Successful marking needs the input of two key elements:

- *Clarity* – a specific territory is delineated that goes beyond pure consumerism and includes societal dimensions.

- *Durability* – signals sent out to the market are not volatile.

Marking is elaborated over time. It results from learning processes and improves through deepening dynamics. It builds on previously ignored opportunities. It is therefore both arbitrary and wrong to consider 1996 as the exact moment that Royal Canin effected a complete turnaround in its marking strategy. Subsequent years were characterized by fine-tuning this marking to make it more precise and, by the same token, to strengthen it. The decision to move away from mass-market retailers had been taken in 1994, at a time when the concept of pet health was not yet explicitly formulated, as it was from 2000 on.

Likewise, marking cannot be reduced to a resolve made at the heart of an organization, even if this seems essential in formulating and legitimizing it. For both Royal Canin and Wal-Mart, marking was developed by an organization through multiple players who were fully dedicated to building it. Reducing this marking to a precisely dated decision taken by a "man at the helm" would be a misleading bias.

Many dimensions of this moral contract remain implicit. Many aspects are never explicitly announced yet appear to be consistently followed. Marking manifests itself through respected norms and shared cognitions, and via the behaviors that organization members adopt. While certain choices and positions are selected unanimously across all hierarchical levels, others are ruled out, never mentioned and possibly not even perceived.

Marking often seems to evolve naturally into a culture that glues the social mechanisms within the company together. Three basic ingredients facilitate its construction:

- common socialization
- crystallizing learning through processes and practices
- cumulative experience over time and across the organization.

Continuity and duration facilitate the success of marking actions and influence fields of marking. Short-term opportunism and trend-driven turnarounds, such as mimicking competitors or falling prey to the pitfalls of management fads, can destroy successful marking. Executives like Sam Walton or Henri Lagarde do not shift direction or modify their strategy because of an early morning anxiety attack in the shower. For commitments to gain credibility, both internally and externally, time, persistence and trust are vital ingredients. The signals that a company sends out to the market have to be reasonably robust. The external world that the embedding company is constructing as both its frame of reference and its target needs an assurance that the company will not blur or muddy its promises through actions that could contradict or negate them. Moving entirely away from mass-market supermarket chains was an essential part of Royal Canin's credibility vis-à-vis specialized retailers and pet owners. The targeted external world – which will ultimately be referred to as the territory – knows perfectly well who the marker is. There will be no bad surprises – ever – because promises that are not respected can mean sudden death. They can kill on the spot, immediately, in far less time than promises that are kept will take to initiate the dynamics of success. And there is no easy way back.

A territory

With regard to business, marking implies a search for distinctiveness. What territory needs to be constructed or occupied to forge a durable profitability? How can the company become not only a recognized player in this territory, but, even more ambitiously, the benchmark? Marking is anchored in a socially defined space. Its strategic dimension is the drive to seek out and master a tightly defined contextualization.

The world of Royal Canin rejects a simplistic vision of selling pet food for dogs and cats. Royal Canin directs itself to people who place a high priority on the health and well-being of their pets. It magnifies the roles of veterinarians, professional breeder associations and specialized media and has become the architect of a world that represents a clear alternative to fast-food-like pet foods, promoting a normative approach and political rights that arguably constitute a "pet charter." The specific segment that Royal Canin targets is not defined geographically, but socially. It offers the same nutritional pet products universally and takes the same ethical position – elevating the status of the pet – whether in the U.S., in Brazil, in Japan or in Europe, and always to a finely targeted segment of consumers.

The world that Wal-Mart initially identified as its prime target was America's backyard: the rural and small-town working class. It understood its rural customers' desire to be given as much respect and offered as much value-for-money in their daily consumption as people living in large cities. Both Wal-Mart's tangible proposition of offering its customers everyday low prices and its symbolic trappings – such as posting "People Greeters" at the entrance of every store – are perfectly consistent with rural and small-town America's economic and social aspirations. Wal-Mart focuses on rather conservative, non-ostentatious American middle- and lower-income earners. Its brand power is reinforced in a vast number of locations because it is the only modern retailer in the area, a situation in which it is often viewed as more than a store, but rather a local institution.

As a management approach, marking does not consider the market as an established and unalterable fact, an external element imposed on a company and which the company has no power to alter. On the contrary, marking understands the market to be a specific configuration of economic players and social practices that the company can to some extent transform and reshape through its determination and willpower, and through its actions. A company may select individuals, groups, or organizations and transform them into buyers, distributors, promoters, or even competitors. It can choose its prime targets, situations, or roles toward which to direct its strategic priorities. The entrepreneur is becoming, in a way, a designer. He tries to create socioeconomic entities that will fit his vision. He is carving out segments from the economic world that will react positively to propositions and their associated lifestyles and consumption patterns. The contractual nature of marking is synonymous with activism and determination. It is constantly nourished and rekindled. Successful marking is an ongoing and structuring phenomenon.

Both companies are strategically geared to having a marked impact on the societies they target. They have both worked toward – and succeeded at – becoming the benchmarks in specific worlds that are far from being purely abstract or incorporeal. They have both participated actively in shaping these worlds via products and services that closely follow a precisely defined objective to stand out from the crowd. These business directions cannot be summarized in terms of a narrowly defined market or a particular set of market transactions.

A company's territory is the segment of society that it wants to serve and to capture, and in some cases help to emerge. It is a spatially anchored social cluster, or world, that the company activates, and in which it represents promised values and mobilizes stakeholders. In fact, behind the market defined in purely economic terms hides society – a dynamic jigsaw of evolving social groups each with its own values and sensitivities, its own hierarchies and its own codes of conduct.

A marked business is a business that is approached through its social components and specific cultural traits. The company identifies, builds, and delineates these. Marking segments the socioeconomic fabric, by determining how to extract durable profitability from it and by making an alliance with stakeholders who really count in the specific context. The company marks a segment of society and, in return, the selected territory has an effect on the company's distinctive image and the products or services it offers. The company is by all means fully embedded in and fully embedding society.

Not all strategies rely on an approach like this. A company may well limit itself to a purely economic rationale vis-à-vis its market, and totally eschew any greater social integration. But in marking, such an integration is the essential strategic axis.

To mark is to forge, and to be supported by, a vision. Marking assigns a company a more general and permanent mission, a kind of idealistic ambition that conditions and guides its strategic progression. The company acquires moral values and new representations of the world and itself that also serve to build its recognition and legitimacy – in a world that the company contributes to civilize. Over time, this missionary stance evolves to a social and cultural identity. Marking, in its purest form, is creating the ties between the company's strategy and its vision, and making this consistent.

The business definition chosen has a strong impact on management devices. The more emphasis placed on marking, the less performance indicators are restricted to a narrow set of financial tools. The social integration that a marking project aims at accords great relevance to the social status that customers derive from their connection with the company. Shopping at Wal-Mart positions the American rural or small-town consumer as a modern customer who is also careful about not spending unnecessary dollars: non-conspicuous, modern consumption. On top of being a local institution, Wal-Mart is perceived as a cultural and moral institution perfectly in tune with Bible Belt American values. In the case of Royal Canin, salespeople in garden centers see their role magnified by the assistance they give to shoppers in the store's pet food section. Moreover, the more the marking project wants to create an entirely new world, the more its frame of reference will evolve and embrace relevant stakeholders.

In some instances, implementation may still follow its own logic, largely disconnected from both strategy and vision. This is especially detrimental when the social dimension of the marking project is sophisticated, ambitious, and complex. Marking, in its strategy and vision, is nourished by shared experiences, by fully and adequately implemented initiatives, and by capturing and feeding back weak signals of change.

How do the company's strategy, vision, and their implementation fit together? The natural reflex is to consider that vision comes first, followed by strategy and, finally, implementation. But this top-down approach is at best a questionable description of reality. Wal-Mart and Royal Canin provide two striking examples – but many more can be found through the systematic observation of managerial practices (Mintzberg 1973).

In reality, the connections between these three components of management are far more iterative and interactive than sequential. Each component, in various ways, nourishes and fertilizes the other two. Wal-Mart's strategy integrated the know-how and the practices that Sam Walton inherited from the Ben Franklin franchises. Likewise, Royal Canin's top management developed a vision heavily influenced by trading with breeders. At the same time, both companies continually listened to their people in the field, through structures and practices that facilitated a hybridizing between the past and the present.

TYPES AND CHARACTERISTICS OF MARKING

While both great markers, Royal Canin and Wal-Mart nevertheless differ in a radical way. The latter imitates while the former invents. This suggests that in business life enterprises have two options available, each giving access to lasting and impressive economic performances.

Generally speaking, two types or approaches to marking can be identified:

- reactive marking
- proactive marking.

Reactive marking exploits and conserves pre-existing social and economic spaces or territories, made up of pre-existing stakeholders. It approaches buyers and users as it finds them, and molds itself to fit into a network of partners – opinion leaders, intermediaries, professional circles, and proximity links – that it did not contribute to shaping. It adheres to their deep-seated aspirations and values. A company is motivated to calibrate itself to an existing world in this way either by a desire to enter a world currently occupied by others that it wants to replace, or through a desire to reconquer a market it had totally or partially deserted. Reactive marking looks to consolidate existing values, socioeconomic relations and lifestyles.

Proactive marking is much more innovative. It favors a different future and the building of a new territory. It means to modify stakeholders' lives and society. It creates, diffuses and legitimizes new values. It puts stakeholders on the stage who had long since ceased being in the limelight. It promotes alternative modes of sociability, and helps the emergence of new ways of living. The proactive marker invents a territory by radically transforming conventions that have guided the existing economic and social space so far. It also permits the company to avoid a simplistic cognitive fixation on the satisfaction of claimed needs when it plans to come up with new contributions, societally based, to the act of consuming. Proactive markings are based on quite another interpretation. They are prompted by a totally opposite obsession. They are about researching and identifying tangible gaps in the proposals made to consumers. These gaps are of a societal nature: the rights of pets, access of middle classes to house furniture of a decent level at an affordable price, and so on.

Both proactive and reactive markings are active. They mean decisions and actions. They may correspond to policies elaborated from scratch. They may also be built up incrementally, through a succession of small decisions made over time while confronting specific events or in reaction to emerging threats – or in grabbing new opportunities.

But these two approaches to marking should be considered as ideal types. Actual business life shows that neither proactive nor reactive marking ever take place exactly as either of these suggest. Observed markings usually blend some features belonging to the two ideal types, and are positioned on a spectrum between these two extremities. Most markings are, in fact, made up of hybrid devices and practices mixing the characteristics of the two models, with variable dosages.

Drawing the marking profile of a given company in no way implies any value judgment. It does not presume that one model performs better, is more desirable, or is more ethically respectable than the other. The specific decision-making context and the company's overall objectives will determine what it requires in terms of social desirability and economic performance.

The reader's guideline provided at the end of Chapter 1 listed seven facets of marking. From seven, and for pedagogical purposes, they may be brought down to three parameters when differentiating proactive from reactive marking: the strategic ambition pursued, its market intelligence and the resulting offers, and the way management implements the intended marking.

Strategic ambition

In the case of proactive marking, this ambition is translated into a vision shared by all stakeholders, both internal and external to the company (distributors, breeders, veterinaries, and so on in the case of Royal Canin). The same source of inspiration and identical references keep these stakeholders close to one another. They live this reference as a common identity builder that glues them together as they face the external world: it stimulates them and makes them proud of cultivating their difference, as a collective property that they manage and enrich.

A company adopting proactive marking has at its center a committed management style. The strength of this center vis-à-vis the periphery derives less from hierarchical authority and control capabilities than from its ability to legitimize norms and values. The values conveyed are of a societal or political nature, political being taken in its etymological sense of life within the city. The center drives, stimulates, and constructs a moral and cultural community within and, even more so, outside of the firm (Koza and Thoenig 2003). This logic of organizational and moral integration enables outside partners to be associated, co-opted and socialized as members of the common project (Selznick 1992). The center is above all a place of institutionalization (Shils 1975).

L'Oréal brings scientific rigor, even a medical outlook, to its hair and skin care products. Internally, this means that its ambition promotes values of innovation and renovation that nourish obsession in its employees, almost to the point of brainwashing. IKEA. too, in its quest to democratize furniture and home decoration, exhaustively codifies its political and even its behavioral norms. Fnac, the French multi-specialist in cultural and leisure goods, positioned itself, at least in its pioneering period, as a "cultural troublemaker." To achieve this it was essential to transform its salespeople into cultural missionaries, transmitting their faith to its target audience – the educated and culturally aware upper middle class. Fnac's pitch was to defend its customers' interest by guaranteeing them the best value for money, a claim based, at least for its technical products (cameras and consumer electronics), on tests performed in its own labs.

Reactive marking is positioned as a complement, a functional expertise, at the service of an overall strategy. This stance does not exclude clear commercial objectives – far from it, in particular when it comes to targeted customer groups. Quantitative goals (such as achieving goals in terms of market share) and qualitative ones (such as image building or revamping) are all consistent with this strategy. Like proactive marking, implementing reactive marking reflects a strong desire for consistency. Strong values are circulated, but they are mostly of a commercial nature. Nevertheless, experience suggests that this excellence-in-execution standpoint is not easy to adopt. More often than not, though, attempts at reactive marking are built around a far more simplistic and fragile ambition, in which the brand is viewed only as one product attribute among others, as one of the product's multiple promotional trappings.

Market intelligence and shaping the offer

Three distinct factors come together in market intelligence and shaping the offer: the spatial, social, and temporal fields that characterize the target market; the type of product innovation that is to be promoted; and the economics of the product's proposed quality and delivered value.

1. *Market exploitation or market creation*
Reactive marking means market exploitation. Inspiration stems primarily from the customers' expressed demands that companies track through surveys and studies, using largely repetitive measurement parameters. Listening to customers essentially means that the company takes the most obvious customer requests or expectations into account, ones that can be empirically captured through behaviors, judgments, observed purchases and declared opinions. What escapes the measurement tool and the majority rule is viewed as either meaningless or not deserving any attention at all.

By simply inventing innovative and relevant market segmentation schemes on a regular basis, and by implementing marketing programs in a distinctive and often resourceful manner, brilliant reactive markings have built quite remarkable and perennial market successes. For example, American manufacturers of cola drinks have been extremely effective in removing, over time, obstacles preventing some customer segments from becoming regular consumers of their product. By developing diet colas and caffeine-free colas they have repeatedly relaunched the product category.

The search for untapped or disregarded consumption and usage territories is the cornerstone of the proactive marking approach. Proactive markers have a quasi-magnetic attraction for *terra incognita*. They are creators of new social and economic spaces.

Unexplored territories may be constituted of customer types who find the current offerings of dominant, and sometimes hegemonic, marketing systems unsatisfactory, either in general or in terms of value for money. Before the inception of Benetton, young people could not find fashionable, well-made sweaters at fair prices. Before the launch of IKEA, the Swedish working classes could not find functional and stylish furniture at acceptable prices.

Unexplored territories can also be identified by observing gaps in the offerings of other companies in terms of customer or user expectations that cannot be expressed in the surveys to which they are periodically exposed. It is then necessary to continuously and meticulously observe customers' lifestyles, or to test customer reactions to innovations. To focus purely on consumer preferences is both inadequate and restrictive. Proactive marking fills the gaps thorough a firsthand, personal knowledge of its consumers, through what is coined as "market creation."

One well-known example of such market creation is provided by the success of Swatch. Swatch watches were launched as "a fashion accessory that happens to tell time." This market creation was both quantitative and qualitative. Watches had been viewed as tools for measuring time. Most consumers needed only one watch, which needed to be replaced only when it no longer functioned. But once watches began to be viewed as a fashion accessory, consumers could have several without feeling any guilt.

But what are the consequences of reactive and proactive markings in terms of prioritizing target customers?

In reactive marking, priority is given to large clients or heavy users, or to customers whose profitability or potential profitability has been identified as high. Those criteria make sense in the perspective of market exploitation. It would be a mistake not to allocate resources primarily to customers who are now or are potentially the most financially rewarding.

In proactive marking, in addition to the financially rewarding customer, major emphasis is placed on "lead customers" – customers who have advanced expectations of their suppliers. These customers show the road to the future. For example, a manufacturer of eye-surgery equipment might place great emphasis on hospitals that are highly specialized in such surgery, and that feel an obligation to be ahead of the crowd both scientifically and economically.

2. Symbolic associations or obsession with tangibility
Reactive marking does propose tangible solutions. However, creating, enriching, and stretching a brand's perceived territory are also part of the ballgame, and are viewed as an essential aspect of a company's competitive advantage and, ultimately, of its success. Companies that adopt this strategy create an image and a message that both allude to dreams and imagination. Marking clearly intends, in these cases, to create brand associations that are mostly conveyed through advertising, as a key communication tool.

Boosting the social status of consumers and users becomes a priority. For instance, companies try to simulate social belonging, so as to cluster together people who are susceptible to entering into the same dream. The brand then becomes a mark of the extraordinary, of social distinction. Indisputably, some brands that have little, if any, tangible or technical competitive benefits, are extraordinarily good in building up this symbolic territory. One striking example is Harley Davidson motorbikes. Although it is difficult to judge the technical achievements of the brand, it is undeniable that it has built up amazing symbolic associations for its customers: it seems you either belong to the Harley Davidson planet or not.

Proactive marking endorses a different approach to constructing competitive advantage. Its normative vision or mission centers on improving the consumer's day-to-day life. And this consumer is meticulously decoded. Day-to-day life is not to be taken as derogatory. What we mean is the capacity to instill innovation and distinction into ordinary, tangible, everyday life. The goal of proactive marking is to make the ordinary extraordinary, to enrich it through a new, concrete proposition, to satisfy aspects of everyday life that remain vastly unexploited, functionally or economically. Proactive marking accesses knowledge and transforms the ordinary on the basis of scientific and technological research, through expertise and through a close understanding of its consumers.

Proactive marking is therefore conducive to the formulation of a very sophisticated offer. Does it mean that any less tangible associations will be totally excluded? Of course not. Nevertheless, these associations will mostly result from users' experience, rather than through extensive promotional actions.

Marking is particularly tricky in the service sector, where the tangible part of the offer is, by nature, quite small. Services are primarily people- rather than product-driven. Success depends much more on how the customer experiences the service. For this reason, companies that sell services are far more dependent upon the quality of their human resources than are other companies. The people who interact with the clients are the ultimate ambassadors of the values the marking company wants to promote. How tangible a company's competitive advantage is will depend on the skills and expertise of these people, as well as on the quality of the service the company provides. In a way, advice and selling go hand in hand at the point of service.

3. *Instantaneous perception or value-in-use*

Markings that perform best deliver perceived value for money to their target customers. In such cases, value for money can be defined as the ratio of perceived quality to perceived price.

Perceived quality obviously stems from the company's offerings of tangible products and associated services. However, it can also depend on the symbolic associations and social codes that the company succeeds in connecting with the consumption or buying acts. Perceived price is also multi-variant. It includes, of course, the purchasing price, but it also integrates promotional aspects of the buying process and, possibly, costs associated with the consumption experience, such as whether the experience is seen to be user friendly.

For proactive markers, users are expected to judge economic value over time rather than immediate or short-term value. Quality is made as tangible as possible. Extremely focused on sticking closely to precise user needs, proactive markers establish quality in a meticulous, sometimes scientific manner. Moreover, proactive markers try to avoid tainting the proposition through price promotions. Above all, the company is selling its customers the product or service's value-in-use, rather than its initial cost.

Since proactive marking is seen as part of building long-term customer loyalty, the company is able to estimate how detrimental a perceived lapse of quality would be, for the customer and for itself. It therefore views non-quality as its absolute enemy. The pressure for product excellence and ease of use is extremely strong. The company tracks in great detail not only its sales but also the actual consumption of its products. In other terms, for such companies, service is the natural companion of products. This creates a total economy of quality.

In fact, in reactive marking, service often appears rather late in the strategic formulation, most often to make up for the loss or erosion of the company's technological advantages when they become insufficient to guarantee market success. In such cases, marketers speak of the product as being augmented, which means augmented with a service dimension. In proactive marking this concept of augmentation is irrelevant, as service is not added to the product, but is naturally integrated into it.

Putting marking into effect

Implementation is the third and last component that characterizes the two types of marking. It can be tackled from three angles: the degree of societal upheaval it creates, the communication style adopted, and how the manufacturer addresses its relationship with its distributors (or vice versa).

1. *Consolidating or transforming the social order*
Reactive marking often delegates consumer and user analyses to a specialized market-research unit, either internal or external to the company. The marketing department then translates this market-research data into consumer aspirations, and transmits this information to the rest of the company to use in future strategic decisions. The market, often restricted to the company's direct commercial targets, is taken extremely seriously. Nevertheless, it is still, in a way, externalized from the inner workings of the company. For the manufacturing, accounting, and supply-chain departments, consumers still remain largely the exclusive turf of marketing and sales people.

This approach also tends to benchmark the company's performance against its direct competitors, and to imitate existing good practices.

Reactive marking leads to a rather conservative or imitative rationale. The company accepts exogenous rules of the game, established or modified by its competitors.

Proactive marking asserts, right from the starting block, new values, and possibly new rights, for consumers or users. To achieve this ambition, it often creates upheaval within the existing societal structure. It identifies and institutes new stakeholders. Some stakeholders who until now have been neglected or looked down upon are given greater status and asked to play new roles. New relationship and interaction mechanisms are developed. New expert agencies are encouraged to give their backing or blessing. Through new schemes of societal regulation, proactive marking modifies the relationships between consumers and products as well as the criteria for social distinction.

To conclude from the above that marketing is *non grata* in proactive marking would be simplistic and a serious mistake. However, what is signified by the word "marketing," which in this context should rather be called "market orientation," does shift. Marketing is no longer managed functionally, as it is in mass-marketing approaches. It is no longer the sole responsibility of the marketing department. Market orientation becomes part of everybody's mission. Marketing may not even appear any longer as a separate organizational function in the company's division of labor, as is the case at Royal Canin. Market orientation becomes an integral part of the company's vision, shared by all organizational functions, and projects.

2. *Communicating to legitimize new perceptions or reassure existing ones*
Reactive marking does not intend to modify the consumer's frame of reference. It is cognitively conservative. What it does is magnify the social status that buying or consumption confers. To attract new buyers, it may also actively cultivate guilt feelings among consumers who deviate, with suggestions they are socially incorrect (as with "Buy British" or "Buy American" slogans).

Conversely, in proactive marking, the company means to sweep away consumers' and users' existing benchmarks, by including variables that have so far been ignored in its propositions and which it anticipates will be features of a potential future demand. Through such objectives, the company is also positioning itself as an educator. This pedagogical construct may involve multiple players, some external to and upstream of the company; far from the end consumer or user. This "education" will spell out the tangible advantages that the innovation will bring to users. It goes without saying that the user is viewed as an active participant in the company's communications, including its advertising, rather than being seen as a passive and indoctrinated receptor.

In proactive marking, push elements are heavily reinforced in the communication pitch. These elements accompany the product through all stages of the distribution channel, through personalizing the way that influential opinion leaders, retailers, and, of course, customers and users are addressed. This is the opposite of the "pull" communication approach, in which manufacturers address end consumers directly, mostly through advertising, to pull consumers into stores where their products are distributed.

While proactive marking appears obsessed by making its offerings tangible, the reestablishment or creation of meaningful benchmarks, and a strong willingness to educate users, this does not mean that it neglects image building. However, again, its approach to image building differs from that of reactive marking. Image becomes a product of the offering's objective quality and the user's positive experiences with the product or service. The paradox is that proactive markers, much less concerned by symbolic associations than reactive markers, over time end up building very powerful images, which become undeniably strong contributors to the company's mark.

Partnerships between retailers and suppliers

Partnerships between retailers and suppliers have significantly grown over the past decades. But in the vast majority of instances, marriages between large retailers and major suppliers have resulted from the impossibility of divorce (Dupuy and Thoenig 1996). In fact, mutual dependencies are often so strong that any conflict that could culminate in the retailer delisting, partially or totally, the supplier, is rapidly revealed as a negative-sum game for both parties. If we cannot hate each other, let us try love. Moreover, consumption in many western countries has been rather dismal in recent years, and with sophisticated consumers increasingly making global judgments in their shopping and consumption experiences, it makes more and more sense to enter into partnerships to get a bigger share of the consumer's heart, mind, and wallet.

Reactive markings may still be, to some extent, confrontational. Negotiations between retailers and suppliers have to take place periodically over terms and joint promotional activities. However, over the past decade, partnership models have been developed to help the partnering spirit gain over forces and impulses inducing conflict. Efficient Consumer Response (ECR) is a popular technique used by suppliers and retailers. Its two major aspects are category management and supply-chain management.

Category management's ambition is to optimize, at store level, assortments of products and brands in order to create maximal shopper and consumer satisfaction. Its vital nutrient is market information. Market research is viewed as the natural "arbiter" of potential conflicts between suppliers and retailers. Category management requires a rather mature attitude from leading suppliers, sometimes selected by retailers as "category captains," that are supposed to be enlightened advisors to retailers on how to grow sales and profits of the overall product category. This may lead them occasionally to sacrifice some of their brands in order to maximize the overall product category's market impact.

Supply-chain management should, in perfect coordination with category management, ensure that products arrive at the right time and with unquestionable cost efficiency at the point of sale. Supply-chain management aims to eliminate the duplication of logistical tasks by retailers and their suppliers and to optimize inventory levels. Other techniques are further improving the efficiency of the supply chain, such as Collaborative Forecasting, Planning and Replenishment (CFPR), which intends to improve the joint ability of suppliers and retailers to forecast demand in quantitative terms, hence improving supply-chain performance.

A key contributor to the proper functioning of such collaboration mechanisms is the strategic alignment of the two partners. This means, concretely, that partners need to periodically check that they still share the same vision of the product category's role with regard to consumers and shoppers. Moreover, from a practical standpoint, it makes sense for each partner to unambiguously define which decisions will belong to the "partnering space" and which ones will remain part of its reserved domain.

For proactive marking, these actions are approached from a totally different angle. The initiator of the partnership, either the manufacturer or the retailer, selects from the beginning partners who are, or soon will be, in harmony with its strategic ambition. Choosing partners is therefore much more selective than in reactive marking. Strategic alignment takes place naturally. Nevertheless, previous partnerships could pre-exist or some intermediaries and opinion leaders may still be unavoidable. In these cases, the proactive marker will need to win these partners over to its cause, and to integrate them in the new space, with the condition that they break away from their previous relational logic and accept new or modified roles. The issue of market forecasting is also of a vastly different nature than in the case of reactive marking, as proactive marking generates totally new value propositions and is played out in a new societal space. Forecasting becomes more a voluntary act and a performance trigger than a statistical obsession.

When compared with reactive marking, proactive marking seems fairly, if not totally, uncomfortable with the survival in its partnership space of existing practices in terms of suppliers and store brands inherited from the past. Brands are assumed to be the federator of the overall network, there to establish a shared understanding of common action and to provide the glue holding the partnership together. This is all the more important when the societal project is pioneering and unique. To label a brand as being a "supplier brand" or a "store brand" can gravely weaken the intensity and the exclusive (when not militant) nature of reciprocal commitments. It shrinks the societal project down to a mere commercial venture. It hints that there are multiple ways of conveying new understandings. It spoils partners' inclinations toward loyalty, by validating individualistic and opportunistic attitudes that can go as far as free riding. The new space that proactive marking intends to build can then become centrifugal, and the initiator of the marking, whether this is the manufacturer or the retailer (generally the company with the most elaborated societal and political dynamics), may then stop carrying the burden of responsibility for the intended construction on its own shoulders. The center might become more a construct shared among various economic and social actors.

To sum up, Table 4.1 presents a systematic comparison of reactive and proactive marking, focusing on the seven factors of the reader's guidelines at the end of Chapter 1.

TABLE 4.1 Types of marking

	Status or source	Proactive marking A vision, an institution	Reactive marking An expertise
Strategic ambition	Who is driving the challenge	Top management	Marketing/commercial side
	Internal role of strategic ambition	Integration	Implementation
Market approach	Exploitation vs. creation	Market creation	Market exploitation
	What needs are satisfied	Filling societal gaps	Needs expressed by consumers
	Which customers feed inspiration	Trendsetters	Most profitable customers
Nature of societal upheaval	Societal impact	Engender new societal, cognitive schemes	Consolidate pre-existing societal schemes
	Who's involved within the company	Everybody: whatever function at whichever level	Primarily marketing
Delivered value		Value of product or service-in-use	Perceptual value
Features of the offering the marking enhances		Tangible characteristics/results	Symbolic stretching
Communication	Objective	Legitimize new cognitive schemes	Respect what has been established
	Customer status	Involved in innovation-building	Respected receiver
Manufacturer–retailer relationships		Common and naturally shared vision	Zero-sum game. Partnering motivated by likely damages of confrontation

TWO ILLUSTRATIONS

How does the marking concept work in concrete situations? We will apply the above mentioned typology to the two case stories presented in Chapters 2 and 3, Royal Canin and Wal-Mart.

Wal-Mart

Wal-Mart has constructed a marking that can be defined as reactive, at least in most of its dimensions.

1. *Strategic ambition:*
   - Merchandising expertise is the key driver.
   - Although Sam Walton inspired Wal-Mart's strategy, his success lay largely in the fact that he was an exemplary merchandising implementer. Later this task was handled by regional managers, who were in full charge of "excellence-in-execution."

2. *Market approach:*
   - Discount retailing existed well before Wal-Mart was launched. Supercenters too were nothing new when the company decided to launch its own in the early 1990's.
   - American consumers had already voted with their feet in making discount retailing a fast-growing sector.
   - Wal-Mart's targeting is not particularly focused. To a large extent implicit, the chain targets America's vast, value-conscious, middle- and lower-income households. The major visionary aspect (and, in this sense, it is somewhat proactive) of Wal-Mart's targeting has been to concentrate, at least initially, on U.S. rural backwaters.

3. *Nature of societal upheaval:*
   - Wal-Mart's main objective was to offer existing discount retail customers greater value for money – by being more clearly defined and professional in its merchandising (in areas such as the range of goods it stocked, the layout of its stores, or its approach to customer service) and much more effective and clear in its pricing (through its "Everyday Low Prices," or EDLP, claims) than its competitors.

- Wal-Mart's non-conspicuous, although very modern, approach to discounting was perfectly suited to, and reassured, U.S. shoppers, especially in rural areas.
- Improvements to the proposition over time were mostly of a commercial nature. Rather than dramatically changing consumption patterns, Wal-Mart's objective was to ensure that its consumers' needs were perfectly met.

4. *Delivered value:*
  - The right merchandise at the lowest price in the store's catchment area.
  - Service is about convenience, availability, and smiles.

5. *Features of the offering the marking enhances:*
  - Wal-Mart offers shoppers the most popular brands as well as its own store brand, at EDLP.
  - It gives due attention (and, ultimately, respect and status) to small towns and rural areas that previously did not have easy access to modern discount outlets.
  - It has proven that customer service is feasible even in a discounting context.
  - This combination of a high perception of quality at the lowest prices has definitely led Wal-Mart to become a "category killer": it has the major market share in the vast majority of product categories it is selling.

6. *Communication:*
  - EDLP requires fewer promotional and advertising activities.
  - Shoppers are not pampered, however they are fully respected.

7. *Relationship with suppliers:*
  - Over time, confrontational relationships with suppliers have been replaced with greater partnership activities (an example is the evolution of Wal-Mart's relationship with Procter & Gamble).
  - Wal-Mart believes strongly in intense information sharing with its suppliers.

Royal Canin

Looking at the period from 1996 to 2004, we see that Royal Canin established a marking modus operandi that has little, if any, resemblance to Wal-Mart's. We selected this case as the closest example we could find of pure proactive marking.

1. *Strategic ambition:*
   - Royal Canin's ambition was inspired by a new vision of the status of pets within society.
   - The expertise activated throughout the marking process was multifunctional and transversal.
   - Royal Canin's CEO led and promoted this marking in a daily, quasi-obsessive way.
   - The marking was the key and the rationale for everyone's daily actions.
   - The ambition nourished and spurred on dynamics of continuous improvement in the company's market approach. Royal Canin never felt that its market knowledge, no matter how good it was, did not need to be deepened and perfected.
   - Implementation did not aim at consolidating "snapshot" market knowledge, but at developing a missionary zeal: greater respect for pets.

2. *Market approach:*
   - Royal Canin never ceased contributing to the emergence and construction of new markets.
   - This ran counterintuitively to pre-existing collective wisdom, that pet foods are a mass-market product.
   - The target audience were pet experts (veterinarians and breeders) and pet owners sensitive to their advice.
   - A scientific understanding of the nutritional needs of domestic dogs and cats activated and consolidated the company. Royal Canin was culturally allergic to overly comfortable or unduly simplistic approaches. This not only ruled out the mass-market approach but also rudimentary segmentation schemes. With this scientific bent, the market naturally included multiple niches.
   - The company did not require artificial stimuli to reinvent itself. Its organizational discomfort with self-satisfaction, originating from a belief that its market approach could always be improved or fine-tuned, was a natural engine of continuous innovation.

3. *Nature of societal upheaval:*
- This marking favored a horizontal logic, networking with breeders, veterinarians, scientific laboratories, and specialized retailers, rather than a linear, top-down logic starting from the supplier, continuing with retailers, and ultimately reaching the customers.
- Royal Canin reestablished the status of stakeholders whose influence, vital with regard to pet health, had been vastly eroded over decades of mass marketing pet foods, giving these stakeholders great visibility and credibility.
- The company both endorsed and enforced a spirit of non-confrontation, of cooperation with these stakeholders.
- By modifying the societal roles of stakeholders, Royal Canin was shaking the political and social status quo. Pets can "make their voices heard" if they have enough dedicated ambassadors who may prescribe nutrition and health good practices (breeders, veterinaries, and so on).

4. *Delivered value:*
- The delivered "value-in-use" is exceptional from two standpoints: qualitatively, in terms of health criteria, and quantitatively. Royal Canin is, in the long run, more economical than competing brands.
- Because the price–performance ratio is considerably better than other pet food products, Royal Canin operates on a rationale of making a breakthrough rather than of incremental progress.
- The marketed proposition is very ambitious. It deals with the health and well-being of pets, and eventually, lengthening their life expectancies.

5. *Features of the offering enhanced by marking:*
- Royal Canin proposed products adapted almost perfectly to each pet's specific physiological characteristics and needs.
- Feeding was no longer left to the pet owner's judgment (which tends to be a projection of his or her own "gastronomic" tastes). The pet was given new status. This doesn't mean that anthropomorphism disappeared, but it was directed at more refined criteria. Pet owners, together with pets, modified their models of nutrition, with the primary objectives being health and vitality. Pets became a community with full respect accorded to their differences.

- The proposition gave the pet owner functional responsibility, as opposed to the emotional status that mass-marketing approaches favor.

6. *Communication:*
- Based entirely on respect for pets, health concerns, and the specific characteristics of each pet (breed, age, weight), the company's communications were entirely educational – it worked to instill a new approach to pet nutrition.
- Communications were circulated by multiple stakeholders: experts, influential opinion leaders, early adopters, and, more broadly speaking, by anyone who advocated pet's rights.

7. *Relationship with retailers:*
- The emphasis on partnerships result from a vision on nutrition shared by Royal Canin and its distribution network. Unlike the reactive marking rationale followed by other pet food brands, Royal Canin did not wait for confrontation to prove to be a failure before considering partnership activities.

THE NECESSITY OF MARKING

When and why does marking become a necessity for management? Royal Canin and Wal-Mart suggest a set of endogenous or internal reasons for enterprises to follow a marking route.

Companies that pursue a successful itinerary evolve, in most cases, within an irreversibly expanding marking context. A branding strategy alone quickly turns out to be too simplistic to carve out a relevant, durable market space.

Two key features motivate managers to become involved in marking: the significant and durable incomes that can result from marking, the organizational integration and cohesion that stem from marking.

Marking is reinforced by growing links between incomes and the quality of the company's rapport with its stakeholders. Marking naturally blurs the distinction between product and service, service being a part of rather than an addition to the product. The quality of relationships is a cornerstone of the process of building and maintaining competitive advantage.

Compared with non-marking, marking deepens the company's relationship to its users (as opposed to mere buyers). The relationship becomes stronger through enhanced service in the traditional sense and a clear recognition of targeted users' legitimacy and social distinction (such as the quasi-political right of small-town Americans to have access to modern retailers and good value for money; or the propagation of a philosophy of respect for pets and their rights to good health through nutrition). Branding aspires, in the best cases, to legitimize the seller and to reassure target customers of the seriousness of their relationship with them, with the balance of information heavily biased toward the seller.

The growing importance of associating products with relational dimensions is fed by several factors.

It starts with the consumer itself. Companies that do not fulfil their explicit or implicit promises are finding that lack of respect for the consumer is increasingly damaging. Even very powerful brands can be "punished" through a loss of market share or melting profits when they stop delivering on their promises. When Marks & Spencer, for instance, failed to deliver fashionable clothes to its evolving British middle-class customers, the consequences were dramatic. Consumers are more and more versatile and picky, and they refuse to be held captive. They express themselves in multiple ways. They "vote with their feet," shop around, and quickly switch away from unsatisfactory offerings. They are vocal and they can make a lot of noise. Consumers also benefit from various sounding boards that endorse their cause: the press, consumer associations, regulatory bodies, the courts (Hirschman 1970).

Another contributor to the increased relevance of relationships is the decline of technology as a source of competitive advantage. We live in a paradoxical period. On the one hand, technology is triumphing. On the other hand, it is not conducive to durable competitive advantage, because of the incredible speed of competitive imitation. With few exceptions, technological innovation spreads through the market extremely quickly, and patents and licenses offer increasingly modest protection. Strong relationships that have been nurtured over time by a company's corporate culture and values end up being a much more robust differentiator than technology.

Royal Canin's "technological" competitive advantage might only have lasted for weeks or months, but its relational advantage would endure for years. It would take an enormous time to replicate its patient efforts to build up and lead a web of opinion leaders and stake-holders, as it created for itself a quality edge in both products and logistics, becoming the benchmark in nutrition for breeders and scientific researchers, and constructing an organizational culture geared at fulfilling these clear goals.

A third factor is linked to a new feature of the competitive game. Companies no longer view the acquisition of new customers as their sole or primary objective. They also try to build customer loyalty, which means they need to delve deeper into the customer's user behavior. Most products are largely comparable with other products, and can easily be substituted. For example, on a construction site, a contractor might hesitate between several alternatives: say, concrete, metallic, or wooden or glass framings. Building loyalty in this case will depend on service quality and personalized relationships.

Successful marking relies heavily upon the quality of relationships with the various territory stakeholders to extract durable incomes. Marking's preeminence over branding is also linked to the status given to brands by many current marketing practices. Marketing professionals are regularly criticized either for isolating themselves in an ivory tower or for exhibiting a somewhat arrogant faith in their techniques and databases, at the expense of listening to the market through weaker, more qualitative – but socially quite mean-ingful – signals. In spite of clear indications that markets are becoming more fragmented or atomized, they can still fall into the trap of the "mass market" approach. Customers tend to feel they should be treated in a much more personalized way, at least from a service or a relational standpoint.

Henry Ford's recipes have become totally inadequate. Customers no longer buy the rationale that personalization would be impossible because of cost considerations: they do not want "less for less" but "more for less." They want their egos to be fully recognized even in large-scale retailing, a card brilliantly played by a leading American department store company. At Nordstrom, salespeople maintain "personal consumer books" on their customers and will call them proactively when they receive merchandise that they think corresponds to their individual tastes.

This quest to personalize offerings is accelerated by the fact that customers are becoming more and more educated and that information on products is now communicated precisely and swiftly through the internet. Customers can and do form a judgment on products or services before going to the store. Companies that rely on superficial differentiation, on brands with little content or products that are disconnected from their service requirements, are finding the consequences can be quite spectacular.

Marking's value-added discipline also has internal implications. It is this obsessive quest for added value creation that keeps top management and all internal social constituencies on the move.

Marking considerably reinforces the desire to work together. It stimulates social bonds and reinforces cooperative attitudes within the organization. Two negative issues may arise, though, which are ultimately doomed to destroy those social bonds and this cooperative stance: bureaucratization and marketization.

The bureaucratization syndrome sees management practices excessively driven by procedures. These procedures in turn translate into an extreme functional specialization and an abusive centralization of hierarchical authority. This syndrome can often be felt in large companies organized around a multidivisional model. It may take many years before solutions to stop this decline are found, as this requires stepping back and considering the causes of the decline. Often a company will spend some years trying to patch up the gaps using outdated techniques and old recipes. Which is, of course, totally wrong – because those techniques and recipes are often exactly what have generated the problems in the first place. It also comes as no surprise that solutions only begin to emerge when top management decides to deal with the problem head-on. In any case, adopting a curative approach is both costly and time consuming.

The marketization syndrome alters the behaviors of management and places the company in an operational mode that favors "short-termism" – the tyranny of quarterly results – and immediately measurable performances – the tyranny of quantification – (Michaud and Thoenig 2003). In this situation the company adopts quasi-market mechanisms to manage interfunctional transactions and interfaces. It substitutes the "internal customer" concept for that of "member of the organization." Relationships between headquarters and business units obey strict hierarchical rules, and individuals are rapidly replaced whenever short-term results are viewed as inadequate. The frequency with which some companies go through CEOs is just frightening! In such a context, the engine of behavior is individualistic utilitarianism, as mutual loyalty quickly fades away. Internal networks driven by experience and identity-sharing give way to a market of mercenaries, recruited externally, who demonstrate no great level of solidarity with their employer's mid- to long-term destiny.

Marking creates an extraordinary vehicle to give meaning to individual acts and to position them in a highly credible, shared vision. It creates elements of a common language that can unite daily operations into a clear strategic game plan. It builds up a socialization space that ties all parties together in a spirit of solidarity, as illustrated by Royal Canin. The moral exhortations of the CEO do not just pay lip service to the marking ambition: they give value and meaning to the practices required.

MARKING CONTINGENCIES

Any slackening of vigilance in maintaining the refined understanding of their environment, or any lack of respect or inconsistency toward the marking logic could very rapidly destabilize these success stories. Marking, whether reactive or proactive, requires that three conditions be fulfilled:

- the marking approach is internalized by the organization and by "external" stakeholders;
- it illuminates each daily action;
- it serves as an instrument through which to listen and interpret the world in all circumstances.

From this perspective, some situations may be especially problematic:

- if the surrounding world changes without the company noticing it in due time;
- if the company stops understanding how the marking process could fail or, on the contrary, succeed, and so becomes unable to accurately anticipate the evolution of its territory. A company that is not endowed, from a cognitive standpoint, with a robust action theory to understand the true reasons for its success is, finally, rather fragile.

Does one marking type systematically perform better than the other? Definitely not, as Wal-Mart, an example of reactive marking, and Royal Canin, an example of proactive marking, show. What is true is that different conditions favor one type over another, and that the key talents or skills differ from one marking type to the other. Proactive marking appears to work best when one or several of the following conditions are met:

- The company is rather new and its founder has a strong influence, as with Sam Walton, or a "re-founder" is given a lot of freedom to reshape the company, as with Henri Lagarde at Royal Canin. Wal-Mart is somewhat bound by the fact that it has improved immensely on retail concepts that had been in existence for some time before its inception.
- The company is relatively small in size. Royal Canin has 2,600 employees, whereas Wal-Mart counts more than 1,300,000 people in the U.S. alone. It is difficult to shake such a big ship.
- The company is not mainstream. It is not viewed as an institution in its economic sector. The risk of arrogance or self-complacency is therefore minimal. Wal-Mart, although immensely successful at its core business, has faced new challenges when it has moved to countries in which it cannot easily export its positioning and systems (see Chapter 6). Royal Canin, however, reflects the extravagant confidence of guys from the remote Gard region in the south of France, doing everything differently from the pet-food giants and their armies of MBA alumni.
- There is a palpable sense of what is at stake. At Royal Canin, the seriousness of the company's financial challenge was felt by most staff. A feeling of potential suffering, of quasi-vital risk linked with any incident, circulated through the organization. This type of anxiety, if there is any, is much more diffused at Wal-Mart.
- The company is not highly diversified. Royal Canin was not diversified across businesses or product categories, especially once it moved away from supermarket retailers. Because it put all of its eggs in the same basket, it was able to become exceptionally knowledgeable, creative and anticipatory with respect to this basket. Wal-Mart, however, has diversified into multiple formats, each of which includes multiple product categories. Its battlefields are numerous.
- The pressure for short-term results is not exaggerated. At Royal Canin, Henri Lagarde sold his shareholders the idea that success could only be built with a mid- to long-term perspective, sincere in his belief that this approach would, in time, lead to a stronger

94

market capitalization. Wal-Mart, whose ownership is still largely controlled by its founding family, similarly convinced shareholders in the early to mid-1990's that the strategic turnaround from discount retail department stores to Supercenters, would require some short-term sacrifices in profitability – in exchange for a brighter longer-term future. This is another piece of evidence that proactive ingredients can exist within primarily reactive marking.

By and large, proactive marking is much tougher on itself when it comes to self-imposed constraints. Its natural reference for success is the long term. Because its promises to society are ambitious and innovative, the imperative to continually renew its project is powerful, as it can never be satisfactory enough in its own eyes – nor, quite likely, in the eyes of its users. If it fails to reinvent itself, the proactive marker is digging its own grave. In such a game plan, the quality of the managers who drive the project and vision becomes crucial.

At Wal-Mart, the replacement of Sam Walton by David Glass, himself later replaced by Lee Scott, does not seem to have created any significant turmoil. What will happen to Royal Canin without Henri Lagarde? This question explains the choice made by Henri Lagarde in 1999 to prepare his departure with Alain Guillemin, his business partner for the past twenty years.

Proactive marking is the more complicated because it is difficult to build two proactive markings one after the other. Once a proactive marking runs out of steam (whether because of the pioneer's departure or resulting from one of the host of constraining conditions described above), is there any alternative to replacing it by reactive marking? Royal Canin may have reached such a level of collective appropriation of Henri Lagarde's ambition, and a collective recognition of all that it requires, that the company could keep up the pace of its success without its former CEO and inspirer.

To sum up, whether it is reactive or proactive, marking is multidimensional, involving action in three areas:

■ Internal management positions and practices characterizing the company's organization. Marking acts are used as a vehicle to establish a reference framework, a positioning (either voluntary or shaped by history), and a strategic and operational project that will guide the acts of the company and its people.

5

THE RIGHT MINDSET

Marking is not the result of accident. Nor does it fall from the gods. It does, however, presuppose a kind of compost, a fertile ground without which it cannot come into being, or will not last. It requires the entrepreneur and the enterprise to develop specific competences and acquire particular abilities.

You don't become a marker just by snapping your fingers. You must have the capacity for it and be mentally prepared. Yes, it is useful to have assimilated the concepts of strategic marketing and to have mastered the techniques of communication and market research, however marking basically relies on something else: the right mindset. This chapter is an examination of this prerequisite, so essential both for individuals and for companies that aspire to use marking as their distinctive competence.

In the jargon of international marketing, the term "suitable mindset" means a turn of mind or state of mind required to fully and completely attain a given objective. More precisely, this expression describes a set of traits specific to an individual or organization. This Gestalt brings together various ingredients: cognitive styles and world-views, moral standards and values, beliefs and convictions, behavioral aptitudes and ways of relating.

The mindset at issue here is the one needed when marking is your ambition; the one that lets you make the broad strokes and bring them into everyday application – as follow-through is at least as important as cleverness. Markers are not just inventors or talented innovators; they are also entrepreneurs, in that they stand outside the norm. Without putting this mindset into action, real excellence cannot be achieved. This is what first and foremost sets apart the people and the companies generally cited as exemplars of marking.

Then again, the right mindset is never just one person's – for example the entrepreneur with marking vision and a plan to excel. A right mindset limited to just one person, and hence never held by or communicated to others, will not take you very far. The great marking creators know how to mobilize their troops and make use of the organization around them. The right mindset is a shared culture. It can be taught, and it brings people together.

The mindset necessary for an excellent marking has six key features:

- Spotting, and knowing the meaning of, nascent phenomena or emerging worlds
- Seeing the outside world (society) more broadly, well beyond the market alone
- Putting oneself at the mercy of adequate information
- Taking a full or holistic picture of the customer
- Being willing to change the rules of the game and stretch the dominant social conventions
- Putting the customer at the center of the business.

We will look at six companies to illustrate how the mindset is kept alive and articulated. Each of them is or has been held up as a model in the world of management and is widely admired by marketing people. Still, these companies are active in quite different industries, have different national origins, and adopt proactive or nearly proactive marking postures. Four of them – Benetton, Club Med, Dyson, and IKEA – were created from scratch on their marking strategy. The other two, First Direct and Tesco, which have both developed through a long history, used marking as a lever for re-creating themselves with fresh momentum. In fact, although Tesco only began its re-foundation in 1986 (apart from some earlier signals of that move in the late 1970's), the company had already been a major player in British food retailing for more than half a century. Likewise, whereas First Direct was launched in 1989, its parent company Midland Bank had been known as one of the "Big Four" British clearing banks since the 19th century.

It is also worth mentioning that the "ending" dates of the marking periods quoted in Table 5.1 are purely indicative. The marking companies continued to innovate and reshape their territories well after those dates (some of them continue to this day).

TABLE 5.1 **Profiles of companies selected as illustrations**

	Economic sector and country of origin	Marking's role in the company's history	Type of marking	Marking period
Benetton	Knitwear manufacturer, Italy	Founder	Proactive	1965–90
IKEA	Furniture and home furnishings retailer, Sweden	Founder	Proactive	1971–90
Club Med	Vacation resorts, France	Founder	Proactive	1955–70
Tesco	Food retailer, UK	Re-Founder	Reactive	1986–98
First Direct (A Midland division)	Retail banking, UK	Re-Founder	Reactive	1989–96
Dyson	Vacuum cleaner manufacturer, UK	Founder	Reactive	1982–95

ATTENTION TO EMERGING WORLDS

The first trait of the marking mindset is that it feeds strategic inspiration with a societal early-warning system. Good markers ignore their company's and the market's accepted conventions. They do not hesitate to believe that the world their company faces is disappearing, and that they must therefore evolve.

Poor marking is based on the features of the present world, which are just so many legacies of the past about to be thrown aside by a future already underway. It aims for spots where the competition is very likely to be entrenched and demand reasonably served. It more or less articulates and guides the company's plans by looking in the rearview mirror.

Executives and managers who build successful markings show very special talent. They combine real boldness with a lot of smarts and quite a bit of luck. When the marking is reactive, they understand that current practices will lose you your foothold in a distinctive or specific territory, so that you must reconquer it and push out the competitors who have taken up the key position. When the marking is proactive, they keep listening to society for the rumblings or weak signals that might become main currents in the near future. Their strategy is to be early. They detect well before their competitors the developing social, moral or esthetic trends. Then they look into their implications, the opportunities they may open up and the solutions their business might develop. The goal of such pioneers is obvious. They want to be the first to serve the trend, hastening its birth if necessary.

This mindset gives a very particular profile to the individuals and organizations that adopt it. The marker acts as a sort of social sponge. He or she takes an interest in nascent tendencies and probable changes in behavior, lifestyle, aspirations, values, and institutions. Their aptitude for decoding signals better than others, or before they do, is strongly correlated with the richness of their background knowledge, and often with the poverty of the knowledge of their actual or potential competitors.

To pick up on these emerging signals, markers use their own antennae, for example, in where and how they spend their time. They spend time with people outside their business. They pay attention to social settings traditionally remote from the business world, and even from market research. They listen to society and for emerging phenomena in the areas of consumption, culture, religion, or living space. They dive into social science and take artists seriously. They pay attention to marginal or underground phenomena and take up forecasting and futurism. They use their intuition and their sensitivity. What makes sense to them is less what their peers talk about and what the figures are showing than what in-depth observation brings out in the way of facts with a future import.

They aspire, moreover, to create and deliver some greater good for society's consumers. They sound like missionaries, if not politicians. They see themselves as people who shape the lives of citizens, who produce value in the broadest sense.

The marker, then, is not some ethereal prophet. Markers do not mistake their dreams for reality, even if they are personally convinced that out of their work they will come true. They cannot be pure-minded zealots with an altruistic utopia, because economic feasibility is their bottom line. Of course, neither are they conformists, too afraid of their own to question the conventions and customs of their little world. Markers transform the habits and rules of the game, the ways of living and consuming, the status of things and their symbols. They elevate the role of the Outsider.

And so: Luciano Benetton was born in 1935 in a poor region of northern Italy. He worked from the age of fourteen in a clothing store in Treviso. Militantly, he sold left-wing newspapers. In 1955, with his sister Giuliana, he started a family business making sweaters, which he himself would sell door-to-door on his bicycle. On at least two occasions he would exhibit a remarkable intuitive sense.

In the late 1950's, a particular phenomenon caught Benetton's attention. The West at the time was experiencing an economic boom. The sustained population growth was creating a horde of adolescents and young adults. Not only that, the general feeling was extraordinarily positive. Italians were looking to break with the gray years of war and reconstruction. This gave them an enormous appetite for anything playful, unorthodox or colorful. Now, at that time there was no such thing as sweaters designed especially for young people, any more than there were relaxed-looking sweaters for adults. No one in the industry offered anything that singled out and satisfied these new customers. But there was an industrial zone outside the city of Prato with a network of flexible, competitive suppliers. This was the alchemy on which Luciano and his family built their innovative ideas about design, production, distribution and communication.

A second strong intuition took shape in 1989. Benetton launched an advertising campaign promoting racial equality. Thought inappropriate even by the standards of creative advertising types, and suicidal in business circles of the time, this initiative embodied, at least in part, one more way for the business to fit in with something it was already familiar with. It was able to identify the emergence of a new anti-conformity expressed by the company's main targets. Young people and adults really seemed increasingly eager to adopt a relaxed lifestyle at odds with the conventions of their elders. Many people found the crude nature of the photography and the openly polemic and political message disturbing and a little shocking. Yet 83% to 95% of the 18–24 age group said they liked this early antiracist campaign. The rate was undoubtedly even higher among Benetton customers.

IKEA officially launched the formula that brought the company success in 1971: furniture assembled by the client, open-floor merchandising, immediate availability of items and parts, and so on. This launch, however, was the result of 20 years' work in which IKEA's founder, Ingvar Kamprad, must have set a record in the furniture industry for trial and error. The 1971 formula took root in the attention he paid to an observation about his immediate environment. The Swedish working class of the day were finding it difficult to furnish their homes with good quality items at affordable prices. This effort to, as they say, popularize home furnishing is summed up by Kamprad in IKEA's mission statement. "We offer a broad selection of furnishings that work well and look good, at prices so low that the majority of people can afford them."

A third illustration of a marking that was derived from a deep, intuitive grasp of emerging societal tendencies is provided by the founders of Club Méditerranée, today rechristened Club Med.

Club Méditerranée was created in the post-war period, in 1950, by Gérard Blitz. Initially it was designed to be a non-profit association – a sports club for friends and mutual acquaintances. The members of this association slept in tents, in sleeping bags, and took turns sharing common chores.

This venture capitalized on a drive to which the established hotel industry, oddly enough, gave no credit, although a new, financially solvent social strata felt it. Blitz detected a considerable appetite among city dwellers for active leisure and sports, provided it was satisfied in a comfortable and carefree setting. He conceived the club formula. His product brought together aspects of a tranquil vacation and those of one that takes people away from the everyday. It banished all outward signs of social status among people in the villages. With participants living in their bathing suits and never handling money, the holiday village honored an egalitarian quality appreciated by modern white-collar people. Club Med provided, as their American slogan would later put it, an "antidote to civilization."

In 1954, Gilbert Trigano, who had supplied tents for the earliest villages and was a friend of Gérard Blitz (sharing his affinity for left-wing politics), joined the Club full time. He turned the non-profit organization into a for-profit business. The chores that had been handled collectively by members would henceforth be given to a paid staff. It seemed plain enough that in a leisure society with rising middle-class incomes, people wanted to get away from housework and the kitchen to live in a truly "care-free" environment.

Our fourth example of marking creation, Dyson, is of a slightly different nature. An inventor by nature and a designer by trade, James Dyson was extremely irritated by the pitiful performance of the vacuum cleaners he used, regardless of their age and price. In his words: "We were all victims of a gigantic con by the [vacuum cleaner] manufacturers. They fit these bags and the bloody things clog up immediately … all suggestions of new technology were merely marketing hype" (Dyson 2002, p. 104). Dyson invented the Dual Cyclone, which used cyclonic separation to replace the bag with a "little typhoon that spun at the speed of sound, in a chamber that doesn't clog" (Dyson 2002, p. 5). But James Dyson says that he hates being coined as proactive, and fairly so, for what the new product did was to overcome a problem that other vacuum-cleaning systems presented.

Dyson's success required years of effort. He formally established his company in 1979, but it took three years and more than 5,000 proto-types for him to create the vacuum cleaner he envisioned. Years of licensing the technology throughout the world resulted at first in only moderate sales, with the exception of Japan where the passion for technology made it a successful niche product. But it was only when Dyson took full control of the engineering and production sides of the product that it was ready for full-fledged commercial success – 14 years later in the UK.

This presentation would not be thorough without mentioning a second ingredient of Dyson's revolutionary proposition: product design. Dyson's innovative designs reinforced the technological distinction of his vacuum cleaners. His utilitarian view of product design stressed that design must be at the service of technology, and not the reverse. This fusion of technical and esthetic features ulti-mately made the product extremely easy and comfortable to use, and caused it to become integrated into our daily lives (Dyson 2005).

Benetton, IKEA and Club Med are good illustrations of a category of companies that from the outset developed their plans by taking into account highly meaningful social forces. Dyson for his part put together a marking plan that was initially an indictment of a whole industry found lacking in terms of technology. Only later did he blend it perfectly with the sociological aspirations of modern, rather affluent consumers.

As for First Direct and Tesco, they provide examples of another type of marking. As heirs to an existing history, these companies turned out to have a special talent, at the right time, for reinventing themselves, finding a second wind and reestablishing themselves, due to their apti-tude for picking up the social signals relevant to their business.

Introduced in Leeds by Midland Bank in October 1989, First Direct is customized retail banking by telephone. It is open 24 hours a day, 7 days a week. From the moment of its creation, First Direct was able to capitalize on the great frustration of many bank customers with the inefficiencies and constraints of branch banking. A poll conducted in 1988 revealed that about 40% of customers found the hours of branches to be inconvenient. Furthermore, about 50% stated they had never met the manager of their branch and that they went there as infrequently as possible. More basically, an increasing number of Britons seemed to care increasingly about saving time. The basic transactions with their bank appeared to them as so much drudgery. British society in the late 1980's was looking riper and riper for any solution to reduce this drudgery. It was also true that telephone installations in the U.K. were widespread enough for First Direct's initial gamble to seem reasonable, both to the company and its customers.

Tesco provides another case of re-foundation. Jack Cohen opened the first Tesco grocery store in London in 1929. The Tesco chain of stores took off significantly in the early 1930's in the aftermath of the Great Depression. Jack Cohen was later on quite impressed by American self-service supermarkets, and he forged a philosophy of "pile it high and sell it cheap," which became the guiding principle of Tesco's strategy for many years to come. By the late 1960's – and largely through acquisitions – Tesco had become a chain of almost 800 stores. However, in the 1970's, Tesco failed to keep in step with British consumers' new aspirations for quality and choice. Consumers developed a negative image of Tesco. The company was perceived as competing almost exclusively on price, with poorly maintained stores and an assortment of items that were often seen as inadequate and of mediocre quality (Waldman and Sood 1999).

The first signals that the company wanted to change came in the late 1970's with the closing of 500 "marginal" stores, the discontinuation of Green Shield trading stamps (which were viewed as giving a low-market image to the company), and the launch of the company's private labels.

But the actual re-foundation only took place in the mid-1980's, once Lord MacLaurin was appointed chairman. The decision to move upmarket was accompanied by a massive investment to transform the exising outlets into modern superstores. Sir Terry Leahy, today's CEO of Tesco, was then a deputy managing director, and was a key architect in this re-foundation. By choosing a consumer-centric approach to rebuild the company's strength, Sir Terry heavily influenced the strategy and the evolution of its corporate culture. At a time when British consumers were becoming wealthier and more sophisticated, he dramatically improved the quality and freshness of Tesco's produce. He also began to increase the proportion of non-food items sold in the superstores. The value-for-money core positioning of the company was firmly reestablished. In 1993, Tesco also cleverly blocked the expansion of hard discounters – who were trying to make inroads in British retailing – by launching its "Value" line, which offered consumers rock-bottom prices on 70 basic products. Tesco was also an innovator in launching its Clubcard loyalty scheme in February 1995. Those efforts ultimately led to Tesco's leadership of the market in March 1995.

A BROAD AND OPEN VIEW OF THE OUTSIDE WORLD

A second trait distinguishes the "suitable mindset" for excellence in marking. Its frame of reference for conducting business is not limited to the market. It becomes society at large.

The competitors of Benetton, IKEA, Tesco, and First Direct gave them room to maneuver because, unlike them, they were really only interested in the current basis of competition. They left to the pioneers the risks of innovation. They based their skepticism on their "realism," which consisted of only believing in what was before their eyes. They thought they could catch up, if necessary, by virtue of their experience or size. But marking implies a broader benchmark, not just a basis of competition as gauged by criteria like market share. The experience of established business people is often, to the great joy of the innovator, a source of blindness or slowness in terms of societal signals.

When Benetton identified an opportunity to introduce a line of fuzzy, brightly colored sweaters, he found this gap completely ignored by competitors big and small. An offering of sweaters for youth and adults wanting casual and upbeat clothing simply did not exist. This only shows how the competition was thinking product while Benetton was thinking customer.

Benetton also took an atypical stance in terms of point-of-sale. He was the first to dare to put up one-brand, one-product stores for sweaters, which automatically gave the product and the brand a prestige that no other retailer had bestowed before. In the face of such boldness, the competition remained doubtful and slow to react. It is interesting to find that even today Benetton has many local retail competitors such as Giordano and Asie, but none of them competes globally.

IKEA continued to capitalize on expectations for popularized furniture because up till then no Swedish producer found this an apt positioning. In fact, from the early 1950's, its competitors pressured the Swedish furniture makers' association not to sell to IKEA – well before 1971 when the IKEA formula was set. The boycott became an opportunity for IKEA, which in 1961 bought furniture in Poland, where it was plentiful and cheap. IKEA gradually built up its own supplier network in countries where it found both low-wage labor and real craftsmanship. Thus the company quickly got into the self-manufacture of furniture. The narrow-mindedness of its competitors greatly helped IKEA to master its trade.

Still, it would be wrong to overstate the coherence and logic behind the IKEA formula (Villette and Vuillermot 2005). It came about more as the result of improvizations, which let the company turn constraints into opportunities. Furniture in parts packed in flat cardboard boxes was first conceived in 1956 as something for mail order. Though the formula failed commercially (the furniture offered was of very mediocre quality), the concept of flattened furniture stuck. And the formula of a store coupled with a warehouse dates from 1971, after a fire in the Stockholm store.

Club Med was able to consolidate its dominance in the vacation club industry over several decades and relatively undisturbed. Numerous imitators did appear as time went on. But none managed to duplicate the fullness of the concept. Club Med fans kept their loyalty to the formula because they could find the same spirit and atmosphere in many places the world over. The number of villages, their diversity and the quality of the resorts were essential competitive weapons. The imitators were pale ones compared with Club Med, which ended up buying many of them. This was the case with Voir et Connaître in France, Valtur in Italy (since resold) and more recently Aquarius.

One other factor helped Club Med to get started, especially in France and many other European countries. Travel agents looked unfavorably upon the rise of the Club. This formula did indeed deprive them of a business activity they considered their prerogative: putting together tour packages. Given this reluctance, Club Med decided to go into direct distribution, through its own agencies and call centers. This gave them more control over their image.

When James Dyson first presented his idea for a cyclonic vacuum cleaner it raised an amazing wave of skepticism from potential manufacturers. Even within Kirk-Dyson – the company he was a partner in, but where his decisional power had been diluted over time – a director told him that his idea couldn't be any good. If there were a better kind of vacuum cleaner, Hoover or Electrolux would have invented it. James Dyson had an ironic comment on this: "You can't imagine a Russian saying to Lenin in 1917: 'Hey! Vladimir, we can't have a revolution. If there were a better way, the Romanovs would have thought of it'" (Dyson 2002, p. 117).

Once the cyclonic vacuum cleaner became a market reality, it was then attacked by market leaders (primarily by Hoover) through a mixture of legal battles and, according to Dyson, distorted advertising claims. Before the British market was "Dysonized," Hoover was still reassuring itself that Dyson would remain a niche product. Self-complacency of historically dominant market leaders can be of enormous help to innovative entrants.

But, first and foremost, Dyson shows that dominant brands have little power when confronted with competitive breakthrough innovation. Once again, the philosophy spelled out by James Dyson is quite enlightening. "Brand is only important when products are identical ... brand dependence was quite simply shattered when the Dyson came along, because it gave the consumer something better. And suddenly the customer had something other than brand to look at" (Dyson 2002).

Broad-mindedness is not the privilege of innovators alone. Why shouldn't re-founders also take advantage of relatively unaggressive competitors and thereby create an undeniable distinctiveness in their industry?

When Tesco began its innovative strategy in the mid-1980's, it was lagging behind the "Grande Dame" of British Food retailing: J. Sainsbury. What were the deficiencies or inadequacies in Sainsbury's decisions or postures that facilitated Tesco's climb to the No. 1 spot?

Historically, Sainsbury's had always been focused on quality, so much so that it paradoxically was much slower than Tesco in sensing the value-for-money expectations emerging among its British consumers. Whenever it finally began price reductions, Sainsbury's seemed disconnected from its traditional quality pitch. It was failing to look at the customer's "whole shopping experience" (*Marketing*, May 15, 1997). In fact, Sainsbury's imitated Tesco rather than making proactive propositions to the market. For example, it launched its loyalty program 18 months after Tesco's. Sainsbury's built itself a follower image well before it actually lost its market leadership. Viewed from another angle, all these elements were clear symptoms of a corporate culture that was far more product-driven than customer-centric.

Moreover, from an even more pragmatic standpoint, Sainsbury's was probably unable to respond to Tesco as aggressively as needed because, in the late 1980's, it diverted a lot of its resources away from the adaptation and revamping of its core UK business. In fact, several expensive acquisitions were made, including supermarket chains in the U.S. (such as Shaw's) and hardware retailers in the U.K. (Texas Homecare). To use a military metaphor, it may be unwise to attack new strategic fronts when you are not safe and robust at your strategic base.

First Direct understood that its market was not, strictly speaking, normal banking but creating a time-saving convenience for its customers, enhanced by personalized interactions. This approach opened up two possibilities. On the one hand it allowed a broadening of its line, to which a product like auto insurance could easily be added. On the other, it guaranteed the loyalty of a customer no longer thought of as an account number but rather as an individual with whom to have an active relationship. First Direct's competitors, even if they did use the telephone as a channel to complement their branches, understood too late the breadth of what First Direct was offering, which allowed it to prosper undisturbed.

PUTTING ONESELF AT THE MERCY OF SUITABLE INFORMATION

Marking calls on a third ability: a fierce and confident belief in the virtue of information. This attitude can in some cases verge on passion. Its corollary is complete acceptance of whatever verdict this information may render, even if it carries a sentence without appeal.

Marking assumes a completely pragmatic mindset. Subjective reality and rationalization do not stand up to facts and their meaning. When it comes to marking, really excellent efforts were and are fed by information. Plans get defined and corrected as they go, by trial and error.

It takes thinking of "information" in the broadest sense. It can be scientific information, such as Royal Canin and L'Oréal constantly exploit. It can be descriptive statistics. It can simply be information coming from firsthand, on-the-ground knowledge.

Of course, information and intuition are not mutually exclusive. Quite the opposite, they enrich and stimulate each other. This is especially true at the very outset of an entrepreneurial effort. Information does not mean giving up on a broader vision, but giving it a full-scale experimental test. Furthermore, it does not mean giving in to the myopia of the short-term, of this month's bottom line. It is about trading off near-term resources against medium-term objectives.

In other words, information has to be a reason to learn, not a support to rigid thinking. It sets off activity through trial and error. The fact that a marking works in no way relieves you from thinking about why it works. Proactive marking assumes that the individual and the company avoid the cognitive dissonance syndrome, which denies the credibility of information contradictory to in-grown prejudices and beliefs (Festinger 1957).

Luciano Benetton, while personally selling the family product line up and down Italy, picked up on consumers' frustrations. He applied his on-the-ground information and worked out a new concept for sweaters. A few years later he noticed something else of strategic use in the analysis of market trends. For example, winter sales at some stores, such as in the mountain resort of Cortina d'Ampezzo, a socially representative place where cold weather came early, permitted him to gather precious information for planning his upcoming production of patterns and colors. He used it to weave an informational net between point of sale, warehouse and factory.

At Club Med, there is a very real belief in information. Nevertheless, it has been limited for a long time to a remarkable tool that measures customer satisfaction in the form of a questionnaire that guests find in their mailboxes when they return home. This questionnaire, called "the satisfaction barometer" in the Club's jargon, has an exceptionally high response rate of nearly 50%. Anyone who knows the importance of word-of-mouth as a business generator in the service sector (65% of new Club Med customers come there mainly from positive word-of-mouth) will grasp the relevance and the importance of this barometer. Still, one of the dangers in overrelying on such a tool is remaining ignorant of non-customers and hence needing more traditional tools of market study.

IKEA also shows an extremely firm belief in the virtue of information. How could it be otherwise for a company that has to manage almost 2,000 suppliers in over 50 countries and stocks more than 200 stores in almost 40 countries? Information for them does one main job. It works as a control on the reliability of an extremely strict system put in place to manage, at low cost and within quality standards, a widespread constellation. What sort of market and customer information is there beyond sales figures? Employees are actively encouraged to suggest initiatives. First these are tested in just one particular store. If successful, means of quickly replicating them throughout the system are put into action. To this end IKEA can play on such advantages as the great geographic mobility of its supervisory personnel, especially store managers.

At First Direct, information is the cornerstone of the system. In fact, the personalized interaction with the customer is possible because the telephone counselors can instantly have on their screens a history of the relationship with a given customer. What is more, this history includes qualitative information about the customer. The men and women working as counselors are indeed trained to enter into the database all relevant qualitative information they can glean about the customer during the phone call. This qualitative data allows the bank to understand the customer as something other than a bunch of statistics.

Information is also extremely critical at First Direct when creating new ways of interacting with the customer. This is why in 1997 the bank ran two successive market tests before introducing an option for customers to interact with the bank from their personal computers. The same thing was done two years later with internet banking. In both cases First Direct made full use of test-customers' response to these new technologies in order to put the finishing touches to their offerings.

First Direct also has an extremely sophisticated operations information system for managing wait times and eliminating as many bottlenecks as possible. This immediate efficiency that the customer can feel fits right into the marketing. A big part of the customer promise turns on the speed of banking transactions.

Tesco is an exceptional case of looking for and using information to guide a customer-centric conquest of the market. This began with a definite ability to identify market trends and to adapt product offerings accordingly. In the early 1990's, Tesco initiated a focus on freshness of food and expanding its non-food range. This priority has continued and grown ever since. Food assortment now includes health and organic products, ethnic foods, and convenience foods (smaller packages, pre-cooked meals). Non-food items now account for more than 20% of UK sales and are growing at twice the rate of food sales.

But in addition to collecting and performing marketing and sociological studies to track customers' evolving lifestyles, Tesco also uses more down-to-earth data that generates powerful knowledge from various information sources to update its propositions to customers.

The company runs Customer Question Time sessions (which 9,000 customers attended in 2004). This communication channel helps it understand what really matters for customers. To keep in close touch with customers, as well as with staff, each head office and distribution manager spends one week every year working in a store through a scheme called TWIST (The Week In Store Together). Last but not least, the Clubcard loyalty program targets over 11 million customers. It provides enormous sources of data for future, more segmented and/or personalized, pitches to customers.

When it comes to information gathering, Dyson is atypical in comparison with our other examples. James Dyson's major source of inspiration is his observation of the hassles encountered in the use of everyday objects. Prior to the cyclonic vacuum cleaner, James Dyson had also marked another utilitarian product: the wheelbarrow. He invented the Ballbarrow, replacing the wheel with a ball, which solved problems associated with wheelbarrows digging furrows in soft lawns, sinking in heavy mud, or losing their balance when carrying heavy loads. As we said earlier, the cyclonic vacuum cleaner also resolved problems posed by traditional vacuum cleaners, such as clogging and losing their suction power over time.

Once the product was launched, Dyson used its customers as major inspirers of product improvement. "We take any complaint very seriously, even if it arises out of the customer's own error [such as a failure to read the instructions properly], and we solve the problem. Customer feedback is our way of foretelling and directing our future and we spare no expense in acting on that feedback" (Dyson 2002).

More generally, the champions who excel at marking have a distinct propensity in their personal reading for works that are not strictly managerial. The personal time devoted to this is sacred, and considered as a prime cognitive investment. When Henri Lagarde chairs meetings at Royal Canin, the briefcase at his side holds as many accounts of ancient Greek military battles as veterinary reports on dog ailments. He also has a small desk used for nothing but reading. The sources he consults can be surprisingly catholic.

These champions also pay attention to the spoken word. They use the "wandering around" technique to see if the weak signals they are picking up have any relevance. In each of these six companies you'll find a strong culture of keeping an ear to the ground. Nothing is more alien to marking than the mythical captain piloting his ship from the cabin and looking only at his instrument panel.

A FULLER OR HOLISTIC DEFINITION OF THE CUSTOMER

There is a fourth ingredient to the right mindset. It involves a fleshed out picture of the customer that is shaped neither by the short term nor exclusively by the salesman's way of thinking. When it leads to excellence, it takes several forms. Rather than reduce customers to the mere level of consumers, the goal is to recognize them and treat them more broadly, as individuals.

IKEA's philosophy, for example, is very clear on this. It is summed up in two expressions that are not just slogans coined for appearance's sake. The first states that IKEA's "goal is not to create value for customers but to call on them to create their own value from the company's merchandise." The second stresses that, "Wealth is the ability to carry out one's ideas."

At Club Med, the president of the American division explained back in the 1980's how he turned a guest into a GM (*gentil membre* or "gracious member"). He explained in a memo that it was a process of transforming a group of ordinary professional people who start off as strangers stuck with each other, into a group of relaxed, lively friends who get so into it that they help the GOs (*gentils organisateurs* or "gracious organizers") in welcoming the next group of people.

For Tesco, retailing has never been, since its rebirth in the late 1980's, a story of selling products. In fact, customer service has always been viewed as the key driver of differentiation. For instance, in 1997 Tesco launched a spectacular and successful program: the "one in front" policy of opening more checkouts when customers had more than one customer in front of them in the queue. In the same spirit, by 1998, 63 stores were open 24 hours a day, taking into account the fact that, at the time, one million people in the UK worked until 11 pm and 300,000 finished work between 2 and 5 am. This obsession to reinforce customer service has never ceased. Today, almost 400 stores are open all day long. Grab n' Go fresh food counters are available in many large stores for customers who want a daily "refill" on fresh products without going through the full shopping trip. All these initiatives are designed to position Tesco as a holistic convenience-builder, and not as an ordinary retailer. This is reinforced by its diversification into services such as Tesco.com, its internet arm that today is by far the largest online grocer in the world, Tesco Personal Finance offers a full range of financial services that have been made simpler and easier to access for customers, and Tesco Telecoms lets customers satisfy all their needs in terms of telephone and internet communication. Chapter 6 will expound more on how Tesco's segmentation schemes nourish the convenience-building process.

At Dyson, two obsessions together created trust relationships with customers. As mentioned, the company is very keen on perfecting how its products are adapted to its customers' daily lives. It even puts moral pressure on itself by "never being satisfied with the product." The second concern is about outstanding service. Dyson considers that *real* service, like *real* innovation, is what people want more than anything. And without a doubt, Dyson is running the extra mile in this area. Customers are free to phone the hotline for as long as their Dyson is under guarantee. If need be, a brand-new machine will be delivered the next morning. Until the guarantee expires, the faulty machine will be picked up immediately, repaired by Dyson and returned by courier.

At First Direct, personalizing and valuing the customer permeates strategy, operations and human resource decisions.

The great markers are chiefly preoccupied with the customer as user. The customer as buyer comes second. He or she is not reduced to being a wallet or a credit card. Because target customers are people who put together their own furniture, IKEA has very advanced thoughts about product use. Since a stay at Club Med is by definition an extraordinary experience, it is the customer who decides on the mix of activities he or she will pursue while in the vacation village. It is First Direct's customers who initiate contact with their bank. Which makes them easily thought of as users. Three months are spent welcoming and educating a new customer. First Direct, moreover, takes pride in not trying to sell him any products or services complementary to the ones he already signed up for, unless the salespeople see a reason for it in his personal history.

Focusing on use leads in turn to the customer's needing more of the selling company's expertise, either from the sales force or the marketing system in the broadest sense. So at IKEA, not only the catalogues but also the point-of-sale signs, the detailed ticketing of products and the store layout suggest and show the products in use in actual situations.

GETTING AWAY FROM THE RULES OF THE GAME

The right mindset is also characterized by non-conformity and a lack of inhibition. Upsetting the existing rules of the game in his industry whets the marker's appetite and stokes his imagination.

Such innovative, even iconoclastic work rigorously combines two things. It proceeds from the markers' intuitions, prone as we just saw them to be, to thoroughly capitalize on consumers' frustrations. And it comes into play as much with customers, the market and society as with employees and business partners such as suppliers, distributors, opinion-makers, political bodies or associations of stakeholders such as consumers.

Luciano Benetton put together a product offering that was, and remains, completely iconoclastic in terms of the pre-existing strategies of sweater makers. His company dared to upend accepted practice of the time and succeed with the unthinkable. It no longer set fashion in terms of pattern above all, but basically in terms of color. Now, relegating pattern to second place was a bit of boldness seen as suicidal by everyone else who made or sold clothing.

Moreover, Benetton's idea for stores was bold and completely innovative. Breaking from traditional clothing stores. Benetton sold only sweaters and only one brand of sweater. With highly visible shop window displays, shoppers could discover the magic of the colors from outside the store. Customers also enjoyed open access to the merchandise.

Advertising was the third aspect of the Benetton revolution. It was oriented to social themes thought to resonate with the aspirations of Benetton's target customers. Even in the supposedly daring world of advertising agencies, images and copy that frankly refer to torture and racism to promote sweater sales do not arise from business-as-usual.

Luciano Benetton also innovated in terms of business relationships. He agreed to give up nominal control of his production and built an industrial zone that tied him to hundreds of sub-contractors in the Treviso area, to whom he gave non-strategic production work such as sewing. He did the same with thousands of retailers throughout the world. If the principle was original for the time, and for a country like Italy, the means used were more so. Benetton relied on trust, not written contracts. Benetton has worked with its French or American distributors by putting together strong long-term relationships based on each other's word. This system obviously makes it possible to maximally externalize investment and risk. Compared with its competitors in the world of fashion, Benetton possesses an extraordinary strategic flexibility.

The necessary trade-off in containing the effects of dispersion depends on an exceptional aptitude for oversight. Here again Benetton dared to break with business routine. In terms of selling, this oversight was entrusted to sales agents. These ambassadors are extremely powerful. Their commissions are based on their sales to retailers. Then they are encouraged to own or partly own certain stores themselves. Still more surprisingly, they have no formal contractual ties with Benetton.

Equally heterodox is the selection of collaborators who are not themselves conformists. Such as the architect who designed Benetton's avant-garde factory, or Olivero Toscani, the longtime creator of the company's unusual advertising.

IKEA thoroughly revolutionized the sale of furniture and household furnishings. The Swedish company set up a new division of labor between itself and its customers, and also between itself and its suppliers. In its quest to popularize this business, it combined four features never before brought together under one roof: low prices; customers taking home their furniture to assemble it themselves; guaranteed functional, good quality products; and open access to the product in large warehouses. In fact, IKEA brought off a feat thought impossible: it developed an incomparable service orientation while operating in a largely self-service environment.

An early innovation concerned the customer's relationship to the product inside and outside the store. IKEA worked upstream of the customer's visit by publishing a catalogue with precise information aimed at questions the customer would have once in the store. Thanks to the advance catalogue, customers could feel prepared for their shopping trip. One doesn't go into IKEA the way one goes into other stores. Furthermore, the layout of the point of sale is carefully thought out and truly original. Indeed, the way complementary products are arranged together is very illuminating for the customer. Products are ticketed in a precise way and customers can consult a salesperson at any time, just by asking. They do not feel abandoned; rather, they feel recognized.

The second ingredient in creating an approach outside the canon of self-service at the time was to relieve the customer of all care while in the store. Baby strollers, child-care areas, and measuring tapes and pencils to measure products are supplied to shoppers. Further, the physical organization of the store is an invitation to take a look at everything in it.

The third ingredient has to do with quality. The network IKEA has built up of specialized product and parts suppliers requires it to produce in huge quantities. The resulting economies of scale enable the Swedish company to offer the low prices that are part of its customer promise. But low price is not inconsistent with quality. IKEA pioneered this through the way it managed specifications and worked out procedures for quality assurance. It was one of the first companies to form a permanent committee of suppliers that would formalize their role. Internally, within the stores and with respect to customers, the procedures are just as rigorous, and the rigor is not incompatible with employee suggestions and initiatives.

Club Med invented a new way to go on vacation, one right in synch with the 1950–80 period; that is, with the new middle classes' massive access to economic well-being. The promise given to the GM is threefold: You will meet people, experience graciousness and learn something.

Meeting people is enabled in many ways. The village architecture centers on an area including the main restaurant, the offices, the shops and the auditorium. The restaurant is organized by tables of eight, meaning that couples and families are seated with people they did not know before. The Club sells beds, not rooms, and several GMs can find themselves sharing a room. The rooms are designed and furnished in a manner that was for many years almost Spartan, without TV or minibar, which encouraged the GMs to get out and join in group activities. Room service is not provided, which also makes the GMs get out and take their meals together, including breakfast. Finally, and principally, each village continuously offers a large number of group activities organized by the GO, which fosters a group experience and the chance to meet people.

Graciousness (as Club Med translates the very French *gentillesse*), which forms the second historical attribute of the promise, is inherent to Club Med culture. It is reinforced by calling people, even in non-French countries, *"gentils members"* and *"gentils organisateurs."* It ties in, of course, to the way GOs are recruited, which is based on personality and behavior and not just technical competence. Thus Club Med makes sure that even its scuba instructors, for all their training and certificates, are not hopeless when it comes to social interaction, and are able to relate to people.

Then there is learning, an exceptional value-added the Club offers the vacationer. The GOs are also meant to be teachers in their specialty, whether athletic, intellectual (computing, bridge, Scrabble, and so on), or artistic.

Club Med is a company selling service in the full sense of the word. This means the business depends for its life on one thing: the quality of its human resources. Studies conducted at Club Med confirm that the success of the villages in comparison with materially similar offerings will always be connected to the abilities of the village chief and the GOs he or she hires, and to the resulting atmosphere and excitement.

First Direct broke all the rules of British retail banking. It married convenience, user-friendliness, personalization and speed, all things that till then seemed impossible to offer. In so doing, the business proved that a chore could be metamorphosed into a positive experience. Their gamble on the telephone as a good channel of personalized interaction assumed a number of preconditions. It was necessary to accompany it with an suitable technological environment (the highest performing software for managing call centers), with a system designed for collecting and using quantitative and qualitative data about the customer, and with human resources with a talent for service. Thus phone counselors were chosen not for their technical banking competence but for their personality. They recruited nurses, social workers, teachers and firemen, all professionals who have presumably learned the required skills for serving people: empathy, being used to working irregular hours, and calm in the face of emotional pressure.

The Midland banking group would play an important part in the First Direct story. It brought financial assistance. It shared services like automated teller machines and the check-clearing system. Above all, Midland had the intelligence as owner to let First Direct reinvent the rules of the retail banking game without trying to get mixed up in the daily work of the new bank in the name of tradition and the conservatism at that time very typical of British banking institutions.

How did Dyson modify the rules of the game in the vacuum cleaning industry? In a way Dyson created respect for his customers. "All suggestions of new technology were [previously] mere marketing hype. The way they [traditional vacuum-cleaner manufacturers] responded to the fact that their product was crap was to bring out a more expensive one, and simply ignore the fact that it was still crap. By the time the public realized, they would have brought out yet another one which the public might believe wasn't crap – until they tried it" (Dyson 2002). Switching from a traditional vacuum cleaner to a Dyson was such a quantum leap in customer satisfaction that users immediately became propagators of the good news. Last but not least, in the infrequent occurrence of a product problem, customer service was truly well delivered. In its industry, Dyson had repaced "crap" with customer delight.

Tesco has modified the rules of the competitive game between large British food retailers in multiple ways. By putting the customer at the center of its strategy, Tesco has shown that the concept of mass retailing was obsolete. It could not be applied to modern consumers any longer. Actually, the so-called mass market is heavily segmented both in terms of price-sensitivity and in terms of mindsets. Not only do Tesco's customers belong to various segments, but Tesco addresses them as individuals, thanks to the massive amount of information supplied by the Clubcard program and to the growing number of interactions with customers that take place at Tesco.com.

Another dimension of Tesco's innovation is its demonstration that quality and fair-to-low prices are not mutually exclusive. In fact, its way of tracking consumer trends, of translating them into store offerings, and its inclination to offer as much customer service as is compatible with the self-service context have never prevented it from selling at very competitive prices. Tesco also makes a point of reinvesting most of its systems savings each year in price reductions, through its "Step Change" program. During the 2004–5 fiscal year, price cuts amounted to £230 million, whereas the Step Change savings accounted for £270 million. Although one may cynically argue that those price cuts were necessary to fight Tesco's recent price battle with Asda, the British subsidiary of Wal-Mart, they have also, and above all, allowed Tesco to build value-for-money for its customers in a way that is almost unreachable for its competitors.

Tesco's approach is to be wherever the consumer is, whenever he or she wants, in whichever mindset he or she is. And it appears to be very successful. The combination of customer-centrism, very high value-for-money and positioning as a convenience-builder has allowed Tesco to shoot for lifelong loyalty from its customers. The idea is no longer to lure customers with one-shot promotions on given shopping trips, but to pamper them with convenient, service-oriented value propositions that induce exciting and repeated shopping experiences. Evidence once again suggests that people are loyal to shopping experiences if they prove to be unlike just any other standard shopping trip.

PUTTING THE CUSTOMER AT THE CENTER OF THE BUSINESS

The markings that we have just gone over all took one commonplace or common-sense trait to an extreme. In each case the customer was omnipresent, even if in some cases this presence remained implicit. Put another way, excellence in marking comes when the customer becomes everybody's business in the company and not just the property of the marketing department.

Club Med, a service company if there ever was one, took involvement with the customer especially far. GMs are key actors in the provision of service. They fit into the collective life of the Club; they participate in the games and the liveliness. The semantics of *gentil membre* and *gentil organisateur* also assume this symbiosis between the company and the customer. Should Club Med fail in this integration and symbiosis, it will become its own enemy – and destroy its customer loyalty. This could set off an uncontrollable process of negative word-of-mouth, which is especially harmful in the service industries. Experience shows that negative rumors are five or six times more powerful than positive word-of-mouth.

The IKEA strategy empowers the customer through a division of labor in which customers become actors and partners with their purchase and use of the product. Moreover, the business goes much further than the mere coproduction of furniture. Its points-of-sale offer singles, couples, and families in particular, interactive advice that enables them to improve their living space and their lives without extra expense. The shopping situation turns these customers into proactive actors. The information they are given about products, about the arrangement of the store, and about terms of sale are all signs of respect shown to them by the company. *The IKEA Store Book*, the employees' manual of conduct, lays out mandatory procedures and attitudes within the store. Three have an almost sacred status and are inviolable at all times: an altruistic concern to educate customers; the provision of accessories, which, for example, allow customers to take measurements themselves; and the service customers receive.

The concept of First Direct was developed to respond to old frustrations among the British retail banking public. It was expressed in the company directing all its efforts at creating the greatest possible satisfaction for its clients. Telephone counselors are trained to conduct conversations in their own words and to avoid standardized scripts. They use and continually add to a database essentially intended to record qualitative items of individualized knowledge about the customers. Procedures are developed to respect that speed of interaction that is part of the customer promise. The call-center technology is itself an engine of speed, particularly in the elimination of bottlenecks, and of user-friendliness, for example by the real-time access counselors have to their customer's personalized screen. Finally, the philosophy of interaction that guides employees stipulates that only timely offers relevant to the customer shall be brought up.

Customer-centrism was the cornerstone of Tesco's rebirth in the late 1980's and early 1990's. It has not stopped since then. Tesco's emblematic motto, "Every Little Helps" (British for "Every Little Bit Helps"), even appears as a subtitle in the company's Annual Reports. It is explained as follows: "It means doing the little things that really matter for customers and staff, in every store, every day," and "We aim to make everybody welcome at Tesco, wherever they live, and whatever their income" (Tesco's Annual Review 2005). The staff's empathetic attitudes toward customers keep being reinforced. Tesco's store staff is trained with skills to deliver better service through a cultural exchange program called "Living Service." Three attitudes describe the way staff should behave when actually delivering "Every Little Helps" in the stores: Know your stuff, Show your care, Share a smile. Store managers across the company work night shifts at least one week out of every 12, to ensure that "Every Little Helps" is the company's focus 24 hours a day. At Christmas and Easter, the busiest times of the year, head office staff join their colleagues in stores to help serve customers.

Dyson seems to be a paradox. Product perfection appears to be as valued as customer focus. However, product technology has been, from its inception, geared at creating a hassle-free solution for consumers who have had to cope with intrinsic dissatisfaction with the overall vacuum-cleaner product category. James Dyson enforces a golden rule of not hiring outside advertising agencies or marketing teams. His belief is that marketing should begin inside the factory and be a process that continues all the way to the consumer, and keeps the manufacturer and the consumer in delicate harmony. Customer service is viewed as everybody's task. Apparently the idea of putting the helpline number on the handle of the vacuum cleaner came from a woman working at the service desk.

As for Benetton, they do not explicitly display how they integrate consumers into their strategy development. The single, yet powerful, sign of their wish to understand their customers' needs is their direct operation of 50 stores they have set up in what they call experimental sites. This gives the company a very clear picture of buyer behavior.

In conclusion, there is something more general that unites the marking efforts we have reviewed here. They are triggered as much by thought as by action. Without the right mindset, no marking can hope to succeed.

6

SPOILING THE MARKING PROCESS

The adequate mindset is a necessary but not sufficient condition. Also required are actions consistent with it and with each other. A marking management drama often plays out when what the business does belies – in fact contradicts – what it says it does or what it believes it does. What businesses do must conform perfectly to what they are, and to what they promise.

Accepting temporary, marginal departures from this practice can be seen as a normal part of business life. The business will compromise, momentarily drop its guard, blink – for any of a hundred reasons, having to do as much with tactical opportunism and outside constraints as with lack of management control and thoroughness. Not only does the believer stray from the path of virtue, he or she opens up the gates of hell.

This chapter conducts an unusual exercise: it teaches mistakes. It makes the case for strict vigilance and committed struggle by the whole company, at every level, against any variances between mindset and practice. Irrelevant actions or operating decisions that make for inconsistent quality can seriously damage, indeed destroy, the effects of the most perfect mental plans.

The first part of the chapter reviews practices that are plainly ineffective. On the surface they look like seemingly inconsequential mistakes and operating traps, by which the business does not obviously violate the right mindset. In the field, alas, such departures turn out to be capable of causing the marking to self-destruct, however slowly or even inconspicuously. Vigilance and firm tenacity are necessary even when the business faces a crisis in sales or, the opposite, seems to have locked in success for years to come.

The second part of this chapter lays out effective practices whose common feature is the harmonization of the right mindset and action. Against Vice will be set Virtue, of the operating kind.

A third part focuses on a special category of error, the kind that can lead to certain sudden death. These consequences affect reactive marking, but especially, and with full force, proactive marking.

Two implications for action and management punctuate the chapter.

The distinction between small accommodations and big departures is relatively fuzzy, perhaps imaginary. Companies thought to be models of success are just as exposed to major risk as other companies, though at the time their misdeed is neither intentional nor visible.

If reactive marking enjoys a little slack in this respect, proactive marking gets practically none. For the latter to make a mistake induces far more damaging consequences than for the former. After all, it promises the virtues and beauties of another world. For this reason its market feels it is all the more socially responsible. Any little tear in the moral contract it has implicitly or explicitly drawn up with its territory is experienced by its stakeholders, customers, employees or opinion-makers more like a shredding. While proactive marking aims to construct new territories and new worlds, it simply cannot act heed-lessly. In this case, to strictly keep its promises the business must become highly dependent upon the society it seeks to shape. Embed-ded as they are in society, proactive markers are much more vulnerable than reactive markers.

TRAPS TO AVOID

Marking of whatever type is necessarily obliged to decode, in detail, the longings of consumers and the market's many vested interests. During the long period of prosperity in developed countries up to the 1990's, many a business played fast and loose with this reality. This posture led them to adopt a rudimentary market approach, to say the least. For a dozen years, the acute or creeping crises that have rocked the world have exacerbated the shortcomings of markings, that is, the traps certain companies fell into. The following list, not exhaustive, summarizes the chief practices that marking companies must avoid, as infringements on the right mindset:

■ Information myopia
■ Simplistic "massification"
■ Excessive symbolization of product
■ Low price or low cost of first purchase as the sole drivers
■ Communications amounting only to promotion
■ Open confrontation between manufacturer and retailer.

Information myopia

One source of error that dogs marking derives from the fact that businesses sometimes almost blindly give credence to biased information. This can ossify the most routine descriptions, rule out facts that suggest making changes, and act as a brake on the marking. A significant fraction of the tools marketers use to gather information actually encourage them to hone existing strategies rather than to instill new ways of thinking.

Satisfaction surveys, for example, ask respondents to assess the reliability of existing strategies. They leave them little room, even with so-called open-ended questions, to offer alternative suggestions. Such techniques also – and this is even more reductive – prompt respondents to talk about the business rather than about themselves. They tend to freeze-frame the world and its economic activity.

The skepticism one must bring to these techniques is greatly supported by recent research that shows, with contributions from neuroscience, that about 95% of the consumer's cognition occurs below the threshold of consciousness (Zaltman 2003). Answers to questionnaires will reveal at best the tip of the iceberg. Words are a feeble expression of thought anyway, which can be more sensitively and better expressed in metaphor than by a complicated and still uncommon marketing approach. What is more, not only is the method underlying satisfaction surveys inadequate in and of itself, but their contents are often impoverished by what managers expect of them and by the uses they put them to. Too often managers are trying only to explore their own hypotheses. Too often satisfaction surveys simply prompt consumers to confirm what the pollsters think they feel. This keeps everyone at the level of confirmation, if not incantation, where managers point with great pride to the remarkable satisfaction rates that so gratify their narrow minds.

Other tools contain other biases that are just as serious. Databases compiling information on customers' supposed buying behavior often come down to a list of products they buy. They do not pick up on customers' attitudes, they neglect their values, norms and beliefs, and how customers express them. Rare is the business that, like the personalized telephone bank First Direct, really takes these things into account. The essential point is that attitudes are not formed by past purchases but by the satisfaction or dissatisfaction felt at the time of consumption. Attitudes are therefore much better indicators of future behavior than indicators that only tell us about past behavior. Moreover, databases dealing only with consumers ignore the multiplicity of actors and influences that create the compost from which every act of consumption grows. There is more to the consumer than just a buyer.

Lastly and more generally, the tyranny of the measurable and the claims of the quantifiable to alone be scientific are likely to inhibit the development of new ways of thinking. It is, in fact, nearly impossible to quantify a new territory – precisely or reliably, anyway. As the territory has no past, extrapolating one to predict and program the future is impossible. Its potential is revealed only as actions are taken.

This was the difficulty faced by Fnac in Portugal. Created in 1954, this French company sells microelectronics, CDs, books, videogames, and photographic, sound and image technology in more than 110 stores in 8 countries, with a turnover of US$6 billion. When it first considered the possibility of having a presence in Portugal, its quantitative market studies resulted in recommendations somewhere between caution and rejection. Its qualitative studies, on the other hand, showed the Portugese would be be receptive to Fnac's concept of offering cultural and leisure products. France's large Portugese community made this especially so, as many Portugese already knew and valued the Fnac name from having lived in France, or living there still and regularly returning to Portugal for vacations. Fnac was smart enough to listen to these qualitative signals and lend them more weight than the statistics. And a good thing it did: today Fnac is highly successful in Portugal.

Simplistic massification

A leftover from the years of the so-called consumer society, the idea of a mass market today comes under the heading of conceptual absurdities. Simplistic massification is living proof that a company's analysis of the mass market, which is in fact largely segmented, has been lazy and just plain inadequate.

The first and most obvious segmentation criterion is the shopper's socioeconomic status, which varies a lot according to a store's location and catchment area. Today's retailers often rely on micro-marketing to incorporate these variations, analyzing customer targets on a store-by-store basis and adapting their product selection where necessary. For instance, Wal-Mart began its store-within-a-store policy in 1986. This policy recognized, supported, and encouraged associates' adaptability in managing their area of merchandise responsibility. Department managers were viewed as managers of their store-within-a-store. The tailoring of assortments to meet the needs of local customers was reinforced when Wal-Mart began doing its own market research (Birchall October 2005). In the same vein, Wal-Mart has recently developed its Store of the Community program, which allows store managers to have even more say than in the past in the selection of goods they offer.

The supposed mass market is also segmented by price-sensitivity. This is why British retailing giant Tesco has identified three sensitivity levels or attitudes to price, and adapted its store brand accordingly. Tesco addresses those who seek quality with Tesco Finest, those who want to optimize the price–quality balance with Tesco, and the price-obsessed with Tesco Value. This is not a segmentation of customers but of states of mind, since one customer can be a quality-seeker when buying coffee and price-obsessed when it comes to mineral water.

Also, the so-called mass market is segmented along sensitivity to the current state of the economy. This is especially strong in certain parts of the population. Such is the case with two-income households or career-minded single people. These buyers try to increase the effectiveness of their routine shopping. They also have a completely different attitude toward products involving their ego.

Some of Wal-Mart's recent strategic moves also illustrate the potential limitations of an unrestrained mass-market positioning and image. As already mentioned in Chapter 3, Wal-Mart's penetration remains disappointing in more fashion-oriented, upscale urban areas. Another probable frustration for Wal-Mart stems from the fact that Target, its arch rival in U.S. discount retailing, has been more effective in catering to its customers' more sophisticated needs, with its sales and margins growing faster in the U.S. than Wal-Mart's.

Another example is Marks & Spencer. This company was for decades one of the most profitable European retailers. What is more, it had achieved truly iconic status in retailing and inspired many companies throughout the world. Marks & Spencer had remained desperately attached to their positioning: safe, British middle-class fashion with a remarkable price–quality relationship – even when the market changed. It was unable to detect that these middle classes wanted more original clothes, and therefore a frequently changing offering, which was exactly what new competitors started to offer, sometimes at more affordable prices than even Marks & Spencer. The flight of its customers to chains like Gap, Zara, or H&M brought the company to the verge of financial collapse. The marking done by Marks & Spencer had been proactive: the company had maintained an image as an institution of British society. Finally, its financial difficulties required it to discard the greater part of its international operations to save the British core market presence. To this day Marks & Spencer is still trying, without definitive or convincing success, to find a style that will recreate its old attraction for British customers.

Defining the product too symbolically

An overly imaginative or unbridled interpretation of the customer's aspirations can lead to taking too much liberty with the concreteness of the offering. This phenomenon, made worse by the quest for drop-dead originality (often exhibited in overly creative advertising), can cause a drift into the non-tangible that leaves good sense behind.

From 1991, Benetton seemed to lose sight of when it was going too far, though it had made great use of advertising as the unifying force of its marking for many years, and rightly so. When the company started using its advertising to promote ethical and social causes – often through militant, provocative visuals against AIDS or terrorism, for example, a number of its constituents expressed serious doubts as to their relevance or effectiveness. If marking becomes a pure act of commitment to civic and political ends, just how far can the business go? When does it pass the socially acceptable and agreed-upon limits of its territory? Can advertising continually keep getting further away from tangible propositions? Proactive marking, even when basically legitimized by its social dimension, does not necessarily give the marker a blank slate to comment on everything in society.

By excessively magnifying its consumers' social status compared with their needs, the marking company can also create relatively dramatic or dramatized social situations that have little bearing on its purpose and that are beyond its competence. A good example of such a misalignment is given by Nike athletic shoes in the U.S. (Telander 1990).

In the late 1980's the U.S. press carried several stories of murders committed in the ghetto in which young men were killed by their peers for their sneakers. For example, in 1989 young Michael Thomas spent $115 on a pair of sneakers that symbolized his hero, basketball great Michael Jordan. When his family urged him not to wear them to school, he replied, "Before anyone takes my shoes they have to kill me." His words were unfortunately prescient. The point is not to demonize Nike or Michael Jordan. Yet in the modern world a company with something like a 40% share of the American athletic shoe market has to recognize that the deep-rooted symbolic forces it uses to support very high prices will have perverse effects on an implicitly or explicitly key target group: poor black teenagers.

Low price as the sole reason to buy

Presenting the price of a product as just its initial cost often signifies an extremely reductive and finally destructive posture in terms of value delivered. There are at least three connected reasons why such an approach is unsound.

You can expect relatively rational consumers to balance out the purchase price with the benefits they will get from the product and its use. With a food product, for example, these will be taste, ease of use, lack of waste or ability to store leftovers.

This can also mean that a business wishing to expand its market has to begin a user-education program. Certain benefits to the products or services it offers are not going to be immediately perceptible.

Playing on low sales price in markets that are not price-sensitive or are unwilling to pay a premium for quality leads to perverse effects. It tends to make the proposition the business offers the market less, rather than more, attractive.

The field of ulcer medications provides a good illustration (Angelmar and Pinson 1998). Smithkline & French, a company that in 1976 had pioneered Cimetidine, which won its inventor the Nobel Prize and became better known by its trade name Tagamet, made a double mistake. It maintained a purely technological product positioning and even scorned image and service. Furthermore, it lowered its price level when the drug was attacked by Glaxo's Ranitidine, known chiefly under the brand name Zantac. Now, Ranitidine, which was not introduced till 1981, was in scientific and medical terms only a very modest improvement over Cimetidine. Yet Glaxo, unlike its competitor, knew enough to show much more respect to the patient and the prescribing doctor. This particularly meant a greater orientation toward patient service (simplified dosage) and a consequently higher price than the competition's.

In this fairly price-insensitive market, especially given that these drugs are (or were, for a long time) completely reimbursed by social security, lowering prices means basically that the pioneering company or historical leader publicly acknowledged how undistinctive its offering was in comparison to the new entrant. In this way Glaxo quickly became the market leader in ulcer medications.

It may be worthwhile at this point to remind the reader that Tesco had its back against the wall in the 1970's in sticking to its old "pile it high and sell it cheap" scenario. It is only fair to say that this had worked beautifully before and after World War II, when Jack Cohen's concept held considerable appeal for Tesco's price-conscious working-class customers. However, maybe somewhat blinded by the multiple acquisitions it made during the 1950's and 1960's, Tesco failed to sense that the world was changing: that British consumers overall were becoming both wealthier and more sophisticated, which meant that limiting one's marketing pitch to low prices alone was becoming insufficient to remain a retail winner.

In the same vein we might mention the relative disappointment felt by the big French retailers in terms of the price reductions orchestrated in September 2004 by France's Ministry of Finance and the Economy. As it turned out, the sales volumes of hypermarkets and supermarkets went up all of 0.6% in the days and weeks that followed. That weak volume meant a net sales decline of 1.8%, in a general context of only a 0.7% decline in spending on staples. This does not mean that consumers are insensitive to price, as is proven every day by the growing role played by hard discounters and low-price store brands. It means that talking about price alone will, by its nature, have only a modest impact.

A close analysis of the hard discounter phenomenon does not destroy this reasoning at all. Granted, a leader like Aldi offers prices on basic products that are extremely low compared with other supermarkets. But price is never traded off for quality. Furthermore, and above all, the huge volumes Aldi buys and the logistical network it possesses spell the difference. Asparagus in Germany is delivered and on the shelves 24 hours after being picked in the field. To its target customers, Aldi really offers "more for less" and so is positioned in terms of real value.

Communication as mere promotion

Another trap a business can fall into, perhaps substantially contaminating its credibility and so the durability of its marking, is to limit its communications to the purely promotional. The effort is often legitimized by a short-term increase in sales. The problem is that this also often plays out as failure in terms of information. That leads at least to a partial deception of the customers and in extreme cases to dangerous situations.

In the summer of 2003, a new cell-phone operator in India, Reliance Infocomm, launched with great bally-hoo an advertising campaign announcing that new subscribers would get 10 months' free calls to a local number of their choosing, and two months' free calls between 10pm and 8am. This deal, however, required subscribers to buy a mobile phone for the equivalent of $12 down and $5 a month for three years.

This blaring ad campaign was hugely successful, drawing in millions of new subscribers. Yet it brought down the wrath of consumer groups. They pointed out that in India, with 40% illiteracy (even higher among the poorer classes most attracted by the Reliance deal), only a small fraction of new subscribers would understand that they were tied to Reliance for at least three years. Of course Reliance answered that, for a termination charge, the contract could be broken. This termination charge proved to be simply prohibitive for the overwhelming majority of subscribers (Marcelo 2003).

A more general lesson can be drawn from this case. Even if it were absurd to eliminate all promotional efforts, they at least have to be combined with clear information and, ideally, be designed as a well-planned educational operation. Because the stakeholders are keeping an eye out for trouble. Should they be called into action, the consequences will not remain purely symbolic or momentary.

Another example of the harmfulness of a purely promotional effort concerns products with an ethical component for some people but about which consumers are insufficiently informed or about whose use the targets have not been educated. A dramatic case concerned alcopops.

Toward the end of the 1990's, notably in the United States, bottled drinks looking like sodas came onto the market: only unlike soft drinks they contained alcohol, especially malt liquor. Since they fell below the legal threshold of 10%, they were defined as "slightly" alcoholic. One group at whom they were targeted, implicitly, was teenagers and young people. These concoctions were easily accessible to them as they were sold from supermarket shelves, and they gave young people the impression that a significant ingestion of alcohol was not harmful.

In no time alcopops were front-page news. People ascribed to them, rightly or wrongly, fatal weekend highway accidents with teenagers at the wheel. The controversy became hot and heavy. Makers of alcoholic beverages, both those who had introduced the product and those who had refrained, found themselves under fire.

Social experts and health experts soon got involved. In 2001, a sophisticated study conducted in the U.S. by the Center for Science in the Public Interest confirmed that the advertising for these beverages had scant appeal for adults but a great deal for adolescents, even though it was theoretically not meant for them. The labels did look like sodas. They caught young people's imagination more than adults'. Evidence of this could be found in their names, like Captain Morgan Gold made by Diageo; in their sugary and often fruity taste associated with a name recalling a brand of vodka like Stolichnaya Citrona; in their TV advertising run at times adolescents would be watching, and in their overexposure in magazine advertising. According to another study made in 2002 by the Center on Alcohol Marketing and Youth at George Washington University, the exposure of young people to this advertising was 1.6 times higher than that of adults and was a contributing factor. Calling a drink that is 9% alcohol "slightly alcoholic" relieved the consumer of a great deal of guilt. Lastly, the study showed a much stronger propensity in young alcopops drinkers to drink alcohol to excess in adulthood.

Alcopops were withdrawn from the market by the spirits industry and its global giants. Its image of moral responsibility threatened to become irreversibly less credible. Behind the memory of Prohibition-era bootleggers lay the specter of Killer of Youth. Though Alcopops represented but a small niche in a vast product line, they became life-threatening not only to the spirits industry but also to beer and wine. By chance or not, a de facto coalition, including in particular the World Health Organization, a leading world soda company and temperance leagues, strenuously urged the European authorities to take drastic measures against the sale and consumption of alcohol. Alcopops' butterfly effect nearly set off a hurricane.

Open confrontation between manufacturer and retailer

Playing on their market share and their massive buying power, large retailers are able to exert considerable pressure to get the lowest price possible from suppliers. Required benefits they ask for are many, such as quantity and volume discounts, cash discounts, trade discounts (series based, and so on). So-called back margins are payments from producers to large retailers in exchange for promotional material, preferential shelf locations (endcaps, and so on) and other services. In countries such as France in which hypermarkets and other large retailers are kept by law from having an unfair price advantage over smaller shops (not being allowed to sell brand name products below cost) large retailers get around the law by selling real or fictitious commercial advantages to their suppliers. These back margins represent up to 40% of large retailers' net profit (Thoenig 1990).

The multinational giants, especially, can also consistently employ a tactic of massive invasion of shelf space with a single product, making competing brands occupy shelves below eye-level – which might appear to be a winning strategy and perfectly reasonable in free enterprise. Yet in seeking out this kind of supremacy, such suppliers, often called "category captains," run a risk: of losing sight of the objective of category management. The function of category management is to optimize the assortment of resellers according to the needs of consumers, so that the whole category will grow, not just the sales of the captain. In theory, a category manager – of men's shampoos, for example – will certainly offer her product on the shelf, with no doubt an extremely favorable placement, but she will also make room for competing products that answer specific market expectations or needs or that quite simply gratify customers' desire for a choice. The wager is that the category manager will be a bigger winner if the selection of products and brands is broad enough to make the category (that is, all brands taken together) even more attractive to the customer. Conversely, a too-narrow range of alternative products discourages the buyer and lessens opportunity for the leader because the whole category is diminished. The monopolistic urge is counterproductive in the end.

One might cite the extremely positive case of a large brewer, especially observant of his role as category captain, who does not hesitate to drop from displays his own listings if they do not correspond to market desires – or do less so than competing listings. The philosophy he puts in practice is that it is better to have 20% of sales in a category that is growing, because it perfectly meets market needs, than 25% of a category with stagnant or declining sales.

In the U.S. in the early 1980's a brutal confrontation developed between two giants, Procter & Gamble and Wal-Mart (Parry and Sato

1996). P&G was using its enormous power to dominate if not control retailers. Its market shares varied between 20% and 45% according to the product category. By contributing to retailers an impressive mass of studies about consumers, the global giant would build arguments for increasing the shelf space given to its brands, such as Tide, Clearasil, Head & Shoulders, or Crest.

Retailers at this time had not yet developed their own electronic systems of information gathering at the point of sale, so they were unable to dispute the P&G analyses. Generally they experienced with real frustration P&G's perpetual quest for domination of their shelves. Wal-Mart, P&G's largest customer by far, was famous for demanding from its suppliers the lowest sales prices on the market. Its objective was to be able to assume its position in its own customers' eyes of "Everyday Low Prices."

Until 1987 the confrontation between these two dominating attitudes was direct and harsh. P&G tried to dictate to Wal-Mart how much merchandise to buy and what to sell it for. Wal-Mart continuously threatened P&G with delisting its products or giving them less desirable shelving. Such a lovely atmosphere was obviously not conducive to information exchange or joint planning and even less conducive to coordination of their two systems. It got so bad that, on the initiative of a third party, the top management of the two companies met and, now aware that perpetuating the conflict was a negative-sum game, decided to work together. It was time for each of them to confirm some obvious facts. P&G needed the huge access to the market that Wal-Mart represented. And Wal-Mart could hardly do without the enormously popular P&G brands to support its own sales.

Nowadays, thanks to an electronic data-exchange system, P&G can continuously watch its flows product-by-product and store-by-store, which allows it to anticipate Wal-Mart's re-ordering. By being familiar with sales, inventory, and prices for different packages of Pampers, its disposable diapers, P&G can virtually eliminate stock-outs wherever Pampers are carried. Not only is the selection of products merchandised guided by consumer demand, but consumers are no longer plagued with the nuisance of stock-outs. The two companies in this way have found obvious gains in terms of increased sales and greater economic efficiency. In many cases, for instance, P&G can deliver directly from the factory to the store, which eliminates the need for intermediate stocking between the two ends of the supply chain. This move created a third winner, the consumer. He or she now enjoys a more apropriate product selection, without stock-outs and at lower prices. P&G no longer tries to sell more to Wal-Mart, it aims to sell better and sell more to consumers through the retailer.

Another example of snowballing conflict liable to harm the effectiveness of a marking is offered by the Norwegian furniture maker J. E. Ekornes (Kumar 1996).

By 1993, Ekornes was suffering from problems arising from adversarial relations with its European retailers. Its situation in France, where its products were sold by 450 furniture dealers, was typical. The forced-march sales philosophy Ekornes had at the time made it sell its product to every dealer who approached it to buy. Because of this overdistribution, retailers wound up having less and less confidence in their supplier. Ekornes felt in return that its retailers did not show enough commitment to make the brand a success. Endless disagreements built up, each side accusing the other of insufficient support. Against this background the brand grew progressively weaker on the market.

Starting in 1993, Ekornes decided to choose its retailers more selectively. The company involved them more in its life, in particular by having them visit Norway. It gave them more financial motivation. And it transformed its former salespeople into retail advisors.

The P&G and Ekornes cases show that evolving into collaboration and partnership is essential when conflict is obviously leading to a lose–lose relationship. It would be wrong, however, to suppose that cooperation is the only solution to confrontation in a supremacy situation. First the two players must be convinced that the other will not try to back out of the cooperation. And each partner must hold cards that make the other dependent on it. It helps to be powerful in terms of sales volume, brand awareness, or image with the end user if you wish to get the partner to play a positive-sum game and escape confrontation or dominating supremacy.

Alternative solutions do exist, as proved by the Royal Canin example. The big European retailers were not able to enhance the market position of its products for pets in any meaningful way. The food industry was a factory for selling undifferentiated, mass-market products based on anthropomorphic impulses. Hypermarkets offered no guarantee of expertise. So the decision was made to leave the big retailers and let the products thrive in specialized outlets. Apart from the suitability of this choice for its entrepreneurial culture, it also put Royal Canin in a position of equal power with its distributors and its network of experts, thus making an ideal win–win scenario.

WAYS TO AVOID TRAPS

For every trap that might poison the marking there is an equally strong antidote. These practices, which we call relevant or effective, apply – and we stress this – to all kinds of markings, whether reactive or proactive. They are spelled out in Table 6.1. We will flesh them out by considering the six companies explored in the preceding chapter.

TABLE 6.1 **Ways to avoid traps**

Traps	Specific ways to avoid them
Information myopia	Multidisciplinary market information Continuous awareness Valuing the qualitative A passion for being at the forefront
Simplistic massification	Precise targeting Finding the right balance between standardization and adaptation Including personalized ingredients
Defining the product way too symbolically	Tangible results Symbolism where it exists reinforces an individual, not a consumer
Low price as the only sales argument	Value in use
Rationale summed up in low initial cost	Consuming/using seen over time
Communications only intended for promotion	Education Dialogue Expertise Marshalling in-house resources
Confrontation mentality between producer and seller	Collaboration Meshing Vertical integration Intermediaries as guarantors of expertise

Multidisciplinary, continuous, qualitative, and anticipatory information

Marking must not shun information and must try not to be purely intuitive. Royal Canin is constantly drawing on scientific information about pets' physiological processes. Even Benetton ended up accepting, after looking at survey results, that its provocative advertising was jeopardizing profits.

Certain approaches to information gathering, however, are more promising in terms of opportunities for new ways of thinking. This is why an in-depth, personalized, qualitative, continuously updated knowledge of the customers is the main axis of effective marking.

An inspiring example is Lafarge, a global leader in construction materials. What this company does is regularly send into the field multifunction teams whose assignment is to talk with the customer. More precisely – and this detail is important – they meet face-to-face with each of the many decision-makers within the customer's organization. The members of these teams have moved beyond the talk-about-me stage and advanced to let's-talk-about-*you*. Experience has proven the lessons from these investigations to be extremely powerful, for they give this company in-depth knowledge of the customer. What is more, since the information gathering is carried out by a multifunction team, the company converts it into solutions faster and more effectively.

Another example is provided by Schlumberger, the oil-field and mining equipment company. Teams that are, once again, multifunctional, and that regularly involve executives in the field, spend whole days with customers and with potential customers. What Schlumberger understands is that to get into the customers' mindset and to discover any lacks, frustrations, or wishes, you have to live at their side (Gouillart and Sturdivant 1994).

In summary then, the information-gathering tools favorable to marking must have five virtues:

1. They draw on disciplines outside management and marketing in the narrow sense, such as anthropology, psychology, philosophy, theology, biology, sociology and history.
2. They favor continuous familiarity with the territory rather than periodic market studies or consumer surveys that risk eclipsing its movements and letting short-lived opportunities slip away.
3. They give prominence to the qualitative and the personalized as opposed to the quantitative and the standardized. Weak signals count as much as, if not more than, strong signals.
4. They involve everyone in the company, all functions together, from sales to product development, from logistics to marketing.

5. Finally, a quest for innovation (in the sense of discovering opportunities) plays the biggest role. In this respect, let us be reminded that one field of investigation is especially fruitful: following up on customers or forward-thinking people who by their lifestyles, sophistication, abilities or drives for expertise, are by nature dissatisfied with the status quo and hence push toward the future.

Precise targeting and flexible implementation

Targeting is the most strategic decision a business ever has to make. Launching an action program, however brilliant it might be technically, can never make the desired impact if no one has clearly identified to whom the actions are addressed. An inadequate or imprecise targeting is a major mistake. It paves the road to come with major difficulties and becomes a basic cause of future failure.

However, the targeting must not be rigid or dogmatic. It has to leave room to maneuver. It has to let the business see what is happening in its territory. The goal is to foster a learning process as to what the business might have missed or failed to anticipate. Any technical or normative baggage it carries impedes the business and keeps it from reacting to a market that is necessarily protean and evolving. Arrogance and orthodoxy are no friends to relevant, effective marking.

IKEA strikes a workable balance between precise targeting and necessary flexibility. The firm's strategic mechanisms and postures for adapting or personalizing product lines greatly attenuate any excessive "massification" tendencies they might have. Its primary target, the one considered the foundation of the business, is apartment-dwelling, urban young couples with children. They, more than other categories of the population, are assumed to be looking for a functional furnishing of their home, due to relative small floor area and a limited budget. This precise positioning does not prevent IKEA from welcoming other groups into its stores; such as older people, who are keener on accessories than on furniture and who may have been typical IKEA customers in their younger days. IKEA has also created within its stores an area meant to attract people who wish to combine good taste and manageable budgets in their professional or home office.

Even if the stores appear highly standardized, the customer, whether from the target group or another one with a profile compatible with the store's line, always has wide latitude in coming up with his or her own creative solution. This is one of the cornerstones of the IKEA system. Thanks to the density of information in the catalogue, the specificity of the in-store signs and the informed advice of sales-people – should they be sought out – the customers can readily put together their own future living space.

At Club Med, the ideal target group is defined psychologically: that is, it is characterized by a state of mind. Club Med is interested in people looking for positive vacation experiences, in which meeting people is more important than traditional hotel criteria such as comfort or room service. A great diversity in Club sites and countries helps keep those who come back repeatedly from feeling any monotony, geographically speaking. Furthermore, the mix of activities (particularly the presence or absence of infrastructure and staff that make babies, young children or adolescents welcome) and of price levels makes it possible to articulate the targeting along a socioeconomic range.

The offer is personalized in that GMs themselves select the activities they will pursue. They can easily avoid the group activities they are less interested in. The French slogan, *"Tout est proposé, rien n'est imposé"* ("everything is offered, nothing is imposed") gives an idea of this approach. The personal dimension is also magnified by the GM's involvement in the actual experience, for instance, acting in the "GM Show" or playing competitive sports or joining in the ceremony welcoming new GMs to the village.

A well-thought-out service is one that adapts to personal character-istics and is wedded to the customer's desires. This crucial requirement at Club Med falls to the GOs. They must constantly exhibit real empathy for the GMs and a taste for interpersonal relations. Targeting therefore supposes faceting, down to the level of the humblest and most ordinary parts of business operations.

Benetton is another business that essentially targets a state of mind. These are customers looking for relaxation, registering their informal-ity and playfulness with their clothing and, at least in the 1960's, rejecting their parents' conservatism. This targeting is amplified, some might say caricatured, in the advertising. Nevertheless, Luciano Benet-ton learned to articulate this philosophy in terms of the demographics he was aiming at, even if his initial objective was 18–24 year olds. Almost thirty years later, in 1995, one could count six different vari-eties of Benetton store. Mega Benetton aimed mainly, though not exclusively, at the young and the very young. Blue Family/Fil di Ferro aimed at a very young clientele, the core of which was adolescents.

Benetton Uomo was designed to attract men, whether young or not-so-young, seeking a casual look. Benetton Donna took the same position vis-à-vis women. Benetton 012 was for the 0-to-12 age group. Sisley, another chain that belongs to Benetton, targets lifestyles oriented toward sports, the outdoors and fashion.

Tesco has been very active since the mid-1990's in targeting its customers more finely according to their shopping expectations. In fact, Tesco, which we described in Chapter 5 as the ultimate convenience-builder, has gone a long way in making available to its customers all the possible variations of convenience – among which they can choose at their discretion: *one-stop shopping*, in its Tesco Extra hypermarkets or in its larger Tesco superstores; *proximity*, in its smaller Tesco compact superstores or in its Tesco Metro urban outlets; *emergency*, in its Tesco Express convenience stores; and *shopping at a distance* in its very successful Tesco.com internet channel. In fact, the Tesco's multiple-format strategy has been largely guided by this desire to cover the spectrum of its customers' convenience expectations. Incidentally, this is once again mindset targeting rather than people targeting, since a given customer may be in different moods or under different time pressures at different moments of his or her day.

Wal-Mart's efforts to distance itself from its excessive mass-market image are also worth mentioning here: for instance, in 2005 Wal-Mart launched Metro 7, a new clothing brand aimed at what it calls "fashion-savvy" female customers with an urban lifestyle. This brand appears in prime position in around 500 mostly urban Wal-Mart stores, as well as on the company website (Birchall October 2005). Similar adjustments are planned for the electronics and home furnishings categories.

In September 2005, rumors had also appeared about Wal-Mart's possible acquisition of Tommy Hilfiger, a financially ailing, upscale clothing marketer, which represented an opportunity to draw more upscale shoppers (Frazier 2005). However, Tommy Hilfiger was ultimately bought at the end of 2005 by Apax Partners, a major investment group.

It is also interesting to listen to Wal-Mart's own view on these recent strategic moves. According to John Fleming, Wal-Mart's chief marketing officer: "We're not going upscale; what we're doing is becoming more relevant to existing customers in more categories" (Birchall October 2005). Once again, the targeting effort is described as better capturing customers or specific groups of customers' mindsets rather than trying to hunt out new customers.

First Direct pursues a policy that is both original and stringent. This internet bank addresses customers characterized by two associated states of mind. It targets people who are dissatisfied with the short-comings or constraints typical of branch banks, people who are typi-cally well off and financially sound, at least enough to manage their ordinary spending. When a new customer applies, this trait is tested through a solvency analysis done by a British company known for its expertise and objectivity.

Why does First Direct select its customers with such care? First of all, inasmuch as the bank offers them a free credit card the moment they open an account, with the real though limited possibility of overdraw-ing the account, it wants to make sure it avoids that particular risk. This is why in 1996 only 50% of the applicants for a First Direct bank account were accepted. But this discipline also ties in with the market-ing plan to the extent that only customers comfortable in their minds and in their current financial situation can be managed by a bank that uses telephones, since a problem customer almost always has to be dealt with face to face.

The good news for First Direct is that the socioeconomic results of this psychographic targeting turn out to be excellent. First Direct customers are wealthier, better educated and more familiar with tech-nology than those of traditional branch banks. And while it is easier to address clients whose state of mind you know, it is not unpleasant to discover that this state of mind correlates with a good portfolio.

Offer tangible results and use symbols with restraint

The offer made to its target customer by an effective marking has a recurring, salient feature. The offer is very easily and quickly made palpable to the consumer. It is conveyed in the sensory impression of the product, the practicality of the packaging, open access to the merchandise at the point of sale, and above all with the uncommon specificity, clarity and legibility of technical information.

The concreteness of the offer can therefore be grasped immediately. This, however, does not necessarily mean that its symbolic dimensions are totally ignored. On the contrary, they are there – but they observe an imperative. If the symbolic dimensions help to amplify the propo-sition, in no way do they constitute the offer itself.

For example, the perception that the Dyson vacuum cleaner, this strange-looking product, was technically remarkable snowballed very quickly among potential customers. Customers who bought Dysons went home feeling they had made a discovery, which they demonstrated to their friends, who in turn came to buy them. In France, a rather recently-penetrated market for Dyson, 80% of sales are currently generated by this word-of-mouth phenomenon (Briard 2005). There is little doubt that, besides being a remarkable technological breakthrough, Dyson has also turned itself into an undeniable social phenomenon.

Furthermore – and this correlates with the concreteness of the offer – customers often only discover the full financial and psychological or ethical advantages by using the product or service. The concept of healthful nutrition promised by Royal Canin is the keystone of its strategy and its success. Nevertheless, pet owners discover when they use the product that it is economical as well. What is more, even if this is not their primary motivation, they take pride in providing something healthful for their pets, rather than merely feeding them.

IKEA offers its target customers home furnishings with three clear properties. It is intentionally functional. It tries to be in good taste, at least if you like Scandinavian design. And, as seen earlier, it turns out to be relatively personalized and personalizable when you get it home. Additionally, and importantly, the prices are low and thus compatible with the financial means of young households.

IKEA lowers its prices and its costs through a new division of labor, whereby the customer handles delivery and assembly. Thanks to its enormous sales volume it also benefits from economies of scale in production and supply line, which it orchestrates perfectly. The relationship of perceived quality and price offered is therefore remarkable. For its target market, IKEA has figured out a business model that, concretely, offers more for less.

At Club Med, the antidote to civilization that the company claims to offer was cannily organized in physical terms. It was established by the beauty of the resort sites and consolidated by their organization. Everything was done to facilitate the group experience, all while allowing an escape for those GMs who occasionally found it too much. In the main restaurant, for instance, tables of eight made the GM meet other GMs at mealtime. However, there were also local-style, satellite restaurants where guests could reserve a table for two or four. The quality of the sports facilities was another part of what makes the offer tangible. In all, everything was done to simplify living and to create a carefree time. GMs used no money for their purchases in the village, but instead used necklaces or a little passbook, which today have been replaced by magnetic cards.

Club Med had a talent for magnifying its value-in-use for the GMs. The invention of the everything-included-and-prepaid vacation made the GM a natural user. GMs were no longer just buyers. The price–quality relation was experienced very positively by the target customers, defined by the company as sports- and leisure-minded. This choice did carry an off-setting consideration for the business that adopted it. The price–quality relation became decidedly less advantageous when the business picked the wrong target. For customers who stayed away from sports and social activities and who always or occasionally wanted a vacation with limited social interaction, Club Med was not only unsuitable but rather expensive. This was not a concept that would satisfy those who felt like spending their vacation in perfect calm, well apart from the turmoil of social life. What is more, the "all-included" concept was for a long time hard to get across to some customers, especially Scandinavians and Germans, who would demand a refund on activities they did not take part in.

At Benetton, the wide range of patterns and colors offered to retailers with every new collection, allows them to choose the assortment they judge best suited to local tastes, given their country and market radius. The Benetton shops, also, are designed to give shoppers freedom of choice. It must be remembered that in Europe at least and before Benetton, there was no such thing as open-shelf merchandising of sweaters. In terms of value delivered to the customer, Benetton offered – and still does, up to a point – good quality at affordable prices, these being very relevant when you consider the youthful cast to the company's target. Not only does this younger clientele have a limited budget, but it also quickly tires of particular colors or styles such that it cannot invest too heavily in a sweater if it is then going to replace it without guilt.

At Tesco, the tangibility of the offering is characterized by a mix of food and non-food products, along with a growing offer of services that are perfectly adapted to British consumers' consumption structure and evolving lifestyles. As we have already mentioned, both the store formats and the store assortments are built to cater to all budgets or price-sensitivities, as well as to match customers' shopping convenience expectations at given points in time. A market-research culture, along with an obsession for listening to customers, facilitates Tesco's anticipation of future customers' expectations. Tesco.com, besides behind a channel for Tesco itself, is also used to test, in vivo, the offering of new products before they are included in stores' assortments.

At Dyson, the reference to product performance is almost obsessive. As Clare Mullin, Dyson's global marketing director, puts it, the company has "a marketing strategy centered on its technological innovation. We're an engineering-led company, not a marketing-led company" (Cuneo 2004). This obsessive product focus is shaping some of the human-resource management policies at Dyson: for instance, all new employees at Dyson make a vacuum cleaner on their first day. As mentioned earlier, engineering and design are not viewed as separate. Designers are as involved in testing as engineers are in conceptual ideas. Finally, it is part of Dyson's corporate philosophy never to be satisfied with the product and to always try to improve it. Saying that tangibility is important at Dyson would definitely be a British understatement.

First Direct also puts what it promises into an abundantly tangible form. Its service is up 24/7 – and it really is – to the point of zero downtime for its electronic and telephone systems since they were introduced. Its speed and personalization, and hence the aptness of its counselors' answers to customers questions or requests, remain unequaled by competitors. First Direct has eliminated all costs it deemed irrelevant to customer relations. Its internal organization is extremely light. Its procedures are both clear and stringent. Its technology is up to date and still flexible. Its workforce is small but competent. It has no use for plush corporate offices, just a call center out in the country that replaces a multitude of branches on busy streets with high rents. In other words, the bank made a major choice. It substantially transferred its cost savings to price reductions on banking services. Following the IKEA example, First Direct also created a business model that offers its target customers more for less. Which is another way of putting together and defining an exceptional ratio of perceived quality to agreed-upon price.

A value-in-use appraised over time

Thinking in terms of results or solutions for the customer, framing his or her satisfaction (and also that of employees and experts who contribute to the marking) in a medium-to-long-term view, and developing the technical side of the product with a service orientation (itself the natural leavening of customer relations) – these elements hardly erase the concept of purchase price but they do make it relative and put it into context. So this price is, for the business and the customer, now just one element in a much vaster proposition. Customers now spontaneously think about value-in-use, which they frequently compare favorably to products that, to a simplistic way of thinking, would be "cheaper."

An even more important phenomenon is that the great, smart and relevant markings wind up enriching or modifying the customer's thinking so much that old points of reference no longer make sense. Let us point out yet again that the Royal Canin offer of healthful nutrition clearly distances it from the "chow" point of reference and so from the prices of such products.

Although Dyson did not actually create new cognitions about vacuum cleaners, it vastly modified the relationship customers had with their vacuum cleaners. Before Dyson, vacuum cleaners had clogged up and lost their suction power very quickly, leading to frequent replacements of one vacuum cleaner by another. This was false technological progress, and the newer version often sold with an unjustified price premium. In inventing his cyclonic technology, Dyson made vacuum cleaners hassle free. Products did not need to be replaced as frequently. Customers were getting original and functional designs and a high level of after-sale service increased their satisfaction. In the past two years, these facts have convinced, to say the least, American consumers. During the 2003–2005 period, Dyson pushed Hoover out from the No. 1 position in the U.S. market. Dyson has shaken the marketplace. The vacuum cleaner has turned from a price-driven environment into one where products are competing on design, technology and performance (Cuneo 2004). In fact, in 2004, Dyson cleaners ranged in price from $399 to as much as $500, an extremely high range when compared with other competitive offers. Needless to say, American customers have fully understood the difference between buying price and "value-in-use."

Even Wal-Mart's success would not have been so amazing if it had just contented itself with offering "Always Low Prices ... Always." Let's remember: when it was launched, it chose to include all major national brands in its assortment and to build a service orientation that made its proposition much more attractive than that of pre-existing discounters. It offered "more for less," at least versus previous industry practices. This value-for-money was even more impressive when applied to its initial prime target, customers from rural backwaters, for whom the only local shopping alternatives were mom-and-pop stores.

Wal-Mart was, and is, facing similar challenges in its European expansion. Without getting into the nitty-gritty of each international operation, it seems that at least four conditions are required for Wal-Mart to be successful:

- a critical size to be able to implement its systems (in this respect, small is not beautiful);
- to bring some distinctiveness to consumers versus local, established competitors playing the low-price game;
- not to be confronted with an overly restrictive or regulated environment, in terms of labor laws and store opening hours, for example;
- some cultural proximity should exist between the host country and the acquired company's corporate culture.

The two European operations of Wal-Mart are inspiring examples of right versus wrong conditions for success.

The Asda acquisition in June 2000 was a perfect package of all these conditions. When Wal-Mart bought it, Asda had an 8% market share in the U.K., and no major player had an EDLP claim in the U.K. Archie Normann, CEO of Asda before it was acquired by Wal-Mart, was a fan of the American giant: observers were saying that Asda had been "Walmartized" before the acquisition. The Wal-Mart culture and the British culture seem to have meshed rather easily. And, last but not least, Asda was a large company with undeniable strengths (fresh foods, the George textile private label). Therefore cross-fertilization could take place between the two companies. In 2004, Asda had a 12% market share (nevertheless, still far from Tesco's 23% share).

Wal-Mart's German operation has been disappointing. Its rather expensive acquisition in 1997 of two local chains for $1.6 billion (which together accounted for less than 3% of the market share) has left a trail of red ink. The company has often failed to understand German culture. What works in Arkansas has flopped in Aachen (Evans 2004). Whereas in other countries greeters welcome customers to Wal-Mart stores, Germans balked at this. Ultimately, the idea was dropped. Moreover, competition in discounting is fierce in Germany: two gigantic hard discounters, Aldi and Lidl, are the low-price winners in that market. Another headache was linked with regulations: selling below cost is so complex in Germany that loss leaders are essentially banned. In 2000, Wal-Mart seemed to have found a rather gimmicky way of attracting shoppers to its stores: it started what it called "singles shopping," where particular nights were designated for shoppers who are single but eager not to be. No matter how successful this might be from a promotional viewpoint, one would hesitate to call it strategic vision!

To make a long story short, Asda–Wal-Mart found the recipe for building good value-for-money for its target customers in the United Kingdom, but in Germany the equivalent never materialized. Therefore, the announcement made by Wal-Mart on July 28, 2006 that it was selling off its 85 German hypermarkets to Real, the hypermarket banner of the giant German retailer Metro, did not come as a surprise.

Lastly, it is worth remembering that value-in-use remains relevant even with low-price strategies, when made possible by revolutionary business models like IKEA's or First Direct's. At IKEA the decisions to popularize home furnishing and decorating set the bar very low in terms of products' selling prices. For all that, what gives value to the proposition is that thanks to the variety of its line, IKEA lets its customers personalize their living space, in a way that is functional and within budget. First Direct understood that British customers, even well-off ones, attached no prestige to paying dearly for basic banking services. But the value-in-use is felt to be remarkable whenever on a daily basis this customer perceives the extreme convenience, user-friendliness and speed of the system.

Communicate beyond the promotional

Communication that is only promotional and, further, centers only on price denotes a business with an extremely poor proposition to the market.

Communication, lest we forget, includes many variables. Points of sale, employees' appearance, product packaging, media appearances by businesses with a societal marking, and word-of-mouth among customers are all part of it as much as, if not more than, advertising. As to advertisements themselves, they can and must, like other marketing tools previously discussed, be true vehicles of information and not be limited to symbolic glitter.

Since one of the chief characteristics of differentiating markings is to change the rules of the game, the primary task for communications in all forms will be to educate the market about new ways of consuming or using a product or service. This supposes a dimension of dialogue with the customer: with experts or at the point of sale, as Royal Canin does, or even in the ads, as Gap did in telling customers, "What matters in fashion is you," meaning that you make your own style with our basic products. Finally, communications have to be gratifying for the marking's ambassadors – the store employees and the sales force. Marketing in-house must always be powerful in a marking business and must come before marketing to the outside world. This prevents overpromising to customers on products or services the salespeople cannot deliver on.

IKEA guides its communications with a profusion of information intended to help customers personalize their selection. The advertising it uses is often centered on results, like the functional arrangement of living space that customers will have once they've made their purchases. Catalogues and stores are themselves part and parcel of the communications effort.

In service companies like Club Med and First Direct, word-of-mouth and reputation work as extraordinarily powerful communication tools.

Club Med noticed during the 1980's that, at least in the Americas, the clientele staying in a village at any given time was, on average, 40% GMs who had been to the Club previously. This loyalty is tied to their high level of satisfaction during previous vacations. To put it another way, in a village of 600 people and more than 120 GOs, 240 former GMs welcome 360 new GMs. The company counted on them as ambassadors of the Club Med culture. The socialization and acculturation process for new customers was consequently highly effective. The company's advertising at this time conveyed in a strong and synergistic fashion its lifestyle and values, like giving customers a chance to learn new activities or take up new sports they had not dared to before.

First Direct also possesses imposing social capital and reserves of goodwill in terms of word-of-mouth. Ninety-four percent of its customers say they spontaneously recommend their bank to their friends and neighbors. Today 40% of new customers come in mainly thanks to this positive word-of-mouth. What is more, the advertising the business pays for is clearly selective. It is meant to attract customers whose state of mind corresponds most closely with the advantages they are comparatively more likely to find at First Direct. They come from the ranks of people highly dissatisfied with their current branch bank. A major theme is, "Tell me one good thing about your bank."

Furthermore, at First Direct the effort to sell complementary products is stamped with a great respect for the customer. The telephone counselors are forbidden, for instance, to offer complementary products or services to new customers during their first three months with the bank. These three months are for socializing and educating the customer while the bank starts accumulating enough personalized information on the new customer so that, when new products or services are offered, they will be relevant and make sense for them at that time in their life. So they never force the customer's hand by treating the customer as anonymous and standard.

Dyson has a golden rule of not employing outside advertising agencies. It is a strong believer in word-of-mouth communication. But how does it build the initial critical mass of good news that is to be further diffused? "We've been very fortunate in that journalists were very quickly onto the Dual Cyclone, tried it themselves and then wrote business stories, initially, and then ultimately product stories that explained why we'd got rid of the bag, and the value of doing that .... A huge advertising spend could have made the Dyson more famous, but it needn't necessarily have made it sell. Only the objective power of editorial was able to do that. Anything advertising can do, true journalism can do better when [we went] into advertising, the 'say goodbye to the bag' slogan was utilized" (Dyson 2002, pp. 228–9). This slogan was critized as being not imaginative enough, but Dyson answered: "Our advertising is not designed to win advertising awards, just to sell vacuum cleaners" (Dyson 2002, p. 232).

Another dimension of Dyson's communication is also worth mentioning: its willingness to carefully educate retailers' salespeople on what Dyson is all about. This is linked with a personal experience of James Dyson's in 1993, in a John Lewis department store in Bristol. Asking for a Dyson, he was "switched" to what he calls a "crappy German brand" by a salesperson who demonstrated in no time that he knew nothing about the products he was selling. Since then, Dyson has been convinced that the antidote to those "switch selling" practices was to better educate store staff about Dyson products.

Tesco's communication talents are multiple. It starts with its overall advertising strategy, which faithfully reflects its shifts in positioning. By the mid-1980's, when Tesco decided to totally eradicate the "pile it up, sell it cheap" image, its ad campaigns were centered on the "quest for quality." In 1993, the emphasis moved from products to the quality of in-store service, with "Every Little Helps." In 1995, a new ad campaign was introduced to personify the "Every Little Helps" strategy, featuring a very demanding shopper, "Dotty," who was always looking to put Tesco and its store initiatives to the test. The Dotty campaigns lasted almost a decade, until 2004. Since 2005, communication has been promoting the breadth of the company's product and service offerings, which has become truly impressive since the product campaigns of the early 90's. For instance, in 2005, Tesco launched a clothing website, clothingat-tesco.com, to drive shoppers to bigger stores. Tesco's clothing business became the fastest-growing part of its empire and was gaining significant market share every year.

Tesco has also made strong use of the wealth of data gathered through its Clubcard loyalty scheme. It uses datamining to deepen its personalized relationships with its customers – with the clear objective of expanding its share of basket. And it seems to be working extraordinarily well!

Last but not least, cause-related marketing activities feed into Tesco's communication power. For example, it has used major advertising spending to support its community involvements, such as "Computers for Schools" or "Sports for Schools and Clubs" – through which customers spending more than £10 are awarded vouchers that can then be handed over to schools or clubs. Similarly, its chief marketer Tim Mason, who is very keen on "responsible business," was an early mover into healthy eating initiatives, one of the most recent ones being the inclusion of a glycemia index (Gi) on food-product labeling, accompanied by the launch of the Gi guide, a lifestyle book to help customers follow a balanced eating plan.

Benetton considers its stores not only as points of sale but also and chiefly as essential communication vehicles. This takes the form of high-density location stores with totally uncluttered shop windows that immediately show the concept. Furthermore, while Benetton advertising is unarguably distinctive, it is also meant to convey a value system adhered to, or thought to be adhered to, by the customer set the company has chosen as its target. In fact, when this advertising centered on anti-racism, it was perfectly congruent with the idea that Benetton designs were a "feast of colors" and with the moral sensitivities of its customers. Then again, as already mentioned above, Benetton went astray the day its advertising themes became overly militant or hard to square with the company's business.

Consistency between manufacturing and trading

Marking has a hard time when a confrontational relationship is evolving between manufacturers and sellers. Making them consistent with each other, indeed symbiotic, is the sine qua non for anticipating, and then responding to, the aspirations and needs of the market, with a view to increasing sales and profits for everyone in the system.

A cooperative mentality between suppliers and resellers, though, can take several different forms. A durable marking seems to require at a minimum thinking like partners in a positive-sum game, each one getting his/her fair share in the exchange. A higher level of collaboration involves the creation of an actual meshing of the partners, held together more systematically and more symbiotically. In the extreme case, the business decides to bring in-house both manufacturing and selling. This is nothing more than vertical integration.

Until the mid 1990's, Tesco's relationships with its suppliers were conflictual. This was largely due to Tesco's competing on price with supplier brands by using copycat store brands. In early 1997, Tesco announced its desire to change this somewhat hostile rapport with its suppliers. The company decided that the focus would henceforth be on partnering with suppliers to conjointly develop a differentiated marketing approach. Tesco was also keen, by so doing, to boost its margins. The Tesco Information Exchange (TIE) was one of the initiatives to put this new philosophy into practice. Through TIE, it started providing its suppliers real-time information about store sales of their products, helping both marketing analysis and logistical planning. However, the new partnering posture also implied that Tesco was looking for suppliers' contributions to improve its marketing efficacy. The partnership could extend into developing specific products for its customers, conducting store-specific promotions or, generally speaking, adapting the vendor's offer to Tesco's customers at a store-specific level. It would be wrong to say that partnering eradicated pressures on suppliers, but those pressures were exercised within the framework of Tesco's marketing vision, with better spelled-out objectives and with the prospect of potential benefits for both parties.

Where do we stand today? Tesco still expresses its commitment to help its suppliers grow and its willingness to share its understanding of customers with them. In its last Annual Review, the results of an anonymous survey, "Supplier Viewpoint," indicated that the situation could be described as perfect – that the majority of Tesco's suppliers think Tesco is professional, committed to its customers, fair, and consistent. Although it would be an exaggeration to describe it as a fairy tale, Tesco's relationship with its suppliers seems to be leaning more toward collaboration than confrontation.

IKEA has gone for an extremely tight meshing with its thousands of suppliers who make all or part of the products it sells. Suppliers write a sizeable volume of orders from IKEA and also get its technical assistance and advice. They also have to observe scrupulously the terms of reference and processes IKEA specifies.

IKEA thus implements a policy of near-integration between the manufacture and sale of its products. Of course, the non-confrontation between manufacturer and seller is marred by its suppliers' undeniable loss of independence. In compensation, IKEA gives its suppliers enormous technological support in the form of advice and training, as well as a big economic reward. Mostly tiny to begin with, they grow with and due to IKEA, who guarantees their longevity. Here again we have a win–win game.

Similarly, at Benetton, a split between manufacturing and sales would not make much sense. The Italian company remains first and foremost a manufacturer of sweaters. But it has adopted a flexible mentality of out-sourcing jobs and costs in functions it does not think strategic for its future. Basically, this means sewing, for which it uses a vast network of sub-contractors. Benetton also has ranches in Patagonia that raise sheep and produce wool, although it uses only a tenth of this wool in its own production. Benetton sells direct only through some 50 experimental stores, it also sells through independent retailers, whom it strongly encourages to use the store names, layouts and products that it, Benetton, defines.

Benetton, then, works through a sophisticated, fairly tight, system meshing the production of raw materials, the manufacture of finished goods, and selling. It participates in every link in the chain, but with the most limited investment possible. Truly, in such a dispersed system, controlling all the actors becomes vital. Now, real control is not exercised through contracts or capital. It is exercised by expertise that comes from the controller's direct operating experience in each task of manufacturing and selling. Benetton has this expertise and therefore exercises the control. The company does know better than to put the suppliers who depend on it in a position of total and humiliating subjection. Many Benetton sub-contractors are located in the Venetia region of northern Italy. They carry out their work along with farming activities. This setup probably mollifies any feeling of dependence that some of them might legitimately have toward Benetton and which would be inconsistent with the spirit of non-confrontation. Cooperation cannot last if negative afterthoughts arise.

For a long time, chiefly in France and Belgium, Club Med sold directly through its own agencies and call centers. More than that, these were often staffed with people from the resorts or who in any case had been trained there. It seemed important that its sales personnel, who were to be ambassadors of Club values, should be able to sense quickly, on the telephone or in person, how suitable a potential customer's state of mind was for the Club. A cultural harmony between sales staff – the local agent – and manufacturers of equipment for the resorts was seen as an essential trump to play. In the U.S.A., however, where Club Med had no option but to use independent travel agencies, it insisted that staff at the expert agencies, the ones selling great quantities of Club Med packages, go through training in a Club Med resort. Club Med created a school for travel agents to learn how to spot the right psychographic targets. The travel agents who had been to "Club Med School" were assumed better able to act as cultural filters. They were expected to keep customers from having bad vacation experiences.

The split between production and selling simply vanishes whenever total vertical integration is achieved as is the case for First Direct. In this case the business produces and sells the product itself. If the two activities are not separate in a legal sense, they still are in an operating sense within the business. This fact is more important than it appears. For in this illustration, the issue becomes how the symbiosis is created within the trade-offs surrounding the single obsession: customer satisfaction.

When a proactive or reactive marking succeeds, the absolute focus on market satisfaction, whether it is first orchestrated by the manufacturer or by the retailer, quickly dissolves any dichotomy or confrontation. Situations commonly find two types of resolution: either cooperation, which does not mean collusion or the absence of divergent interests, or mutual avoidance, by relying on alternative channels.

A DEADLY SIN

Proactive markings have loftier ambitions than reactive ones because they aim at putting together unknown socioeconomic territories, thus positioning themselves, rightly, as vehicles of social change such as alternative ways to consume, new modes of interaction between buyers and sellers or innovative ways to use time. The results can turn out to be extremely spectacular and long-lasting.

But glory has its price. The enterprise has to hold itself, in detail and at length, to the explicit or implicit promises it has made to the market. It runs the risk of being seriously weakened, perhaps of dying, if it betrays them. When you are the proactive marker in your industry, you may play with fire by committing acts against moral and professional authority.

A famously proactive marker, Club Med, for instance, made a huge impact and had commensurate success for over a third of a century, roughly till the end of the 1980's. What followed was another story. To appease the anxieties of the financial world after the first downturn in its earnings, company executives decided to considerably increase the responsibilities of the resort managers. This decentralization, intended to trim costs and bolster productivity, unfortunately undermined the enthusiastic, festive qualities that resort managers had been known for. In fact it caused strong and visible erosion in the distinctive nature of the Club Med formula. It poisoned its image and its societal territory.

Longtime GMs, who made up the core of their customer base, suddenly became worried about what could be seen as a lurch toward banality for the culture they had known and loved for decades. The early 1990's brought to light what seemed to several stakeholders as the weaknesses in a less-than-rigorous strategy. Heavy financial losses occurred in 1996 and 1997. Naturally, since then the company has made several attempts at reestablishing itself. Nonetheless today Club Med remains a business far from its roots and its pioneering vision of what a vacation could be. Its management maintains an upscale positioning, quite opposite from the egalitarian vision of its founder, Gérard Blitz. The jury is still out in the announced expectation of a return to respectable profitability in 2006 (Cambon 2001).[1]

Transgression can occur elsewhere, too, for example in the behavior of the marking's founder. Such is the case with IKEA, whose owner, Ingvar Kamprad, always presented himself as the supreme incarnation of the values of the company he created. His official image as a simple, modest, even thrifty man would be chipped away at by the Swedish and international press. Several times since the 1990's, bits of information on his way of life have produced dissonances. His supposed fishing cottage in Lausanne turned out to be a luxurious 300 m² villa. The austerity of his lifestyle seems to include a 240 ha property in the south of Sweden and a 17 ha vineyard in Provence. Granted, such outward signs of wealth are not surprising for a man thought by knowledgeable observers to have the 13th largest fortune in the world. Granted, too, nothing at IKEA is comparable with the frauds and other scandals such as took place at Enron. It is true nonetheless that these are spectacular departures from the exemplary values Kamprad was supposed to have breathed into his company. They lie far afield from the messages that come through what the company says officially. They become flagrant counterexamples and a source of real embarrassment. They have not added up to outcomes for IKEA one could call catastrophic, but bombs going off too loudly can shake a business to its foundations (Truc 2004).

This is what almost happened with The Body Shop in 1994. Created in 1976 by Anita Roddick, this company is a chain of boutiques selling natural hair- and skin-care products. The Body Shop occupied a leading position in cosmetics. It also made itself conspicuous by making social responsibility the cornerstone of its identity. What is more, Anita Roddick was known for taking extreme, passionate and deliberately moralizing positions. Animal rights, fair trade and environmental protection figured among the causes she espoused.

This positioning of the business crowned by the extravert personality of the founder acted as a powerful point of reference and a source of inspiration for the company's employees as well as its customers. At the same time, the resulting image constituted a source of vulnerability. In the mid 1990's, in an atmosphere of scandal, business practices called hypocritical were uncovered. Sarcastic notices appeared in the press, while associations of "responsible" consumers let loose their fury upon the gap between the company's social ideals and its actions.

An article (Entine 1994), widely commented on elsewhere, brought accusations confirmed a year later (Clark 1995) that the so-called natural products of The Body Shop contained cheap, petrochemical ingredients; it added that sloppy quality control had led to contamination of some products and that on average The Body Shop donated less money to charity than other British companies. Lastly, it was accused of making threats to journalists who had the nerve to criticize it. Other critics (Watchdog 1994) alluded to unfair contracts The Body Shop made with certain groups of employees and its franchised distributors. Despite its promises, The Body Shop allotted only a relatively modest share of its purchasing to Third World suppliers. And then it came out that The Body Shop used vitamin E from Hoffman-Laroche for inclusion in its sun screens. Now, it seems this product, like a multitude of pharmaceuticals, had been tested on animals, a practice The Body Shop denounced in its charter.

If you stand back to consider these practices, they appear overall to be relatively secondary in the total life of the business. And yet they were nearly fatal for the company, its marking and its financial performance.

By introducing New Coke on April 23, 1985 and that week stopping all production of the original formula, Coca-Cola drew vehement and nearly unanimous rejection from the American people. The surprise to the company was only made more dramatic by the fact that studies slavishly conforming to the orthodoxies of modern marketing had concluded that this sweeter, more sugary product would appeal to the consumers sampled. Coca-Cola had spent more than a hundred years convincing North Americans that its product was an integral part of their lifestyle, their cultural heritage and their national identity. Taking away their original Coca-Cola was therefore not just about taste. It was a bit of its soul that the giant from Atlanta had cut from its territory, which included more than just consumers of the drink. The business had committed an error in terms of the right mindset by announcing that the new product replaced the old, when it should have been treated as a variation on the historical product. On July 11, 1985, just 77 days after the thundering introduction of New Coke, Coca-Cola decided to withdraw it immediately from the market and reintroduce the old product under the name Coke Classic (Gorman 1985). A giant had nearly destroyed its main asset.

Transgressing the right mindset is a serious error that results in the business's momentary or enduring decline. Yet it does not necessarily mean a swift and certain death. Club Med, The Body Shop and Coca-Cola have all survived and eventually become successful again, however great their real or potential suffering. However, French company Chevignon, a business that was emblematic of the 1980's in France, was not so lucky.

Chevignon's aviator-style clothing and accessories had by the 1980's become icons for teenagers and young adults. Galvanized by its success, it seriously debased its status and its image by signing an

155

agreement with Altadis (then Seita) to make and sell cigarettes under the Chevignon name. Chevignon broke off the agreement in 1991. But the general outcry it prompted, at a time when the fight against teenage smoking was at its height, left an indelible stain. The brand was no longer fashionable, and it soon fizzled out. It would be bought by the Naf-Naf Group in 1995. The societal tidal wave that Chevignon represented at its moment of glory is long gone. The company is gone and the name remains merely as a trademark. Its territory has been bled dry, at least in contrast with the promise it initially showed. Naf-Naf's attempted reintroduction of the brand began with their apologizing for the cigarette episode (Nicolas 1998).

The general lesson to draw from deviations – big or small, intentional or not – in the area of proactive marking is that absolute consistency in the marker's actions is required to create absolutely consistent perceptions. Society in the broad sense, or at least a segment of it, inevitable takes its revenge when proactive markers betray their correct mindset and break their promises. Nothing is forgiven of those who transgress, in even a tiny way, their mindsets, the worldviews they promote, or the contracts they affirm.

Diverging from one's mindset is a real danger for a proactive marker, but it is not without risk for reactive markers either. Recent events at Wal-Mart illustrate this. In 2005, Wal-Mart was confronted with a string of assaults; some political, some legal, some community-driven. The company was hit with about 8,000 lawsuits (of which two-thirds were injury-related). One of those lawsuits, launched by six former Wal-Mart employees for discrimination against women in pay and promotions could concern 1. 5 million plaintiffs if elevated to a class action.

Wal-Mart's anti-union posture is also raising a lot of anger. The largest union in the world, Union Network International, announced at its 2005 meeeting in Chicago that it was preparing a global one-day protest against Wal-Mart. The objective was to force Wal-Mart to accept unions or to soften its anti-union stance (illustrated once more by the May 2005 closing of a Canadian store that dared to allow union representatives). This anti-union posture also explains to a large extent the battle that took place in New York to keep Wal-Mart out of the city (Grimes 2005).

This situation ended up raising concerns from some investors (Birchall June 2005). Two leading UK investors formed a transatlantic alliance with Illinois and New York City pension funds to urge Wal-Mart to carry out an independent review of its legal and regulatory controls. Their letter to Wal-Mart focused on three problems that had seriously stained Wal-Mart's image: an 11-million-dollar federal penalty for allowing sub-contractors to use illegal immigrants ; violations of laws on under-age labor ; and the grand jury investigation into the expense accounts of Thomas Coughlin, a former Wal-Mart vice chairman – not really in conformity with Wal-Mart's claims of honesty and frugality! Some analysts insist that, unless the illegal conduct of top managers is systemic in a company, it cannot or should not severely damage the company's image (Colvin 2005). Although Wal-Mart has admitted that there was voluminous evidence of Coughlin using corporate funds for personal expenditures, Lee Scott sought to counter the damage by saying that this only demonstrated the strength of the Wal-Mart culture, and that Wal-Mart was committed to acting properly, even when it hurts (Birchall July 2005).

Late 2005 was no more pleasant for Wal-Mart. An internal memorandum on employee's health insurance was leaked to the press, confirming that the health insurance coverage of Wal-Mart employees and their families was meager, to say the least. A documentary released in November 2005, "The High Cost of Low Price" did not reveal any new criticisms of Wal-Mart, but definitely added to the negative publicity surrounding the company.[2]

Three factors make it imperative to avoid deviating from the right mindset and thus complicate the observance of effective practices.

The more a company, an industry or an economy becomes involved in marking dynamics, the greater the probability that departures, intentional or not, will appear – and the heavier the wages of sin for those who do. Put another way, not marking obligates the business very little. Reactive marking obligates it substantially, and proactive marking obligates it very heavily. The marking business then fosters an increase in potential sources of vulnerability. Failure is more costly the higher the bar of virtue is set.

The territoriality of marking inhibits competitors, putting them on the lookout for the slightest chink in the armor. The competition can also opportunistically exploit the weaknesses of others in terms of keeping their promises. The right mindset and its translation into everyday operating terms are invisible assets whose weight is often ignored. They can be destroyed in far quicker time than it takes to construct them.

Stakeholders in businesses are growing in number. They are more ready to stand watch over and swing into action against marking businesses than other merchant businesses in marking economies.

Customers, opinion-makers, press, special-interest associations, consumer groups, the courts, regulators, not to mention employees, all make up so many little groups waiting to topple the marking business when it is found at fault, rightly or even wrongly.

When business executives are confronted with a downturn brought on by being lax in their promises, they can be inclined to turn into a safety valve what should be an alarm signal: the defection of customers or outspoken stakeholders (Hirschman 1970). Such executives feel it is effective to disarm their customers and their stakeholders by imposing one and only one option: blind and mute loyalty to the practices of the business. They show scorn to those who speak out against them, or silence them with controversy and discredit. They hope to prevent defection through advertising or pricing. All that because they judge, wrongly, that their short-term interest needs a bit of room in which to maneuver. In fact, this only hastens their decline.

The correct response is very different. Defection and outspokenness serve as so many signals that the business must align its promises with its practices. Ensuring a marking is durable and consistent demands two attitudes:

- To not defensively deny, with technocratic arrogance, the validity and legitimacy of stakeholders who defect or speak out. Respect or listen to the points they make.
- To not push stakeholders into line with company practices. Rather, the business must show some humility by trying to win them back with responses that are acceptable to each.

7

SOCIETAL EMBEDDING

Embedding companies aim at more than just having a business impact. Beyond their short-term financial performance, their ambitions and actions are driven by another overarching target: to shape a broader and lasting specific world of their own. Their success comes from being simultaneously the architects and the epicenters of new societal, cultural, and social spaces: the ultimate benchmarks and common denominators of all involved. We call this process "marking a territory."

This chapter is devoted to a better understanding of a territory as a special kind of organized economic and social structure.[1] We examine its distinctive characteristics and their implications on building and sustaining a territory. To understand the process will require a proactive marking perspective.

The main difference between reactive and proactive marking is simple. Reactive marking conserves and makes use of pre-existing social and economic territories, with identifiable stakeholders. Success in this case derives from the business's ability to insert itself into, and fit, this territory. Proactive marking, however, looks to build new territories that the business can design and grow from scratch. These new territories are based on new understandings. Proactive marking involves new stakeholders or modifies the roles of existing ones. New values legitimize the conquest of new frontiers. Businesses that mark new territories also invent other ways to link exchanges between upstream and downstream. They are driven by an unconventional mindset which rejects conventional wisdom. They act as societal reformers. Their management is driven by a societal cause that it wants to legitimize and to establish as a source of economic wealth. In a way, it advocates a certain vision of the future and enters an engineering process to realize this vision.

While the term "territory" usually refers to a geographical and spatial dimension, in the context of business and management it refers to an economic setup embedded in a specific societal context. The term "market" may not be adequate enough.

The purpose of the first section of this chapter is to show precisely how this wording change is a value-added action. It defines a territory as a concept and reviews key cognitive differences between territory- and market-based interpretations. Territory as a way of naming and understanding managerial action enriches the identification of opportunities for economic differentiation and social innovation.

The second section suggests that, like other economic regimes such as hierarchies, markets, and networks, territories are action sets. They are outcomes of proactive coordination projects linking production to consumption, upstream to downstream, in economic exchanges. At the same time, building and governing a territory require a wide array of specific managerial capabilities that differ from those needed for other economic regimes. Institutionalization, domination, and civilization are some of them.

FROM MARKET TO TERRITORY

Words matter. They lead to action. They are representations of the world – of what, how, when, and why. They set standards, criteria for behavior. In a way words provide theories. If I do this now, that is likely to happen. Causal linkages of this kind rely on definitions of the world and of effectiveness that decision-makers carry in their head.

Terms or words used in everyday speech, while they might be considered as shortcuts or proxies (reality being far more complex), often become self-fulfilling prophecies. As we fall into the habit of using a term, in our thoughts or our speech – we believe it is relevant in any situation, that the theory it implicitly conveys is of use at any time, and that no more inquiry is needed to understand the specifics of a certain situation, to check the truth or the fallacy of its causal links. Terms become normative habits, never questioned, that express the right and the wrong way to operate. An additional danger arises when these wordings are shared and agreed on by those around us, as we feel more comfortable using them unquestioningly.

Such is the case with "market"; one of the most commonly used words in business, not only in day-to-day discussions, but also as a key reference for action taking when making strategic and marketing decisions. "Market" quite often becomes a catch-all word for the outside, the environment in which the company operates. The surprise is that in a number of cases it raises more problems than it provides solutions. It may, for instance, give an oversimplified view of the world the company is facing. It can lead to overestimation of the weight of economic drivers or processes in solving a problem or generating change. It may just be too vague to lead to clear action. While such facts are familiar to managers, the surprise is that representation of the world as an action set remains overwhelming. This is why substituting the word "territory" for the word "market" is not just a question of semantics, an amendment to the way we talk at the coffee machine, but is a mindset or cognitive revolution for action taking. Both do not cover the same theories about what lies outside the company and how to be successful.

Where does the difference lie? The word market makes a lot of sense when used in a macroeconomic sense. It provides a way to understand (and a theory to define) equilibrium and optimal conditions. It is also relevant in dealing with prices in a given sector with a given competition structure, from a short-term perspective, all other things being equal. From a micro-economic perspective, a single business can use the concept to adjust its production function. Managerially speaking, market favors a merchant perspective. Its reasoning prefers adaptation and exploitation rather than regeneration and innovation.

The difference between market and territory has to do with their cognitive components. Household appliances provide a good example of the value a territorial perspective adds to action-oriented knowledge. As in many countries, including the U.S. or the U.K., the French household appliances sector (washing machines, dishwashers, ovens or refrigerators) is characterized by a mechanism one may call the "meeting of the few." In the mid-1980's, three manufacturers supplied more than 60% of the total sales in this sector in France. Seven distribution chains sold slightly more than 55% of the goods that millions of end customers annually purchased. Since then, the concentration level has increased, three major retailers now selling close to 70%.

According to orthodox economic analysis applied to price-fixing, such a sector should be considered a juxtaposition of two separate interfaces or markets. Upstream sees a confrontation between two oligopolies: manufacturers and major retailers. Downstream offers quite a different vision: several retailers face a crowd of individual, unorganized buyers.

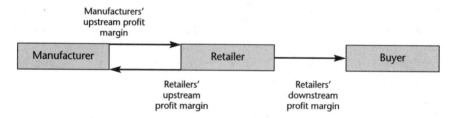

FIGURE 7.1 **Market reasoning applied to household appliances**

Each interface or market is organized according to different princi-ples. The key assumption is that what happens downstream does not spill over into what happens upstream, or vice-versa. Both worlds are separate, as if there were a wall dividing them.

Observation, nevertheless, shows that this separation may not be so clear. Major distribution chains participate in both markets. They simultaneously generate profit margins downstream – through sales – and upstream, from their buying power. The upstream profit margins can be massive, representing up to 40% of their total profits. Such large retailers acquire products at a cheaper price than do traditional independent local retailers, as they order between 100 and 500 times the volume of goods. Can a manufacturer, even if it is one of the big three in an industry, really afford not to be on the shelves of a distribu-tion chain that sells annually half of what its major factory produces?

Despite such facts, orthodox reasoning argues that what happens upstream – such as the profits made by manufacturers or retailers – has no impact on the dynamics of the relationships and the power of the partners downstream. These should simply be considered transaction costs, at least in the short term. But in the long term one might expect that what is at work upstream could induce some effects downstream. Ten or fifteen years on, we would expect that, because national distri-bution chains control access to end customers, the pressure of the market would impose its logic, its competitive dynamics, on both groups of oligopolists: large manufacturers and mass distributors. In other terms, prices should decrease and costs lower. End customers should benefit massively, as should the largest commercial and indus-trial companies.

Such reasoning, despite its elegant deductive structure, may not exactly fit the facts, which have been seen to contradict it. In France, the prices of electronic household appliances have not decreased in a spectacular manner, even when compared with other similar sectors; when they occasionally do, consumer behavior is not the main vehicle or driver. Two facts are striking. As consumers, households do not really benchmark prices and products. It is as if they face difficulties in doing so, or are in a state of cognitive confusion. Price opacity is high. There are a great many different types of products on offer, although the three major brands do attract a high level of awareness. Also, the profit margins that major distributors extract upstream through their purchasing power are to a large extent (85%) not transferred to their end customers.

To understand such practices, it is helpful to remember the presumptions on which the concept of market is based. In essence, market exchanges are very similar to barter exchanges. The term "market," the representation of the world it assumes, provides an appropriate structure with which to predict and manage economic relationships when, and only when:

- Transactions involve no cognitive, informational, or technical complexity. They are simple enough to be understood and handled by all;
- Transaction costs are low. They do not matter much and are not relevant for either of the parties involved;
- Transactions are settled in a direct manner between the two parties. They involve no third party playing a mediation role;
- The content and terms of the exchange are easy to specify to users;
- Users are assumed to behave in an identical manner under any circumstances;
- Transactions are achieved without any additional investment apart from a minimum level of information on prices, which is easy to gather.

Experience suggests this framework relies on premises that in reality do not often exist simultaneously. It assumes that, in everyday life, a certain number of conditions are simultaneously present and satisfied, such as:

- Markets are considered as a kind of natural state, pre-existing trans-actions and parties, and the business has no other option than to embed itself into what already exists. A business cannot invent and mold such a world from scratch;

- Price levels are used by the business as the ultimate criterion with which to generate transactions;
- Exchanges and transactions are considered a game linking two parties, and two parties only: the business and the end buyer. No other stakeholders matter;
- The two parties involved are free to withdraw at any time, exchanges are spot exchanges, not repeated patterns between long-term interdependent players.

Such an action theory implies that markets evolve and function as if they were abstract, impersonal worlds. That economic agents are foreign to each other, except during spot transactions. That all markets behave and function in a similar manner and according to identical criteria. That whether a business marks with a proactive approach or relies on a reactive one does not matter. That economic mechanisms are alike.

But a territory refers to a very different image of the economic world and to an alternative type of action taking. Reality "out there" is considered as comprising differentiated worlds, each one unique. Lasting relationships are seen to often link interdependent parties across long time periods. Past experience is recognized as shaping repeated interactions. Action arenas are understood to be social constructs open to the domination of strong wills and power dynamics. Economic actors are viewed as operating in contexts that run hot, filled with passion, greed and prejudices.

A reinterpretation of a groundbreaking social economic study on household appliances in France suggests this (Dupuy and Thoenig 1996). In terms of organized action systems, the study showed that the sector did not function or evolve as a juxtaposition of two distinct markets. The sector instead had to be understood as a single entity made up of multiple interdependencies and complicated interpersonal relationships, in a social and economic space comprising highly integrated parties.

Many actors are involved in the process of providing household appliances to the market and society: manufacturers of components and spare parts, private brand producers, leading public brands manufacturers, high-end public brand manufacturers, traditional retailers, wholesalers, discounters, kitchen retail specialists, specialized retail chains, food mass retailers, buyers, consumer associations, fair trade public agencies. In France, 32 different types of actor shape in a relevant manner the socioeconomic context of transaction and exchange in this business sector. Each one plays a distinct role or set of roles. Each one is driven by specific vested interests.

Obviously some stakeholders or economic actors matter more than others in shaping the market. They exert great power and massively influence transaction contexts. Their domination has direct implications for other players who are far less dominant. The latter may have either to adjust their own interests, strategies and acts to those of very influential players or to leave the system even more. Compared with Japan and the U.S., the case of France suggests that the number of players, the influence each has on the economic game and the outomes for the users are amazingly different. Globalization of products and brands in open economies does not imply that national markets have become identical across the world.

At the periphery of the French household appliances business sector are public institutions dealing with fair trade enforcement (this is quite the opposite in the U.S., for instance), watchdogs such as consumer associations, single buyers (here again it is less the case in the U.S., at least in household appliances) and private brand manufacturers (mostly located in foreign cheap labor countries). They may be rather powerless despite their formal resources (law for fair trade agencies, voice for consumer activists). They may also deliberately withdraw from the main game by creating a distinct action system, for instance by linking the producers, the retailers and the users, as is the case with high-end public brands such as the German company Miele. In this case of selective distribution, while being in command of the niche, Miele as a producer may offer to traders such as kitchen retail specialists, protection against the volatility of competition on the main market.

Somewhere between the periphery and the core are economic actors who are neither marginal nor dominant. This is the case for traditional retailers and wholesalers, leading public brand manufacturers, and non-specialized mass retailers. They may be quite important players. Nevertheless they face constraints they cannot handle by ignoring them. They also may build coalitions of interests with third parties but are not in a position to amend the dynamics of the market and be leaders in setting the rules of the competition.

The core of the French system is not in the hands of the leading public brand producers (as it is in the case of Japan) or under the control of a subtle tripartite coalition (leading national brand producers, non-specialized mass retailers, and consumers, as in the U.S.A. One particular figure holds a clearly dominant position: the mass retailer specialized in household appliances who uses a consumerist approach. Darty is by far the leading national retailer of household appliances and electronics. This company offers, or at least aspires to offer, the biggest choice of brands and references at the lowest prices, holding the dominant position.

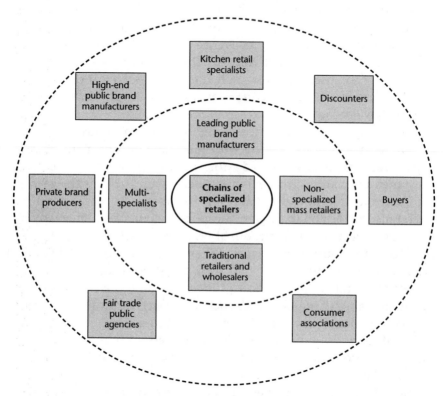

FIGURE 7.2 **Core–periphery reasoning applied to household appliances**

The specialized mass marketer dominates through its capacity to create the rules of the game and of the economic transaction, in the short and in the long term. Other stakeholders must adhere to its rules. The distributor becomes the linchpin of an intricate system, the glue that holds the system together – it marks a territory largely structured around itself. Its domination rests on three major resources.

Although selling at a loss is prohibited in principle, the mass consumerist distributor can circumvent the prohibition and use brand leaders as loss leaders. Second, despite self-service, the specialized mass distributor employs salespeople in its stores. These personnel are paid on commission. Positive or negative bonuses are calculated so that when confused customers ask for advice, the salesperson will direct them toward private brand references that are offered at lower prices, but with a larger profit margin. The salesperson's influence is very effective, because a choice of goods induces anxiety in most customers. Buying a washing machine produces a higher level of anxiety than buying an automobile, making the customer more receptive to the salesperson's arguments.

Finally, to the extent that shopping areas are local, the big retailers' mass buying gives them the power to rapidly eliminate competition by slashing prices. Competing retailers can adopt one of three solutions. The first is to withdraw from the household appliance field altogether. This is the case for mass-market supermarkets that use large household appliances as occasional loss products to attract customers to another section and induce impulse buying. The second solution is to become a specialist by following Darty's model, but always staying a step and a size behind. The third solution, which many small independent retailers adopt, is to regroup themselves and their purchases.

Like retailers, manufacturers can adopt a wide range of behaviors. They are constantly put under pressure. To get shelf placement for their products in hypermarkets and gain the market shares that will give them life, manufacturers must accept high discounts. Otherwise they must take refuge in smaller distribution channels such as kitchen specialists. Manufacturers of private brands do not deal with marking: they take on a production function only. They depend on extremely low costs (which explains their implantation in foreign countries where labor costs are lower) and their success is never assured to last.

The three major manufacturers of large household appliances in France, the top-of-the-line brands, keep their share of the market and their production tools through a combination of three different techniques. They try to maintain a direct relationship with end buyers through advertising, through which they try to impose their reputation on the buyer and short-circuit commerce. But while this strategy might work against small, independent businesses that generally only carry one or two leading public brands, it stands no chance against the big retailers and bait-and-switch practices used in their stores. Public brand manufacturers also rely on functional and technical innovation, although unfortunately technical innovation is expensive and only guarantees temporary success. Finally, they produce specific private brands and references for specific, specialized consumers, making them even more dependent on their products. In other words, the manufacturer's marking becomes a difficult strategy to carry through without strong allies or the support of credible opinion-makers such as consumer advocate groups. Buyers, on the other hand, are marginalized. Only retailers hear their voice. At the same time retailers, and not producers are in a position to channel the customer's wants. For they control the place of sale.

Through advertising, the big retailers present themselves as defenders of household purchasing power, using the "low price" argument. In this way, any potential intervention by the public sector to reorganize downstream practices is kept at bay; downstream practices constitute approximately 40% of their profits.

The status of supplier or demander masks more subtle situations. Not all retailers are alike. Leading public brand manufacturers do not adopt the same strategy as competitors who manufacture retail or generic private brands.

Systemic reasoning goes much deeper than market reasoning. It explores what is at stake for each participant, and considers participants' behaviors, resources, and constraints, and how these are linked through interdependencies and transactions. Participants have numerous criteria for action-taking and decision-making. They find solutions in situations that seem without solution. Surprisingly enough, interdependencies, even asymmetrical ones, do not exclude the possibility of alliances between the dominant and the dominated. Large retailers cannot ignore leading public brands without the risk of losing credibility in the eyes of their customers. Smaller, independent retailers, however, can use the larger stores as wholesalers to benefit fully or partially from the low purchase prices consented by manufacturers.

Economic sociology research studies shed light on differences between the products offered and on consumption and buying habits. In France, a system dominated by specialized mass retailers has implications which differentiate it from other countries (Dupuy and Thoenig 1996).

In Japan, the dominant actor is clearly the national mass manufacturer, which uses a relatively proactive marking strategy. Not only do its public brands enjoy such overwhelming brand awareness that foreign brands are simply ignored, but it also positions domestic appliances not as durable tools fulfilling household services such as washing clothes, but as objects that make a statement about fashion or lifestyle. Manufacturers are constantly inventing new features and functions for these appliances. The offer is updated two to three times a year. Retailers are extremely dependent on manufacturers of recognized public brands, as commercial developments in Japan, when controlled by local authorities, are very hostile to specialized hypermarkets.

Consumers are the weakest players in the game. Japanese consumers replace their appliances far more frequently than do consumers in France or the United States. The Japanese change their washing machines every three to five years, regardless of the appliance's condition or performance level; accordingly the economic system that governs the household appliance sector is characterized by great stability over time.

In France, this sector is a lot less stable, a lot more commercially opaque, and relations among its members tend to be contentious. Manufacturers play a smaller role and the location of their plants is a major cost factor. France is a country in which technological innovation is highly developed: with increasingly light, compact appliances that consume low levels of water and energy, and so on. At the same time, technological innovations, which are most often marketed by public brand leaders, are seen as loss leaders by the big retailers. The goal is to attract customers to the store through brand leaders that finance major advertising campaigns by offering a lower price than a neighborhood store, and by using the commission system to sell private brands that are less technologically innovative, but also less expensive and yet more profitable for the retailer.

End customers as well as retailers find it difficult if not near impossible to compare prices and brands across the market. Shoppers are offered a wide spectrum of alternatives. For instance a leading brand may not sell exactly the same product to specialized and to traditional retailers, or even inside the same channel of distribution, to Darty and to one of its competitors. While 98% of the content and features of a washing machine may be identical to another carrying the same brand, whatever the point of sale, an automatic emergency mechanism may be added to the machine when sold by Darty while a special washing cycle for delicate fabrics may be added to the same machine when sold by another specialist. A store may also change its public prices every half-day during the week. Therefore comparisons are hard to make. Shoppers face confusion and opacity more than they benefit from transparency, this in a market dynamics that is dominated by a core actor, the specialized retailer, who paradoxically refers to consumerist principles (free access to the shelves, availability of all brands existing on the market, and so on).

THE TERRITORY OF THE ENTERPRISE

Territories and marking can be found just about everywhere: in commerce and in industry, in goods and in services, in low-tech and high-tech, in English-speaking countries as well as in French-speaking ones, in both global and local contexts.

Territories refer to spaces or inhabited worlds. These spaces do not exist in a bubble; they are embedded in society. These worlds emerge as a result of actions taken by a business. While territories can be understood in terms of a spatial component, their true nature is not essentially determined by geography or physical proximities. Their nature is economic, social and even political. It is made up of stakeholders and actions, relations and interests, dependencies and transactions, norms and identities.

Territories are real in social and relational terms. They are action sets. They are not just symbolic or imaginary. Such a perspective differs significantly from theories developed by semiologists and philosophers who underline the importance of the networks that major brands create as humanizers of the world, making it lively and interesting to experience. In their opinion buying a brand is acquiring a specific space, a particular pleasure, a way of life, a celebration. There's certainly a price for everything, including classical music. Consuming Beethoven can be costly. However, Beethoven provides a particular vision of the world that is dear to many people, that has a value because it makes them believe in their spiritual dimension, it recreates the magic of a concert hall and it gives them the feeling that they are members of a selective club. While brands socially distinguish their buyers, they also allow them to inhabit a space. The same goes for shoes and hamburgers. These worlds signify more than they are. They cannot be reduced to just the object itself, even if this object is beautiful. They have rules that buyers play by, that persuade them of the quality of the brands. Complacency is part of the brand game. Everyone knows the worlds created by brands are not real; yet we appreciate whoever organizes those worlds, and we know they are not evil.

Our perspective states that territories, the worlds and activities they induce, result from a management process called marking. Marking translates the way companies use an active and deliberate approach to enrich the relationship between a product and a purchase. But companies do not rely entirely on fate, nor do they passively trust market forces. Marking companies create dense relations that have nothing to do with bartering, or with its more sophisticated form, the market. The substitution of the concept of market with the concept of territory is not just a simple rhetoric trick or an academic coquetry. A territory is an intentionally organized project which has to be sensed, understood, engineered.

There are several organized forms of economic action, the most well known of these being hierarchy, market, and network (Powell 1990). But a marked territory is a unique form that resembles no other. Having already mentioned the market characteristics, a few comments should be added about network characteristics and why they are not identical to territories as such.

An interorganizational network is an answer to existing dependencies among companies (Pfeffer and Salancik 1978). It can take different forms to stimulate the success of its members: joint ventures, administrative exchanges, associates, cartels, social relations. To attain this goal it builds partnerships – finding common ground between them through, for example, the transfer and sharing of resources and training, thus creating reciprocal confidence, lowering and sharing risks. A network ensures the durability and reciprocity of relationships among its members and the clarity of member obligations.

One of the best known forms of network is found in industrial marketing (Hakansson 1982). A business-to-business connection links the provider of raw materials, the manufacturer, and the customer together. Cooperation through the network proves to be much more efficient than market competition, as the mutual acquaintances and confidence it provides ensure a win–win situation among network members. The resources and skills that create value and that each member controls are strongly connected.

The territory as a managerial project differs from the network on several levels:

- Members are integrated in a denser, more durable fashion;
- Territories operate on levels other than simply those of utility or lowering transaction costs – they tend to have a more global vision, with strong ideals, clear codes of behavior, common identities;
- Territories never presume the pre-existence of social relations in transactions. Instead, they seek to create solidarities and links where there are none;

- The business involves other stakeholders in its initiative: consumers, non-profit-making associations, opinion-makers, regulatory bodies, traders, and so on. Through an assimilation process, the business internalizes the values, priorities, and habits of other environments into its own project, so that its economic success becomes tightly linked to the success of a larger social segment in which it operates;
- Management takes on causes important to other stakeholders. In this sense, the business becomes a kind of representative or governor of a world comprising federated parties.

Marking a territory takes the gamble that transactions that are integrated into a world in which members share common ground will be more efficient than purely commercial transactions. Beyond just creating strong social ties among a few actors as a hierarchy of authority or a legal contract does, studies in sociological economy show marking aims to develop weak social ties among many actors that otherwise might not be linked in (Granovetter 1985).

A territory can be equated to a contextualized business submitted to a specific societal order. Royal Canin's territory is one in which participants – pet owners, veterinarians, various associations, specialized media interested in pets, and so on – construct and share a non-anthropomorphic approach to cats and dogs. Wal-Mart's territory comprises mid- to low-income earners living and working in American rural backwaters: consumers who avoid conspicuous or undue spending.

A territory can be more or less socially dense, in terms of the number of stakeholders within it, the parts they play, and how it is governed. It is enough in this respect to compare the standard pet-food territory with that of the nutritional and health-conscious pet food.

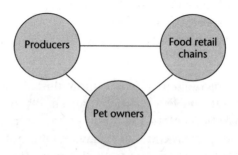

FIGURE 7.3 **The territory of basic mass pet food (stakeholders)**

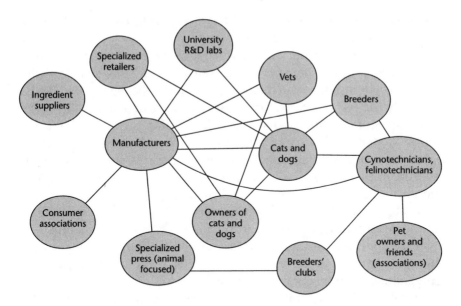

FIGURE 7.4 **The territory of nutrition and health pet food (stakeholders)**

TABLE 7.1 **Comparing pet food territories**

	Basic mass pet food	**Nutrition and health pet food**
Number of stakeholders	Few	Many
Role differentiation	Low	High
Governance	Hegemony and competition	Cooperation and coalition

It is amazing to compare pet food to holiday packages presented in Chapter 1. In both cases the markers, Royal Canin and Club Med, have built a specific territory with different groups, co-opting many stakeholders in quite differentiated roles, and around different governance patterns.

The term territory refers to a segment of society and a collective dynamic that the business wants to serve, to capture, and – if need be – to help materialize. The business activates or creates this world's identity, while serving its values and helping its stakeholders to emerge and take sides. Marking invents or identifies this world, it constructs or reinforces it. It segments not only the market but also the broader social tissue. Marking is everything that socializes the business and the way it confronts competition.

We can easily imagine definitions that would restrict territoriality to mere geographic components – such as physical area and logistical infrastructure. For instance, when looking at cement, the logic would be that it is only the physical proximity of the customer that allows for a delivery of tons of cement at a good price. The reality is that this logic only works under specific conditions: in sectors with a low capacity for competitive differentiation and whose evolution is slow, or in sectors that are restrained by quasi-monopolies (access to quarries, high costs of production machinery, and so on). Cement is protected only as long as concrete remains an essential product for construction. There are already numerous substitutes for concrete, such as steel, wood, and plastic.

A territory does not limit itself to selling. Knowing and incorporating the customer in the marking process is a way for the business to integrate itself more completely in the society it is part of. Consumption is defined in the broadest sense of the term, its definition ranging from the consumer's way of life to the sense the citizen gives to the future of the world, and in the industrial sector, from the customer's client to the final user. Marking mobilizes social and economic, normative and behavioral, public and private, moral and functional factors. Marking aims to impose certain patterns on relations between the product and its use, and to eliminate others. It reinvents the market by substituting it with other forms and processes. In its most accomplished cases, marking is a project that transforms the economy and society, not simply a way of influencing sales.

Social sciences define a territory as a distinctive and unified space. It is separated from other spaces or its environment by barriers. It has a specific social organization; the territory creates a common frame of reference for its inhabitants. These inhabitants share an identity that defines their actions and preferences. A territory also has its own political life, a center that governs it on the basis of what almost amounts to a social contract, a moral pact at least.

The idea of territory as a form of organized economic action parallels the social sciences definition. First of all, it refers to a population that inhabits a common social and cognitive area and is united by processes of governance and social control. The marking business creates and maintains relations, identities, challenges, and references that lead otherwise heterogeneous groups and individuals, functions and arenas to become sufficiently interdependent. The territory provides common denominators for its various stakeholders, which are distinguished by the different external worlds they belong to. On top of this, the marking business unites the members of a territory via a common governance core.

Marking a territory is, to a certain extent, a matter of social control. More precisely, it is a vision of the world that is rationalized by the business, and incorporates both its external environment and its internal organization. This vision gives meaning to the business's actions by defining what behaviors are appropriate and how to interpret and to direct this world. Marking determines the business's strategy, its organizational structure and power.

One of the most spectacular results of a vast research project on major American companies sheds light on the marked world (Fligstein 1990). Companies run by directors with strategic marketing backgrounds are the most likely to be both directed and led by the pressure of short-term financial gain as their main priority. The flipside of this type of social control or world vision is that the company has no territorial base. It is stateless, each market being equal to the next. Its greatness lies in its unbelievable capacity to adapt, leaving one market to open up on another.

The term "territory" also refers to a business's area of competence, or jurisdiction. Within a territory, stakeholders have the authority and freedom to deal with issues relating to these areas of competence. For a business, marking a territory means exercising an authority that allows it to integrate independent actors involved with heterogeneous situations and activities.

Lastly, the territory refers to a defined world that is independent from third parties. Where customers and products are concerned, the business takes advantage of a reserved zone, protected from exterior threats. Barriers aim to prevent entrances and exits, in order to keep out predators and competitors who won't respect barriers should they find a way to cross them.

Marking is an intentional action. It is a project that stems from finalized action, conquest, expansion and a policing function, in the broad sense of the term. The business's territory is neither won in advance nor acquired once and for all. It requires continued and deliberate action.

Marking a territory coincides with the business's interests – in a financial sense, of course, but in a broader sense as well. There is a desire for hegemony and the dynamic of power, the goal being to erect the business at the epicenter of the territory. While it might be founded on and legitimized through altruistic ideals (for example improving users' comfort, recognizing the legitimacy of animal rights, promoting fair trade), marking a territory aims to establish a dominant place for the business and to make it the hub of events. The territory seeks to have authority over the products and activities that it controls even partially.

This work is never complete, and if a business thinks that way, its territory will quickly fall apart. Everything must be done to ensure that the business doesn't lose its lead. The marking and construction of a territory requires time and consistency: it is a sustainable development project.

In an economy where distribution takes precedence over production and in a context where regulation drastically restrains income protection via cartel practices and commercial protectionism, marking prevents the business from being a pawn that can respond only passively to the contexts in which it finds itself. A business can give itself the means to reduce its dependency on the prison of its context by creating new contexts for economic, social and cultural action. Through marking it can become involved in many different areas, exposing itself to public debate and giving itself a civic responsibility that goes beyond just conforming to the norms of good governance or of ethics.

Territories last. They may also collapse. This is because they are actor-centered and action-dependent. They exist because they are embodied in individual acts and concrete transactions. To underline the importance of the fact that territory builders institutionalize their action sets is not just a mundane gesture of labeling ordinary or obvious requirements for economic achievement and success. As societal reformers, proactive managers do one thing that differentiates them from reactive marking: they construct, from scratch, resource situations and opportunities, for themselves as well as for stakeholders. Territories do not fall from the sky. They are not just there, waiting for some magician to bring them to light. Human activities, social interactions, and ethical and value changes give rise to them from the ground up.

The marking manager becomes an institutional entrepreneur, a center. He or she produces institutionalization (Shils 1975). He or she creates and transmits norms and values that shape the future of social and political arenas on levels other than just consumption and employment. By deciding to control its own fate, the business will also play a part in shaping the fate of the territories and populations that it addresses.

As institutions, territories both restrict and facilitate behaviors. They allow alternative or new values to be taken into account that were not previously considered or addressed. They also create iron cages, build constraints to limit human action. Institutionalized economic territories function not as objective, impersonal machines, but according to the meanings participants attribute to them as they engage with the business's project.

A territory consists of different groups of actors who come to share some common knowledge in relation to specific situations. Without such a minimal level of shared knowledge, and its ongoing modification through learning, no territory would ever last. Within a territory, stakeholders group recurrent actions by their typical features. It is this typification that makes it possible to attribute meaning to their actions (Berger and Luckmann 1971). When typification does not occur, economic goods designed to bring customers added value will not fall under their radars. Institutionalization, which means the attribution of value, transforms these goods into practical resources. It is not because Royal Canin markets high-quality dry pet food that it has achieved sustainable success. It is because it has developed and structured a territory, a culture – or, to define it better, a new meaning understood and shared by multiple actors – the moral and value backbone of which is respect for the health of pets as the basis of behavior that is also pragmatic. To buy, sell, or recommend dry pet food makes sense as a means to conform to these values and meanings.

Price, packaging, and communication are just a few components among many that are part of typification. What really matters in a managerial perspective is to combine behavioral patterns that usually would not be linked (for example feeding pets and making them healthy) or even vested interests that are perceived, rightly or wrongly, as incompatible (for example the pet shop as the place to buy pet food at an acceptable price) so that these combinations induce functional consequences (in this case, for the end buyer and for the vet).

Social reform via the creation of new territories implies that companies consider it a priority to examine and to reform concepts, values, and meanings in society, not just to manufacture and sell another product among so many already available. Ethical sentiments can sustain economic exchanges and enable the proactive marker to achieve legitimacy.

A business doesn't just ransack a territory and leave. On the contrary, it manages, civilizes and pacifies it. It provides infrastructures and services that legitimize its profits and protect its authority. It also establishes and maintains order. The territory's borders can reveal themselves to be porous when faced with active enemies. Consequently, the company must pay great attention to its allies and citizens – in order to maintain their often volatile loyalty and to prevent them from emigrating. Keeping economic war at bay is one of the company's priorities.

Force, propaganda and economic opportunism are not sufficient tools to enable territory builders to get third parties to join them and share their typifications. Functional harmony must be fostered and its origins, rooted in tacit meanings, must be established by the business and by its stakeholders (Weick 1979); this is why the creation of a new territory is such a difficult stage. A territory is co-constructed. In other words, its behaviors and transactions require explicitly or implicitly negotiated meanings. As long as typifications remain volatile or fluid, the risk involved in establishing this new world is high. Once knowledge begins to be shared, volatility decreases dramatically.

Managers as institution builders usually spend most of their time, and direct most of their attention to negotiating meanings and to socializing their partners. As the most successful builders of new territories have experienced throughout history, conquest is not enough. Colonization matters. Brute force, in the form of economic violence or relentless propaganda, delivers dismal results over time. On the other hand education, interaction between the center and the periphery, a capacity for self-government that is negotiated between the territory's citizens and its leaders, and a center that defends the territory's integrity, by their combined virtues ensure the welfare and well-being of its citizens with peace and harmony; thus they are critical to successful territory building.

A marked territory is therefore characterized by a relatively long-lasting social arrangement between numerous stakeholders who are linked together by shared knowledge or conventions that state the means and meanings of doing things; the business at the center playing a predominant coordinating role by the use of reputation, consensus creation, and governance by confidence. A well-constructed territory manages itself with not much interference from the outside.

8

BUILDING AND GOVERNING A TERRITORY

A market is generally thought of as an action space that relies primarily on pricing for its organization. Businesses in the market essentially have a commercial function alone. By contrast, a hierarchy is based on principles of legitimate authority: asymmetric relations are established among its specialized areas, imposing an action plan on them (Thoenig 1998). A network, another space of economic action, can be structured around the business's capacity to occupy a structural void once it has successfully polarized numerous relationships with third-party partners that it otherwise wouldn't have had any direct contact with (Burt 1992).

The territory, defined as a project for organized action, builds an economy in which quality plays a major part. The marking business calls upon external mechanisms that can serve, directly and indirectly, a number of purposes, and establish long-lasting ties of cooperation, exchange, and interdependency.

Goods and services do not circulate by themselves. They are diffused because members of the society they target undertake to diffuse them. Marking is born when the market is no longer sustained by the business as an intangible concept, but is managed by it as a socially malleable entity. To sell their electric products, Edison General Electric, Thomson Houston and Westinghouse required a market for electrical goods. To achieve this, they financed the construction of power stations.

Marking is distinct from a pure marketing approach because it requires and mobilizes a crowd of participants, mediators, and other stakeholders. It also fosters common ground rather than competition.

Various components, tools, and devices are required to construct a territory, to civilize its stakeholders, and to hold them together. The active cooperation of third parties is a key factor in this respect.

The company and its management cannot achieve sustainable

government if they reason with only the short term in mind, if they behave egoistically, and if they do not promote the well-being and interests of their partners. Special skills are needed to defend the boundaries of the territory from outside threats, to police its other stakeholders, and to be considered as legitimate by them at the same time.

Management skills needed to create, grow, mark, and defend a territory facilitate the framing of an innovative representation of the world and of its own contribution to it as well as the targeting of clients and stakeholders in line with the representation of such a world. Managers also allocate lasting attention to relevant information and weak signals. The organization they head cooperates with partners and clients through win–win arrangements. The company aims at full domination within the territory. Every operational detail fits the overarching framework.

DETECTING A SOCIOECONOMIC VOID

Creating or occupying a territory comes from the desire to fill a consumption gap. Benetton identified a gap in the availability of sweaters for the young and for fun-loving adults. Marks & Spencer seized upon the absence of an economically acceptable offer for the new working class. IKEA noticed that the Swedish working classes only had access to furniture that was either too expensive or mediocre in quality. Virgin Atlantic answered a twofold desire for pleasure and reasonable pricing in the area of air transportation.

To meet their goals, marking businesses must achieve a high degree of innovation. L'Oréal invented modern marketing almost unconsciously, with a staff that had practically no previous sales experience. Swatch transformed the Swiss watch into one of the attributes of modern life, even after everybody had given up on it. The recipe for success lies less in a major discovery than in the capacity to leverage new ideas and to integrate them into everyday life earlier and faster than the competition can.

The marking business selects its battlefield, it doesn't submit to it. It doesn't tailor its vision to pre-existing practices and visions. It rejects them and creates new ones. At the same time, it capitalizes on speed and essentially never slows down the rhythm of its development. One of the most visible examples of this is the constant launching of new products and added-value services without ever diverting from its objective. Consequently, the marking business forces the competition into a delayed imitation. This represents a decisive advantage in a world defined by specialists as an economy of hypercompetition.

The marking function brings to society something that was missing and that transforms it. Take, for example, L'Oréal's democratization of personal hygiene and beauty care. Or Swatch's giving youth access to Swiss watches at low prices, thanks to a marriage of advanced technology and design. The business is more than just an opportunistic supplier, anonymously distributing ordinary products through mass channels without any reference to the service or the customer. Companies that make a difference become benchmarks in history: Apple's Macintosh, Du Pont de Nemour's (DuPont) Nylon and Teflon.

Listening carefully and with continuous vigilance to society is a key component of marking companies. To govern a territory requires an intense and bilateral relationship with its public authorities and its citizens. A territory grows thanks to the keen intuition of its members and their ability to anticipate new values. It calls for an openminded attitude – permanently – and thorough scrutiny of the weaker signals it receives. More generally, markers must be adept at establishing relations with multiple independent actors while still controlling the social situation they create. Management must move out of the office and still call the shots.

OFFERING ALTERNATIVE CONSUMPTION PATTERNS

Territories are built through unorthodox approaches. Benetton differentiates its sweaters by colors, not by designs. Marks & Spencer initially began with market stalls and products at a single price. IKEA defines quality first and foremost as functionality, and modified the terms of the exchange with its customers, who deliver and assemble their furniture by themselves in return for low prices. Virgin Atlantic transforms the waiting period at airports and services on board into fun experiences, using techniques that almost coddle its customers.

Markers have only one reference in mind: consumption. They deliberately ignore their competition and their colleagues. In other words, the territory shows an iconoclastic logic with regard to existing offers. But it is deeply rooted in consumption.

Marking businesses sense new needs while they are still nascent, working primarily on reasoned intuition. And they react fast, because no one has exclusive rights on good ideas and initiatives.

L'Oréal and Swatch would never have become champions of economic profitability and introduced new understandings of civilization in their fields had they been managed according to good practices borrowed from competitors, or relied on mercenaries hired for short-term missions. The business that makes a difference is a complex mechanism. It doesn't resemble any other because it creates itself without imitating others. This complexity gives it its strength: rejecting it would be nipping its dynamism in the bud.

This is not an easy attitude to embrace. Refusing to imitate your peers, especially if you are a small fish in a world of big fish, requires audacity and, above all, a capacity to make the vital cultural break essential to the development of alternative forms of local knowledge and unorthodox views on customer relations, internal organization, and tactics to counter competition and hierarchies. This cultural break is a cognitive process. Is it a coincidence that the executives of Royal Canin did not go to the same universities and business schools, did not read the same marketing books, did not listen to the same consultants, and data taken from the grocery sector, unlike their peers in the big multinationals?

A cultural break doesn't imply careless economics, on the contrary. The business is launched before fixed costs are created. Benetton externalized its investments and risks by sub-contracting production and by establishing a pseudo-franchising system for its retailers. Marks & Spencer built up its outlets only after having generated a respectable volume of business from market stalls.

The more complex the territory the marker is aiming at, the simpler his or her proposition should be. Marking requires a blueprint, even if its outlines shift with each new extension or change. For its creator or reinventor, the territory is not a vague nebula, a world without order or stability. What the marker offers consumers is crystal clear. There is nothing esoteric in Benetton sweaters.

TREATING CONSUMERS AS STAKEHOLDERS

Consumers, who are not limited to buyers alone, are given opportunities to voice their expectations through strategies that encourage their opinion. They are welcomed and treated as citizen consumers. The marking business refuses to pay attention to the purchase act alone, to its shopping component. It talks about purchasing and consumption in a much richer way, stressing citizenship and ethical, even philo-sophical, components regarding fair trade, the urban lifestyle, or respect for one's immediate social environment.

Buyers bring other societal and civic roles of their own into play. They become stakeholders. Securing their loyalty depends on satisfy-ing their expectations, but also, and most importantly, on the respect the marker gives them. For instance, they will be actively and physi-cally co-opted in the formulation of the marker's strategies. They become part of the marking certification process.

The result is a definition of the offer that is not purely economic or to do with basic consumption alone. The vision translates to a politi-cal project, which means the business wants to weigh in, to improve or modify the lifestyle of its territory's citizens. Fnac transformed itself into a cultural agitator in the name of a societal ambition to improve the status of the cultural goods it provided. Royal Canin uses pet's rights to confer a political status to consumers of its dry food. The democratization of consumption is the raison d'être of IKEA and Marks & Spencer. IKEA promotes the maxim that true richness lies in the customers' capacity to satisfy their own needs. Gap developed variations on a project which began with "you create your fashion with our basic pieces."

CO-OPTING INTERMEDIARIES

Marking often means cutting out intermediaries, shortening the supply chain, as Benetton and IKEA have done. Such initiatives cannot be explained solely by the goal to lower costs. The expected gains are of another nature: bypassing or lifting the opaque barrier of retail that hides downstream opportunities and signals from consumers and society, effectively blinding suppliers and segregating them from their targets. Publicity does not provide an effective substitute to intermediaries. Most markers are aware of the fact that abolishing intermediation is not possible nor desirable. In the territo-ries they create and govern, markers build or rebuild new forms of intermediation. To be more precise, they construct interconnections within the territory without monopolies and without zero-sum or negative-sum games. Marking businesses integrate stakeholders that have been neglected, and establish them as rightful partners. To give some examples, these are the hairdressers and the pharmacists that L'Oréal brought in, or Swatch's specialized retailers, designers, and engineers.

The world is becoming richer and more evolutive because businesses are now taking other skills and knowledge into account and integrating new moral concerns. Royal Canin accords great attention to professions and sectors such as dog and cat breeders, veterinarians, and researchers in this field. This interaction constantly goes well beyond just promotion or marketing or the usual logic of public affairs. It is a role that falls onto the company's executive management. The image and the future of these sectors and how they approach and promote the concept of rapport with pets are what matter primarily to the company. For these reasons the company encourages perennial partnerships and guarantees openness of decision-making, often moving upstream. It gives extreme attention to anything that could affect the future of each stakeholder. Leaving mass retailing to enter specialist channels requires something in return: the business must be able to co-opt these channels into its territory.

The business never acts alone, but with and through other businesses. Third parties are mobilized and integrated in one's territory in a rather peculiar way. The marking enterprise creates new alliances and sets up exchange relations having in mind the goal to make them endure, hopefully, over the long term so that some form of shared socioeconomic project binds and civilizes the various parties involved. Contracts and deals are not enough. Marking is done hand in hand with stakeholders. Its organizational engineering allows for, and even leads to, open confrontation between different points of view. Territory encourages learning processes – the marking business is in permanent contact with, and listens to, other stakeholders.

The marking business doesn't create its territory by decree. It doesn't integrate populations through brute force. It organizes a territory without establishing a formal or hierarchical organization, through vertical integration techniques, for example. It does not rely solely on developing a dense fabric of networks, it animates a world. It gives flesh to this new entity and is not afraid of bringing its different parts together. The marker takes action logics and roles that are in principle heterogeneous and integrates them to make them compatible – all this with multiple players who otherwise would have nothing to do with each other and who in the past were thoroughly compartmentalized. The built-in territorial economic exchange draws its strength and legitimacy from its cultural, political, ideological, and institutional components.

QUALIFICATION, EVALUATION AND PRESCRIPTION

Supply and demand can meet when mechanisms or actors have a minimum amount of agreement on the product's attributes. And price is not the sole or even the principal vector of the exchange. Quality is a major operator in the exchange (Callon, Méadel and Rabéharisoa 2002). More than prices, it is a judgment of the perceived quality of the products that limits their interchangeability and segments the space of consumption and economic exchange, creating profitable niches by coordinating and adjusting the desires of both manufacturers and buyers. The marker and its stakeholders who make up the territory give great importance to quality. And because quality is uncertain, some ad hoc adjustments and judgments become necessary, even sometimes cardinal.

Quality plays such a big part because of the uncertainties that products and services entail. To eliminate these uncertainties, it is essential that suppliers and customers share cognitive references, without which individual points of view would be incompatible. Hence the importance of existing conventions and relations that link the seller with the buyers.

Educating the public through the recommendations of experts plays an important part, as economic interest cannot be relied on forever, nor can it always be readily harnessed without tackling ambiguous complexities. Building consensus between human or impersonal resources that will form the opinion of economic agents is a crucial phase for territory management, especially when choices are complex. More than a free-trade economy, the modern economy can be described as an economy based on the recommendations of perceived experts (Hatchuel 1995). The conquest and government of a territory seek to assert the preeminence of a particular opinion to establish it as a lasting source of profit within the territory.

The function of intermediation plays a key part in territory development, linking the product to its intended user. Marking a territory has one very distinctive characteristic. It does not resist the function of intermediaries. On the contrary, it tends to favor it and to legitimize it as a third-party guarantor and source of credibility. The marker pays close attention to third parties, especially when intermediaries cut across several types of judgments. In this respect, independent mechanisms, in terms of intermediaries and transactions between manufacturers and users, play a key part. To rid quality of all uncertainties, a proactive marker will favor agreements, nomenclatures or conventions that will produce an unequivocal definition of the product's quality or of a person's professional qualifications.

The quality of a product or a person is not unique or immanent, but multiple and constructed. Two tasks, identification (or qualification), and evaluation (or judgment), help master uncertainties that impact quality in a relevant way.

Qualifying and re-qualifying both allow users and customers to identify and singularize. Qualifying is about establishing equivalences that are conventionally shared. An innovation creates new ways to qualify, yet uncertainties linked to evaluation, to judgments of the attributes that define the product, still have to be reduced.

Hence a second process: creating or reinforcing mechanisms to judge and become engaged with the marking process on the basis of personal or impersonal trust, through which the exchange is made possible while offering a choice. An agreement on price not being of much help in eliminating uncertainties, markers must encourage the sharing of cognitive references that become social conventions, thus allowing coordination between the parties involved in a set of transactions (Thévenot 2001) . Social sciences call this process an investment in conventions and practices. Such investments involve trust and personal networks (Karpik 1999). Notions such as usefulness, judgment or preference are important. This is because, to evaluate an offer, it must lend itself to evaluation, either through the characteristics of the product, or through social conformism forms such as fads.

More concretely, marking means mobilizing entrepreneurs of ethics. These individuals, sectors, institutions or professions are used as guarantors. They impose new ethical codes on third parties, users or intermediaries, without necessarily being in charge of enforcing them. Equally they impose new constraints on rational economic action. As such, these entities must have credibility in political or ethical arenas, such as the standards of good citizenship. Intermediaries as well as conventions must be credible throughout the entire process and across the full network of stakeholders, including the media, lobby groups and the public sector.

Intermediation takes on several forms. It can draw on opinion leaders, for example on the expertise of specialist distributors. It can make use of the credibility and social status of expert roles, for example by cultivating opinion leaders within particular groups of users.

Guarantors are explicit. This is evident for the technical workshops for goods sold by the French retail chain Fnac. They can also be implicit. The importance of culture in France in the 1960's and 1970's, and in neighboring countries, coincided with the take-off and spectacular expansion of Fnac. Not surprisingly, Fnac has also been successful in countries where culture is seen as part of the non-commercial sphere, channeling the collective identity of a group or expressing the collective imagination of a society. The company's territory would probably be minuscule in countries such as the United States or Great Britain, where books and DVDs maintain, overall, a status of transactional goods for individual entertainment. Fnac's long-lasting success is reinforced by the fact that commercial expressions of culture are perceived as collective goods when they refer to artists, works of art, or intellectual celebrities who also fill functions of heroes or symbols of culture as a value in itself. Another example of an implicit guarantee is the democratization of consumption, which started in Scandinavia in the 1960's before spreading to other countries, a democratization that provided a favorable base for the development of IKEA.

Participants and associated groups that defend ethical causes are often co-opted and integrated by marking enterprises into what sociologists call hybrid forums (Musselin and Paradeise 2002). Issues such as sustainable development or the rights of social minorities are addressed by ad hoc consumer group meetings or more permanent arenas. A wide variety of forms of economic intermediation and of mechanisms are used to create links and retroactions between supply and demand, and mediations between different networks. Guides and classifications, for example, are frequently referenced to formalize quality requirements, to diffuse them to a large audience, to build consumer confidence in the product or to lower uncertainty and anxiety feelings among the purchasers.

LOCAL INDIVIDUALIZATION

The territory acknowledges the heterogeneity of its stakeholders. It looks at populations in separate and differentiated ways. The individualization of consumers is not only accepted but encouraged. From this viewpoint, mass-media advertising, which brings standardization, can be counterproductive. Being able to create differentiated relationships is a major competitive asset that provides insurance in establishing the business's authority in the long run.

The territory favors individualization of the product. Buyers pay to become the owner of goods whose properties have been adjusted to fit their particular world, so that they can make it their own. While markers can use a variety of methods to single out their offer, depending on the circumstances – patents, manufacturers' brands, packaging, style, location, or personable salespeople, to mention a few – the process of individualizing that offer really comes down to human variables, such as a particular good being seen as attached to a particular person. The danger for the company lies in an absence of product individualization. Nothing is worse than ignoring the importance of these human variables. Adapting the offer so that it is differentiated is a major challenge, and marking makes it its first priority. From this point of view, hypermarket grocery retail and related trends in mass consumption do not make a favorable context for the creation and sustainability of territories hinging on individualization of customer demand and use.

In practice, the territory is analyzed through the relationships that connect sellers to buyers. Individualization can begin at the development stage, can operate through the mechanisms of commercialization, and can mobilize customers or beneficiaries' social networks. But it is primarily downstream, at the most local level, that the offer is readjusted and broken up into narrower, more individualized terms.

BENCHMARKING: THE 6 Cs MODEL OF TERRITORIALITY

The creation, management and marking of an economic territory can easily be summed up in six points. The "6 Cs" can be used as a model to prepare the ground for managerial action. It is easy to apply to the situation of her own business by a practitioner, in order to find out what she should need to do differently.

The interaction between the 6 Cs, so long as it is coherent, activates and regenerates the business's territory.

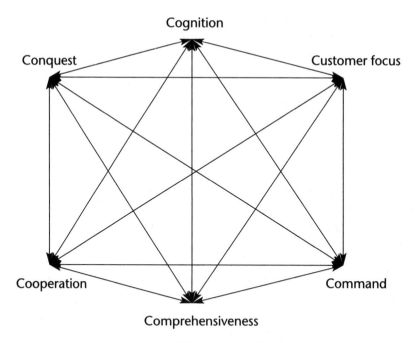

FIGURE 8.1 **The 6 Cs**

Cognition deals with the company's representation of the social, economic, cultural and political environment that it acts upon, and the role it would like to have in the future of this environment. This decoding process can be conventional. If so, it privileges an established, even traditional world, entrusting the business to monitor or even consolidate pre-existing social values and behaviors. In this sense commercial cognition is an action theory that adopts the traits of an existing world and imitates patterns considered normal. But decoding can adopt a different position. It can convey a new societal vision, in which case the business is seen as an agent of change, a reformer in an evolving world. Territorial cognition deals with emerging worlds. It capitalizes on socioeconomic gaps that the business seeks to bridge, an ambition that it shares with its targeted customers, expert intermediaries, third-party guarantors, and of course, its collaborators.

Customer focus translates the way in which the business selects its partners for transaction and action. A marketing business adopts a narrow vision, essentially limiting itself to the immediate customer. A marking business has to make the first move, taking a number of third parties into account and not just the immediate or final customer. Proactive marking even incorporates potential partnerships. The business is customer focused so that it can target its offer and coordinate its propositions with the right mindsets. It is precise and personalized. It constantly endeavors to make customer focus congruent with offer, and vice-versa. Proactive marking requires an uncommon competence: the ability to serve a multitude of partners in diversified ways.

Command deals with the tools used and the information gathered by management. The marking business has a great aptitude for collecting data, explaining it, and anticipating events and the consequences of its choices. Command limits uncertainty. The business also adopts a management style that encourages a truly obsessive attention to research and other sources of information. This is because only a multidimensional decoding of the world is deemed to be pertinent for action. The marking business does not settle for measurements taken at one given time. It remains open to social and to cultural phenomena beyond buying and consuming. By the same token, knowledge gathering and assimilation are not discrete actions, but a continuous process. Knowledge will be considered pertinent if it is multidisciplinary in form and nature. Territoriality looks well beyond the usual studies and research of traditional marketing.

Comprehensiveness refers to the way the business anticipates, covers, deals with and closely follows up events and impacts of its own actions within the world it has chosen. It shows an extreme eye for relevant and grounded detail. Its marking is implemented daily, exhaustively and consistently. Quality and relevance of information matter more than quantity and precision of data. Quality is monitored, regenerated and refined by the whole company, and by all its opinion-leader partners. Territoriality naturally relies on the invention and the renewal of propositions. And, just as naturally, it views products through their use. Finally, it manifests itself in a medium- or long-term perspective.

Cooperation is what management practices to ensure that stakeholders work together. Territoriality demands a high and continuous level of cooperation. A anticipates the consequences that its actions will have on B and C and vice-versa. Any eventual incompatibilities are exposed and conflicts are openly discussed. A vision must be clear for all in order for it to be shared. All actors and stakeholders, both internal and external, are valued according to their palpable contributions to systemic success. Notions of confrontation with intermediaries are not considered pertinent to the marking process. Internally, hierarchy does not promote transversal initiatives as they are expected to occur spontaneously between the different trades and services.

Conquest refers to the business's ambition to dominate and to extend its territory. These necessarily go hand in hand. The horizon seems infinite and the ideal is never fully attained. Territorial extension is important as it stems from innovations and allows new customers or actors to enter its cognitive system. The goal is not only to attract buyers, it is also to see the new cognition promoted by the business become that of the numerous stakeholders in its territory. Here again, it is the quality and the narrowness of the propositions that enable the territory to be extended.

The 6 Cs model of territoriality allows management to characterize a business and to evaluate its marking. To illustrate the simplicity of its

TABLE 8.1 **The 6 Cs of Tesco and Sainsbury**

	Tesco	Sainsbury
	Marking enterprise	*Merchant enterprise (1990's)*
Cognition	Wants to be a convenience builder	Considers itself to be a self-service retailer.
Customer focus	Segments consumers in terms of mindsets. Customizes the offer.	Directs the customer toward the products (even if the products are high quality).
Command	Extremely sophisticated database. Decodes different lifestyles.	A weak culture of market research. No proactive policy.
Comprehensiveness	Manages service as a natural extension of product. Value added to the customer, at any price level.	Faces difficulty in translating offers in terms of value for money
Cooperation	Is a pioneer in partnerships with suppliers. Uses transverse logic to steer all projects.	Was once a pioneer in category management, but quickly stopped applying it in an adequate spirit.
Conquest	Multiplies formats to constantly enrich the convenience of the offer. International development, on the condition that territoriality is respected. Diversifies significantly into convenience-driven services.	Makes diversifications that are not linked to a territorial vision framework.

use and its robustness for management, it will be applied to three companies mentioned in previous chapters – Tesco, First Direct, Royal Canin – whose markings were or remain significant references, representing major innovations on pre-existing practices in their sectors of activity. To emphasize their originality, they will be compared with companies whose profiles in their sectors have been dominant while following conventional marketing practices or developing weakly territorialized models.

TABLE 8.2 **The 6 Cs of First Direct and banks with branch network**

	First Direct	**Traditional retail bank**
	Marking enterprise	*Sales and customer administration*
Cognition	Common bank transactions should be easy and fast.	Customers are taken care of during business hours, and the branch remains the cornerstone.
Customer focus	Customers who do not accept the constraints imposed by banks on their branches. Customers without financial problems in everyday terms.	Covers a large socioeconomical spectrum, even if a segmentation can be planned later.
Command	A fine reading of time-saving expectations of broad segments of the population. Intelligent databases (on attitudes, and so on).	Statistical and aggregate databases.
Comprehensiveness	A very clear business model while pursuing the "more for less" motto. An exhaustive service orientation.	A proliferation of products. A low legibility and transparency of fees by clients.
Cooperation	Harmony between marketing, operations and human resources.	Frequent tensions between front line and back-office.
Conquest	An extension to the channels that enrich convenience (internet, cell phones ...). Only services that are compatible with its territoriality.	Diversified distribution channels – telephone, and so on – with occasional coordination and compatibility problems.

TABLE 8.3 **The 6 Cs of Royal Canin and "mainstream" pet food companies**

	Royal Canin	"Mainstream" pet food companies
	Marking (push)[1]	*Marketing* (pull)[2]
Cognition	A nutrition/health offer. Respect for and knowledge of pets.	Offer is a food product. Capitalizes on the affective emotions of pet owners.
Customer focus	Consumers that are highly sensitive to nutrition. Breed and age conditions of pets.	Consumers who are not very sensitive to nutrition. Segmentation is used only if it can generate large sale volumes.
Command	Scientific study of the contribution of food to health. Keen understanding of networks of experts.	Classic market research (buyers, brand recognition, and so on).
Comprehensiveness	Coherent and exhaustive quality approach. Attention to usage value. Service is a given.	Marketing-mix of mass distribution. Priority on product price.
Cooperation	Offer built through multiple partnerships.	Some partnerships with big retailers.
Conquest	Quality and refined customer focuses. Imposing one's standards of the relevance of products, segments, prescriptions, and so on). Shortest time to market processing.	Market shares in mass distribution. Standardization of the offer and preselling of the product through mass advertising.

9

ORGANIZING A MORAL COMMUNITY

Generating a vision of the business would seem to be a necessary condition for conquering and marking a territory. A vision would be absolutely tied to one person, the leader or the creator – whose legitimacy would be dependent on having a charismatic personality. All it would take to rally the troops would be one exceptional person; a visionary, non-conformist innovator. Historiographies speak at length of original advances made by leaders with irresistible managerial drive and powerful egos. These proverbial heroes would be omnipresent in their companies. They would work hard. They would live in states of perpetual fever, their projects never far from their minds. They would have an insatiable passion to convert everyone they spoke with to their cause. No one would be able to escape from it. In return, they would demand unconditional, submissive loyalty from their disciples or followers.

This description seems a little narrow and far from sheer fact. The presence of even a brilliant or inspired leader is a useful condition, but by no means sufficient. Moses did not do everything all at once and on his own. Having followers so spellbound that they are inactive is not just inadequate, it becomes a heavy burden, a serious handicap. An enthusiastic sermon does not guarantee that action will result. The fact that individuals hold beliefs or that small groups assert their confidence in a particular vision of what is desirable does not necessarily result in behaviors that are in line with these beliefs and these perceptions. Conversion is only one step. Something more is needed, and the hardest part remains to be done. To be persuaded is good: to put one's convictions into action is even better.

Marking a territory requires the collective effort, dedication, and imagination of a large number of people within the company. It would be a grave mistake to attribute the territory of a marking company to the work of one single charismatic leader. Quality of organizational management requires reasoned decision-making, action based on strategy, and pragmatic indicators that are compatible with the dynamics of territorial marking.

This chapter deals with a facet of management, people and organization which, in the case of marking, is not micro-management as usual. For two lessons can be learned from the observation of real life:

- Successful marking approaches require a very high degree of cooperation between the various parties involved, inside the enterprise, and also between them and other parties of the territory;
- Building ways and managing processes to simultaneously achieve functional cooperation and moral integration are top priorities at all levels inside the marking enterprise and its territory. Micromanagement matters quite a lot.

BUILDING A MORAL COMMUNITY

Marking organizations follow in many respects obvious and well-known patterns of good management as far as staff and tasks are concerned.

When considering the eight companies covered in this book, none of them could really be described as a bureaucracy, ignoring the customer, overwhelmed by centralization, proceduralization and specialization, and giving a premium to staff-free-ridership. On the contrary, they show recurrent patterns and characteristics that will be summarized below and that do not require unusual skills from seasoned practitioners.[1]

Before considering marking a territory, though, it is necessary to debureaucratize the company, and that takes time and attention. For instance the advantage gained by Royal Canin over Nestlé or Procter & Gamble is not simply a question of vision and strategy, which it might have achieved relatively quickly. It is a much more permanent advantage that capitalizes on the vitality of its members and the strongly cooperative relationships between its internal functions. Originality in the way an organization operates and is managed is a major invisible asset. It sets up an entry barrier to the marking of the territory by companies lacking such a resource.

Which type of organizational functioning, if any, should markers conform to? The cases reviewed in previous chapters suggest a clear conclusion. Lasting marking ventures are organizationally managed in a rather recurrent manner. At least five characteristics capture their essence:

- The socialization of its employees by the organization is intensive and spread over a long duration;
- Close cooperation shapes the relationships between the various parties or members, and it is experienced as something obvious, even as a moral duty;
- Mutual loyalty is encouraged along the operational units with regard to the enterprise and to its territory;
- Confidence in oneself and in others is rather high whenever problem-solving is concerned and target-reaching is at stake;
- Internal networks and communities of intuition and culture provide the main channels for policy-making. These common references are characterized by badgings, by processes of recognition that allow the various parties to identify each other.

Such a profile is close to the definition of an organic type of model (Michaud and Thoenig 2003). It characterizes enterprises focusing on the medium term and betting on their own capacity for regenerating a business sector.

Organization management is aimed at creating and at making compatible two different worlds within the same enterprise: a world of rules, structures, control and morality, and a world of initiative, participation, creativity and commitment. The fact is that both facets are fairly well developed in marking enterprises.

Rules and structures relying on control and morality allow us to distinguish between acts, conducts and errors that are acceptable or understandable, and those that are unacceptable, between successes that are normal and those that are exceptional. Initiative and participation are of a different order. Relying on creativity and commitment, they elaborate moral motives of obedience: moral means that they imply the joint integrity of individuals and of the community to which they belong.

Available data such as opinion surveys and direct observation of some of the enterprises studied in previous chapters clearly indicates that great attention is given by management to developing such moral motives, human resources being a priority not only for staff experts but also for line managers at all levels. In most cases this persistent attention induces strong impacts. Individuals appropriate these motives. They deliver behaviors that reflect their imprint. They act in an accountable way. They feel responsible for what they do and how they do it. They care about the consequences their own behaviors have for others. They refer to the firm as a community to which they belong and feel duties.

Chapter 6 listed a few cases of marking failures by enterprises not sticking to their promises. These deviations and mistakes had an immediate impact on the moral facet of their organizational management. Such had been the case for Club Med for instance. Recognition by executives of the ability of some employees (GMs) to participate and make decisions affecting them and the community directly dropped. Employees became less likely to consider the moral aspects of their own acts affecting de facto peers and other members of the organization. They refused to endorse any responsibility for these impacts. In other terms they stopped playing collectively. They basically minded about their own turf and vested interests.

A marking enterprise without a world of rules and structures may quickly become a centrifugal army without vision and integration. A marking enterprise without a world of moral motives of obedience may never take off or may lose its territory, as Club Med experienced for a number of years.

Why should markers not only be strong business leaders but also strong community leaders?

One main advantage brought by moral commitments between individuals and their enterprise is to help employees be both dependable and disposable. Managerial decisions are often based on obscure contents. These obscure contents as interpreted by others (employees, peers, and even superiors) require managers to create a guarantee that employees will obey without questioning too often the exact reason for the decisions made. Such factors are very relevant to success in proactive marking, when market relationships are still uncertain or obscure, when decisions have to be made in uncertain conditions or when the rules applied are often still not absolutely clear. Learning fast by trial and error implies a strong moral community inside the organizations. It is no coincidence that Sam Walton, Henri Lagarde, James Dyson and other founders of successful marking enterprises, if not some of their successors, have, each in their own way, been outstanding moral leaders.

SHAPING ACTION TAKING

Culture is a term often associated with organizational excellence. The problem is that, having become a catchword, it may mean just about anything and lack managerial relevance.

Marking organizations in a sense have a strong culture of their own, which they may share to some extent with other stakeholders inside their territory. Three characteristics or nuances should nevertheless be kept in mind.

Culture is far from being just a set of founding myths, heroes and stories. People do not behave like malleable and passive robots, as if they would be dominated and indoctrinated through drill techniques. For a marking enterprise, its culture means that in no way does it ignore the outside world.

Instead of talking about culture, and to avoid the danger of reducing it to an almost metaphysical state of emotional fusion, we will use different wording: sense making, cognitions, integration. The topic of this section is to show that marking organizational management is action-oriented, interactively managed, and integrating outsiders. It is probably the most valuable intangible asset a marker may need to develop.

Management as sense-making

Marking enterprises create a lot of financial value. The paradox is that complying with financial figures, budgetary indicators and PNL goals does not seem to be the ultimate reference for action taking. Something other than mere selfish money incentives is at work that drives behaviors, stimulates pride and pushes people to go beyond opportunistic selfishness.

Building a lasting territory is quite simply impossible without one fundamental condition: meaning must be given to the work that each member does in his or her particular area. This meaning is not something that miraculously falls from the sky. Lengthy and skillful management processes are needed to induce meaning. Managers use various methods and specific activities to produce this meaning: they create ethical and cognitive standards that, because they apply them to their own actions, become credible for their employees to the point of taking them on as their own.

To give meaning consists of attributing sound reasons for one's actions. I do A and not B because I think that in doing A, I will obtain something more or something different: it is this "something more or something different" that drives me to act. In other words, meaning is produced through the same knowledge and rationale on which the business is based. This is far from the management style that focuses only on short-term, financial incentives; command and control; or charisma. It counts on the employees' ability to think, and not on their opportunism or on their feelings. It makes sure that individual commitments to the common project result from community-building mechanisms.

Why do certain organizations respond more quickly, more easily learn new ways of doing things, and see more cooperation from their members? One main reason is that individuals within such organizations have fewer possibilities to retreat into themselves, to avoid such contact with others. The creation of territories works when the organization operates internally as an action-oriented community, and not as a dogma-focused guardian.

What in the case of marking organizations does community pressure mean? It is the way moral reasons are elaborated for individuals to obey and to conform. This moral nature manifests in various ways: a concern to behave responsibly, giving attention to the consequences one's actions may have for others as well as oneself, showing respect for others, or experiencing feelings of belonging and identity. These motivations become irreplaceable organizational factors when the business finds itself in particular situations, such as when it faces an unstable and uncertain market. In fact, in such a business context, decisions must be taken without being able to refer to any precedents.

Success in marking, particularly in proactive marking, demands a style of leadership that is capable of creating meaning, certainly for the outside stakeholders, but also in the eyes of the company's staff. Relayed by the middle levels of management, marking leaders devote themselves to creating a true cognitive structure that incorporates the various internal functions of the business as much as those of its customers. Royal Canin offers a textbook case.

A first remarkable fact is the time allocated by its CEO to constant and informed reading: publications that deal technically and scientifically with dogs and cats and publications that discuss management application of research in the social sciences or on military strategy. This attention is not the fruit of chance, a simple hobby or pastime related to work. Henri Lagarde uses this intellectual capital as a lever for the collective action of his business, because it feeds into a second remarkable fact.

As CEO, Henri Lagarde constructs cognitive references that he persistently circulates through the company and makes his troops participate in – ways of thinking and planning for action, theories of success. In other words, he creates meaning. This meaning serves to explain the world that his business is seeking to change. It allows him to rationalize his business decisions. It provides a clear frame of reference that unites the employees in a lasting commitment, one that stimulates consistently reliable performances.

Sense making is a preoccupation and an important skill for managers marking territory. They have to devote much time to this and keep it up for the long term. Thus Lagarde, since taking up his role, and throughout his time in this position, has conceived a new definition and understanding of pet food that outright rejects any anthropomorphic approach.

The creation of meaning is a work that unfolds on three levels:

- the formation of a general theory about the world in which it is acting;
- the development of management instruments with which to articulate this theory;
- and fostering a process of collective learning (Weick 1995).

In the first place, the cognitive architect develops a new understanding, a new theory of economic action. Through its founder or its re-founder, the company builds, devotes itself to, and explains an original interpretation, totally new and with general application, a new way of viewing the world and of working within it. In the case of Royal Canin, and as already emphasized in Chapter 2, this interpretation rests on the moral and social status of pets in our society, on the function of feeding them and on the attention that is paid to them by their owners.

A prerequisite is to make this unconventional interpretation look credible. It must become so much more plausible, therefore credible, because it runs contrary to the frameworks previously established in the business or the benchmarks in the sector. At Royal Canin, this explanation was developed from facts observed and observable in the field. Patiently studied from beginning to end, they end up making sense, looking plausible, credible and with general relevance. They have the effect of showing the explanatory framework to be robust and empirically based.

In the second place, sense making implies a process allowing management tools and models to be set up, adopted or invented from scratch that are compatible with this explanation. These tools and models are practical results employees derive from observing and interpreting facts. At Royal Canin, one such result is the segmentation of types of pet food according to the pet's particular specialization.

A key point is that these segmentations, if they are used for some time and prove to be effective, reinforce the value of the general explanation that produced them. Employees and also outside partners trust their relevance and their effectiveness. They become true believers. As time goes by, the strategic intuition carried by the executives – which at first might have seemed to be a subjective opinion, more or less arbitrary, perhaps fantastic, or even suicidal – acquires an intersubjective value. It is progressively appropriated and shared by the members of the organization. They believe in it not so much because they cannot choose to disbelieve – a sin condemned by the hierarchy – but because it has become part of their way of thinking, of their cognitive perspective.

Arguably, in the long term this demonstrates an effectiveness that is both tangible and economic. But, and the point is essential, such representations and cognitive lenses also become identifying factors. They signify the belonging to a community: their own company, which is unlike any other.

These meanings are therefore quite different than indoctrination by propaganda, pressure from moral preaching, or a conviction obtained because the individual is compliance prone. To accept them is an expression of the fact that employees no longer feel the vision and its management method are external to them, but rather see them as something of their own, a rational and pragmatic model that they have taken on as their own, that they have internalized. Instead of a dogma imposed by third parties in positions of authority, command and control, and who have to be respected to avoid trouble, employees move to a conviction, a truth to which they adhere with a feeling of being the owners and guardians of it.

A third facet of the work of sense making takes the form of a progressive, continuous, and collective learning process. The meaning that has been created amplifies weak signals from the external world.

Royal Canin dismissed the strong signals it had relied on up until the middle of the 1990's. This rejection represented a groundbreaking and resounding action. First through its CEO's authoritarian decision, then through progressive staff support, the business turned its back on the management conventions currently in force in the pet food industry. These conventions and beliefs originated in, and derived their authority from, the mass marketing and distribution of grocery products.

This process requires a pragmatic attitude. For instance Royal Canin's CEO, then his management team, and finally his employees, observed contexts in which small details that had not been noticed before, or had been considered marginal and anecdotal, started to come together, were shown to be connected, and began to make sense. The members of the business interacted and exchanged opinions with each other, not to interpret conventional market studies and quantitative indicators, but to expand, compare, and validate their intuitions.

Lagarde and his management team devoted a lot of time to developing these opportunities – through formal staff meetings and, above all, by making a point of talking to their employees one-on-one whenever a situation gave them the opportunity: when an offer was to be made to a customer; if a mistake occurred in terms of quality; when giving sales talks; or when launching a new product. In this way, the business grew collectively more confident even though it was regarded with skepticism and considered a maverick by the rest of the industry. But as the particular facts it was dealing with began to come together, the initial explanatory framework – to move away from mass grocery retailers, eventually refined to respecting the health of pets – suddenly enabled it to reach a more general level. The conclusions Royal Canin drew from it in terms of business actions became more and more exact and effective (Weick 1995). In brief, the meaning was reinforced in practice.

In other words, individual members and their roles become integrated around a common challenge that they had constructed together and freely agreed on, even though there was strong and constant moral and operative pressure on each of them. Management actively fostered socialization throughout the year, and won loyal relationships. Problems were resolved through a horizontal network. Errors and conflicts were brought out into the open, not hidden away.

Leaders of missionary organizations know that mistakes are an integral part of innovation, and provide opportunities for learning and innovation. They do not ignore mistakes, they treat them as occasions for explanation. They do not manage their subordinates by praising them, but by analyzing, by interactively explicating the reasons for the outcomes. In doing so they earn empathy. In a way, markers are pedagogues, not preachers. They teach by interaction (Farson and Keyes 2002).

Managers as cognitive architects

Markers are cognitive architects. James Dyson at Dyson, Samuel Walton and his sucessors at Wal-Mart, Lagarde and his executive team at Royal Canin, Walter E. Disney at Walt Disney, and many others have forged inside their enterprise and its territory a common language which unites in a robust and lasting manner their staff as well as their outside partners, so that the vision is expressed in identical standards of action without these needing to be communicated. On top of behaving as heads of an authority hierarchy and as policy-makers, they also manage their organization and influence their outside partners as cognitive architects.

Building and diffusing common references are means to an end: action taking. Marking organizations are organizations sharing the same language for action (Michaud and Thoenig 2003). Such a language has nothing to do with what is sometimes called jargon, a special vocabulary and collection of expressions that would only be understood by insiders. It does not depend on linguistics. It is not a speech or a discourse. It is a special kind of cognition managers and staff carry quite implicitly: criteria for action taking.

Such criteria are used as rules of thumb for decision-making purposes, as tacit theories linking a consequence to a specific cause. If you do L, M results. Or, in order to obtain M, L must be chosen. For instance, to increase sales one should rely basically on the prescriptive influence of vets (Royal Canin), on monopolistic control of the shopping area (Wal-Mart), and so on.

Possible criteria of choice are many. For instance, what is the ultimate and convincing indicator to consider: potential global demand (in volume), local opportunities, or a gap in the range of products? Does term really matter or not, and if it does, is the short or the medium one that should prevail? What are the strategic engines to give priority to: wants of new types of consumers, acceptability by the distributors, or functional breakthroughs?

Whenever a common language for action exists, the various parts of the organization (and the various parties of the territory) develop a strong mutual understanding. Common knowledge develops mutual trust – I know that you know that I know.

Common does not mean that no other specific may be used by an actor (downstream or upstream) that would not be shared by the parts she is in interaction with. On the contrary R&D is in charge of tasks whose logics of action are different than marketing's, just to give an illustration. But the fact that some basic criteria are identical helps integrate the business perspectives inside the social fabric of the enterprise.

An organization sharing a common language is not to be confused with a totalitarian community, with managers acting as censors of deviations to the party line. Deviations are sins to be punished whatever their economic consequences while acts are experiments to be assessed by referring them to the enactment of the enterprise vision and strategy. Ideology leads to the reverse of common language. It destroys information and rigidifies knowledge. Markers are aware that arrogance and fundamentalism destroy moral communities and kill business success.

How to grow, model and adjust, when required, a language for action taking?

The markers as cognitive architects build criteria for choice in an endogenous way. They discard any exogenous influence such as imitation of competitors or benchmarking. They go even further in avoiding any influence from the outside. It is amazing to see how most if not all the eight enterprises covered in detail in this book favor the recruitment of "autodidacts," and do not hire seasoned experts. They grow their own people. They keep their distance from established standards and technical conventions issued by professional milieus such as marketing or strategy, even when to some extent they rediscover some of their fundamentals. Keeping a distance encourages non-conformity. It widens the search for alternatives that may lead to new business models. No surprise that markers are also management innovators in their industry.

Endogenous language building takes time. It is not governed by decree. Four main tools are available and used in developing endogenous action criteria.

1. *Operational units are empowered.*
Efficient empowerment addresses operational issues. Units are put

under conditions that do not allow them to sit back. They get the actual power to act. They also become fully accountable for the tasks under their jurisdiction. One limit is put to empowerment processes. Operational units are not allowed to become strongholds out of control. Marking companies also avoid the use of overspecialization as an organizational tool. They do not subdivide tasks, jobs and functions in an exaggerated manner. To park marketers, controllers and other professionals in specialized departments and to give them exclusive jurisdiction over their function chops management up into bits. A landscape of vertical silos is designed that induces low cooperation between them because they shut themselves apart.

One solution to fight the emergence of monopolies is provided by allocating quite a wide jurisdiction to each unit. Specialization of tasks is not high. Overlap and redundancy are considered acceptable ways to fight inner monopolies. Redundancy makes it easier to rapidly correct errors that inevitably occur in the marking project. It also ensures a high level of reliability. A redundancy of skills and knowledge and the overlapping of tasks no longer represent costs that must be controlled, but are sources of quality in terms of the company's capacity to be reactive or proactive when confronted by turbulent or uncertain environments (Landau 1967).

2. *Urgency is used as a threat mechanism in order to engender a climate of steady and strong mobilization inside the organization.*

Urgency is not just a word or a state of mind. It has to be linked to relevant aspects for the organization. It also has to be linked somehow to the moral community identity and dynamics. For instance, to be excellent in time-to-market delivery for new products is not just a matter of compliance by the plants to the instructions of the headquarters. If Royal Canin persistently performs as it does, it is also because workers and foremen share to some extent the same action cognitions as their hierarchy. Pride adds some salt and pepper to it: small people from "nowhere" feel proud to outperform established multinational corporations.

3. *The executive level focuses its attention on controlling the business's major uncertainties.*

Executives move around, inside and outside their organization, as well as rapidly through their agendas. Two aspects are of importance in this perspective. Low turnover of managers and internal promotion to senior levels stabilize trust and facilitate fine-tuning evolutions. The organization tries to keep its employees for the long term, not to lose them quickly. Incessant turnover runs the risk of losing distinctive knowledge or weakening the cooperative spirit that determines economic performance. The marking company can make only limited use of external mercenaries recruited ad hoc (consultants, executives brought in at short notice, and so on). Laying out the game rules is not something that can be improvised. Socializing newcomers is considered an investment that takes too much time and is too costly to be wasted. A careful and transparent mechanism of succession for the top position in the enterprise is needed. Growing successors takes time.

Top markers are aware of one truth. Cognitive architects have to be considered as vital assets. They master tacit know-how. They also personalize territories they have built up. Executives who join the marking enterprise from the outside would not have the same legitimacy to govern the territory or as effectively understand the implicit shared cognitions.

4. Networks are activated.
Management helps build many networks, inside the organization and with the other parties involved in the territory, putting together varied origins and experience and treating them on equal footing, covering diversified topics, with fuzzy boundaries and wide corridors of action.

Managers as credibility and legitimacy achievers

The rules of the game should be transparently clear. They should also consistently be respected by the executives who themselves abide by them. They are designed to encourage collective integration and communal identity in an environment where the threat of major players competing has a humbling effect and spurs on performance.

The social dimension of the territorial development strategy inculcates a sense of its own role and a vision of the future that stimulates, inspires, and mobilizes the collective in a way that involves more than just the value added to shareholder investment.

An effective marking company is an organization whose management is felt to be legitimate by its members ands by the stakeholders of its territory. Its leaders are not satisfied with limited quantitative reporting and "objective" methodologies. Even if the organization does look like a hierarchy with the usual inequalities and selection processes, it bases its authority on more than impersonal figures and individual performances. Above all, it calls for a cohesion that connects the rulers to the ruled. This solidarity toward a common vision of the future is anchored in a territory to be conquered, for which each member feels some responsibility at his or her level. The members of the organization expect and receive from their leaders two complementary things: a project that influences society and ensures the sovereignty of their business on this territory, and the capacity to apply the decisions that have been made. Defining the future in identical terms is a key ingredient for successful marking.

Organizational management of marking businesses also emphasizes the value of two factors: persistence and example. For something to be seen as moral and remain so, leaders must show proof of their own integrity.

Persistence consists in constructing the territorial development strategy, instead of in the unrelenting rallying of employees, so much so that it becomes the defining principle of the organization. For at least three times a week for nearly eight years, management at Royal Canin continually presented, adjusted, and updated the diverse facets of this shared vision and identity. This persistence was relayed to all the company's sites through decentralized presentations run by middle management. In this way, everyone involved could be part of the choices being considered and understand the reasons for them. References to Epaminondas, Moreno, and Maslow became widely understood at all levels. The discourse this has produced is effective because the hierarchy has shown itself to believe in it and to adhere to it consistently.

Respect for the customer and care about the product will remain empty slogans if they are not passed on through the organization and legitimized by being clearly illustrated in practice. In this lies the essential role of management. The hierarchy has influence because it sets the example. Its own behavior serves to profoundly influence the culture and the practices of the entire company. Managers practice what they preach.

The business's daily life is another area in which it teaches by example. So that everyone identifies with the project, they all, from the bottom to the top, are subject to the same conditions. From factory workers to the CEO, everyone at Royal Canin flies economy class, rents bottom-of-the-range cars, or travels by second-class train. To remain humble is not just a remarkable attitude. It serves an organizational and business effectiveness purpose.

207

INTERNAL ORGANIZATION AND EXTERNAL TERRITORY

There is a wide array of ways and means to integrate outside actors belonging to the territory in which the marking enterprise is embedded.

At Royal Canin for instance, R&D is entrusted not to basic academic researchers, but to applied researchers working in veterinarian fields. R&D is managed not according to any upstream model in which the different disciplines are carefully separated, but according to a downstream and service-oriented logic.

Technical training and professional qualifications also matter. At Royal Canin they prioritize knowledge about pets rather than knowledge about buyers. The idea here is to diffuse among prescribers, sellers, breeders and many more stakeholders the segmentation of pet food and to use them as relays to reach the pet owners. The aim is for those who are directly in contact with customers to in turn convey to cat and dog owners the company's values of respect for pets and its focus on an understanding of their needs. The marking of the territory is completed with an enormous editorial production of technical brochures and encyclopedias in which Royal Canin's name is mentioned only on the title page.

The messages spread internally through the business are also those that are spread to the outside, among the territory's stakeholders. Exemplarity and persistence act as markers. At Royal Canin, the territorial development strategy shared by the staff of the company is also shared with its partners. Company directors give the same presentations of business vision and policies to both audiences.

The marked territory is defined not only in economic and normative terms. Social relations and social values are also reflected in how a marking enterprise organizes its physical space.

Building design is an important lever, for example in the production areas. Royal Canin's plant in Aimargues is designed so that manufacturing and development activities are physically close to each other. Workers, veterinarians and dietary researchers are not separated physically or socially from the rest of the business. R&D is carried out in close proximity to the kennels and to the production plant.

Merchandising is used in retail outlets to create a physical microspace that expresses, visually and practically, the idea of a territory. Royal Canin proposes a global design to veterinary clinics that promotes pet nutrition in the four customer areas: reception, the waiting room, the consulting room, and at the sales desk. For many years, the veterinary profession considered the sale of foodstuffs as demeaning to its professional image. But Royal Canin offers clinics a concept that incorporates a comprehensive merchandising approach with a new design for the entire clinic, not just the sales shelves. The clinic becomes a credible place in which to sell food for all pets, not only for sick pets. This design is apparent on entering the clinic, and continues through the customer's visit. When a customer asks for advice on his pet's health, the nutritional information provided is closely associated with the pet's diet. None of the clinic's four client areas distribute conventional advertising materials, only sophisticated and educational nutritional information is available throughout the customer's route through the clinic, and the point of sale is clearly visible from the three other areas. The business impact has been considerable. Veterinary clinics that have adopted the concept have doubled their product sales.

Whether marking is proactive or reactive, we find similar traits. The construction of push type territories for specific trades serves as a socializing force both within the company and within the territory it occupies. Taking this idea to its limit, inside and outside the company become one and the same space. For all that, the business does not dissolve away into its territory: quite the contrary. The facts show an apparent paradox. Marking businesses that incorporate other stakeholders into their project and place the customer at their center function on the model of a community organization.

Some organizations show themselves to be self-sufficient when it comes to their decision-making systems. They do not bring in representatives from the external environment in a show of respect for accepted procedures of good governance. What would be the use of including a strong proportion of outside directors on their executive boards? Their independence, often cited as grounds for including such directors from the outside, is relative. This is corporate governance in name only; the board's real role is to be able to dismiss the CEO. It does not ensure any superior performance. Companies that are strong proactive markers and create new territories seem to manage with relatively little call for outside directors. Neither Canon nor Toyota has even one on their boards, both of which are distinguished by having a very high number of members. Compared with their rivals whose level of marking is much more modest, these marking businesses also seem to be far less obsessed with creating shareholder value, yet perform better than companies with weak marking. Moreover, these companies also regard their staff as priority stakeholders.

FUNDAMENTALS OF MARKING ORGANIZATION

Marking organizations do not refer to the machine as the standard to emulate. For machines are rigid and proceduralized technocracies that induce partitioning and mutual avoidance. Instead of breaking problems down to their narrowest specializations, marking organizations learn and think by pushing their members to be sensitive to the market and society. They also do not conceive the marketplace as a machine, but as a living and complex organism.

Marking organizations encourage employees to see old problems in new ways. They favor intuition and imagination to better anticipating emerging wants and societal norms. At the same time they do not consider that the psychological and interpersonal well-being of their employees is the ultimate goal to reach and satisfy. Marking organizations are not pastoral workplaces. On the contrary they put employees under strong pressure. Free riders are not welcome. Nor are persons who may not really share the societal vision and the economic model. The territory as a whole, including the outside stakeholders, and not the system, is king. It legitimizes the mission to fulfil. It integrates the parties as a team. People fight battles and share common destinies not because they conform to authority. They do it because they feel driven, as is also their hierarchy, by challenges linked to societal embedding as well as to sustaining economic success.

Marking enterprises definitely are of a special kind. They act as moral communities. They share their values and their faith with outsiders. They function like missionary orders.

In a way a common destiny and a shared moral project unite their members. Their aims in promoting their project are societal in scope. They know how to gain the allegiance of stakeholders in their territory so that they feel like participants in the project, even part owners of it. These businesses construct a morally internalized collective challenge; they convey an outlook and a representation of the business that continues using specific management instruments while never ceasing to mobilize the input of everyone involved. This approach ensures all stakeholders are relevant, beginning with the members of the company.

All the same, their faith is not blind and the ideas promoted are not oppressive or dogmatic. The marking business in no way resembles a doctrinaire sect of fanatics. Fanatics have no rules: the reasoning behind their actions is drawn from the sacred, based on principles viewed as absolute truths, set in concrete. But the marking direction develops and evolves by being put to the test. On principle, the organizational style of management that the business adopts does not suppress deviation. It values pragmatism and the learning process, and collaborating with its stakeholders to construct new meaning.

In summary, the building of territory proceeds from the center of the company and respects certain basic precepts.

- Territory building and managing results from collective action. Several stakeholders, the business's staff being the foremost, cooperate and make their stakes compatible.
- A specific leadership style is required which promotes trust, transparency, the sharing of the project, and complete adherence to the utopian principles that give meaning to its actions. Management must set the example in its daily operations. It is essential the business's leadership shows itself to be beyond reproach.
- Zero deviation is assumed where its promises are concerned. One of the principal virtues of the marking business is that each person constantly pays meticulous attention to the smallest details. Competence is certainly indispensable, but it is not sufficient. An attitude of respect and modesty makes all the difference.
- Love of the product is a shared priority across stakeholders. The product is always genuine but never considered as perfect. Innovation and development assure the enthusiasm of stakeholders, which is vital.
- Time and continuity are requested. For its staff, length of service is highly regarded. Resorting to mercenaries recruited ad hoc for a short-term mission is looked upon as a mistake.
- The evangelical community acts in symbiosis with the stakeholders in its territory. It does not abandon them for insignificant reasons.
- The marking enterprise vigilantly defends the integrity of the territory against centrifugal forces and plundering attacks.
- It maintains a position of permanent alertness. Awareness of its fragility and vulnerability vanishes when the perception of an outside threat wanes, when management settles into comfort and certainty.
- Strict hierarchical divisions inside the marking company are ignored. It combats internal monopolies and administrative strongholds. Strategy, marketing, management decisions, to give only a few examples, do not belong to anyone in particular or exclusively.

Instead, it favors horizontal approaches to problems that are appropriated by the collectivity.

■ Organizational excellence is managed as a key asset hindering competitors from catching up. Solutions are not regarded as good just because executives or experts proposed them. Messages are attended to and their content is considered independently of who sends them. Suggestions are adopted because their content is appropriate, no matter who expresses them.

Companies good at building territory function in a relatively complex manner, combining flexibility and uniformity, integration and initiative. They mobilize a broad range of actions that they develop as they go along. They impose a strict model with a basic game plan in which all members have clear parts to play, while dealing with unexpected events and molding themselves to the particularities of their territory.

There is no one best way, no one best model that will work for every situation. First Direct is not IKEA, which is not Royal Canin. Each company has its own history and culture, which, through local roots, nourish its rise to global status: Swedish working classes and urban references for IKEA, rural and anti-elitist connotations for Wal-Mart. Whether it is a beginner or whether it is recreating its marking, the marking company constructs an external territory that is peculiar to itself, and to invent a territory needs creativity. Marking takes the company's positioning and unique project into account internally, in the way the organization functions. Each marking company has something that is unique to it.

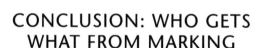

CONCLUSION: WHO GETS
WHAT FROM MARKING

Appropriate marking creates value, and does so for various stakeholders.

FINANCIAL VALUE

In financial and stock-market terms, the point of reference is the shareholder. In terms of share value, marking pays and pays well, even in markets reputed to be exclusively short-term oriented.

The criterion of goodwill value expresses the market value of a company's equity minus the book value of its total shareholders' equity. The facts show unequivocally that marking businesses carry a high value. In October 2005, to take only the U.S. giants, the highest goodwill values accrued to Google (96%), Yahoo! (86%), Coca-Cola (84%), Microsoft (82%), and IBM (77%). The ranking of French companies that are on the CAC 40 Index is revealing as well. As of April 8 2005, the three highest goodwill values belonged to a network television station, TF1 (84.5%), a manufacturer of health and beauty products, L'Oréal (80.4%), and a food producer, Danone (73.1%) – average goodwill for the 150 largest capitalizations on the Paris exchange was 52.6% of share price.

Companies that have been and remain marking models earn high goodwill values. Royal Canin's goodwill value reached 92% in 2002. In light of its accelerated growth since then, there is every reason to think it will only get better. This observation can be generalized. Thus the global ranking of retailers by their Q ratio – the ratio of their market value to asset value – puts Starbucks in first place, ahead of Amazon.com (Deloitte 2005).[1] Starbucks and Amazon undeniably belong in the category of creators of durable territories, and beyond that, leaders in their respective segments.

One argument is commonly made. The valuation of intangible

213

assets favors services and high-tech companies. Manufacturing companies, by contrast, will see their value much less affected by the valuation of such assets. But the rankings suggest this is not the case. L'Oréal and Danone have their feet firmly planted in manufacturing, so often portrayed as the heart of the old economy.

Interbrand's rankings validate the implications of goodwill, although they only evaluate certain major brands. In France, though retailing and wholesaling contribute 2.3 times the value creation (in GDP) of the industrial sector, only six service brands rank among the 30 top-valued trademarks (Hit Parade 2004, Interbrand). Worldwide, only 19 service brands appear among the 100 top-valued international trademarks (Global Brand Scorecard 2003, Interbrand).

These observations lead to rather happy conclusions. Any company – big or small, local or international, in any industry – can be a marker. And any type of marking, whether proactive or reactive, is able to generate high goodwill, dominant market share, lasting growth and spectacular profit rates. Proactive marking is in no way the only solution to create value.

Reactive marking does not seem as fancy and glamorous as proactive marking. It does not build from scratch and constitute societal territories that never had existed before. Reactive marking may be characterized as the way to embed the company in a territory it had abandoned in the past or competitors had invented before it.

Management best sellers legitimize such stereotypes. For instance blue ocean strategies are assumed to sustain much higher performance than red ocean strategies (Kim and Mauborgne 2004). While the former are characterized by innovation, entrance of uncontested and non-crowded industries, and the refusal of conventional trade-offs between value and cost, the latter are defined as competing in existing market spaces, trying to beat crowded competition, and exploiting existing demands. Red ocean strategy in this regard is close to what we call reactive marking.

Evidence questions the absolute supremacy of innovation niches. Wal-Mart, Tesco, and Dyson are illustrations of reactive markings that have delivered, in a lasting manner, spectacular economic and financial results. They are success stories of the same magnitude as proactive markers such as IKEA, Benetton or Royal Canin. The type of marking does not make the difference, the quality of marking does. Wal-Mart, Tesco and Dyson are outstanding implementers rather than radical innovators in their business. They have copied formulas competitors had invented. But they assembled and applied them with much more rigor and depth. Economic excellence also derives from excellence in marking implementation and operational management.

SUSTAINABLE GROWTH

The value created by good marking is substantial; by mediocre or confused marking, it is paltry. This partly explains why big international banks, despite their size and substantial annual earnings, lag behind in the goodwill rankings. Lazy or hesitant marking penalizes a company's value.

A marking, however, can never be taken for granted. When a marking starts to fail it destroys a great deal of value, sometimes brutally and swiftly. The Ford Motor Company found itself at the end of 2005 with a negative goodwill value of –8%, when in 2002 this had been a positive +66%. The market penalizes bad quarterly results, of course, but also, and especially, markings that have become obsolete, having dozed off or sinned by violating their promises.

Marking is an invisible asset that allows markers to rebound from difficulties better than the company that merely trades. For the territory can be mobilized, bringing success where others would simply give up. Apple with its iPod is a spectacular example (Kumar Mylavarapu 2005, Yoffie 2005).

At the turn of the millennium, Apple held about a 2.5% share of the world PC market, vs. 1% back in the 1980's. The company was clearly not through losing share, either. It was in crisis. Meanwhile its board had fired two CEOs in a row. But it would rebound in spectacular fashion where no one expected it: in digital music. The iPod is a memory-based music player. Young people who saw it and heard it just had to buy it. For most of the major players in music or computing, music looked like a business about to die, threatened by the open access that computer pirating made possible. But Steve Jobs won the crazy bet he made at Apple. With the iPod MP3 player, originally priced between $250 and $500, Apple became the uncontested market leader of this new sector. Total company sales climbed to $3.5 billion for the last quarter of 2004 and earnings to 8.5%, the highest figures in over 10 years. At the end of 2005 42 million iPods had been sold.

An invisible asset that Jobs mobilized for the iPod was the pioneering territory his company had put together in the mid-70's when it was launched, in an insane challenge. Dwarf that it was, it attacked IBM, then a giant in size, market share and sales power in the computer market. Yet it would succeed beyond all expectations, because it deliberately created a new territory: that of the elegant and well-designed, user-friendly machine, in a setting of social opposition to monopolies and mainstream lifestyles, as typified by the hippy era. It was characterized by, among other things, small exposure to virus attacks, fierce loyalty from its users, a spreading communitarian spirit that capitalized on the symbols of alternative lifestyles, and a specialized sales network incompatible with PCs. In short, by a democratic and welcoming image that stood in contrast to IBM's PC, yet with higher prices, which in contrast seemed a bland, inhuman work machine imposed by a corporate hierarchy. The Apple Macintosh, the personal computer released in 1984, would be Apple's legendary perfection of its mark.

To the great surprise of knowledgeable observers, Apple then went into a gradual economic decline. One major reason explains this reversal of fortune. The company went commercial. Its management became a little less interested in product development and turned its back on its socioeconomic territory by adopting practices that were not compatible with its old community values. Its executives – one of whom came from PepsiCo (that is, the food industry) and tried to import into the Mac and Apple culture the best practices of the mass market – hastened its decline.

The success of the iPod is primarily one of returning in 2001 to the territory of the 1980's. It was Jobs's good luck that the executives who had taken over at Apple (Jobs had been forced to leave his own company in the early 1980's) did not have enough time to irreversibly destroy these values and this community, in particular in the music and movie marketplaces. iPod created a music territory where there had been none: paid access with high-tech, portable, computerized machines. This new community in a new generation looked very much like the Mac territory.

The marking approach insures sustainability beyond compare with the fragility of the trader's approach. To go back to an indicator like goodwill value, the companies that ranked at the top in 2005 (except for Google, who only came onto the market in 2004) were right there four years previously, in 2002: Coca-Cola with 87%, followed by IBM with 82% and Microsoft with 81%. On the Paris exchange, two of the three top companies in April 2005 were the same as of March 25, 2004: TF1 with 85.9% and L'Oréal with 82.9% – excluding Aventis and Sanofi-Synthélabo, which were involved in a hostile takeover.

SOCIETAL VALUES

Shareholders and owners do not have exclusive rights to the benefits from the value created by a marking company. The company also creates financial and non-financial value for its environment. It does not content itself with targeting the right consumer; it remodels society and the social and cultural roots of consumption. It does not restrict itself to selling; it shapes the social, cultural and political environment that gives it meaning. The value created by the market in favor of the business is only durable and sustainable if it becomes value for consumers, and perhaps for the greater societal entity called a territory.

The business and its stakeholders – from creative artists and music publishers to resellers and customers, for iPod; from pet owners and breeders to pets, for Royal Canin – are all invested in the territory. Values added lie on a broader, less selfish or opportunistic plane. Marking businesses are more diffuse and societal than ordinary trading companies. The stakeholders in a marking make something more out of it, and do it well. Marking companies do not do their job in quite the same way as their competitors. Each constructs a world that is about more than just trading, and which includes a dimension of community or identity that tightly binds its stakeholders to the center the company occupies. Marking companies do not do their job in quite the same way as their competitors. Their world is about more than just trading in as far as it includes a dimension of community or identity that tightly binds its stakeholders to the center the company occupies.

Bill Gates at Microsoft, Eugène Schueller and François Dalle at L'Oréal, Samuel Walton at Wal-Mart are often cited as models of markers. To keep their work from becoming ordinary, the members of a territory, starting with the business, are motivated by a worldview of which they are the architects if not the inventors: the popularization of beauty products, to take L'Oréal as an example, or access to modern mass consumption for American rural folk, in the case of Wal-Mart.

The evidence is that marking entrepreneurs and enterprises doggedly include societal evolutions in their remarkably anticipatory visions of new patterns of consumption: the world wide web as a new service area for communication, access for the working class to paid vacations and self-care, access for rural consumers to large-scale retailing. Their brands have become tremendously well known and famous, their communications are now cited as examples in business schools and professional journals, their strategies are something their employees strongly identify with.

A considerable proportion of top markers inducing societal change processes find their source of inspiration in a private stock of books, covering social sciences or broader sources of inspiration. These managers take the time to read novels, biographies of conquerors, treatises on military strategy and battlefield leadership – Clausewitz, Napoleon, Epaminondas, Sun Tse or Stendhal. The ideas presented in books on management often strike them as too simplistic and too far removed from the realities of the business world.[2]

It would be unrealistic to think of marking companies as having unlimited influence. They will never remake the world in the image of their own will, however dangerous and immoral or generous and imaginative it may be. Societies are too multifarious and complex to accept just anything.

Successful markings obscure those that failed. Building and managing territories are not set in stone, in terms of either their content or their payback. Largely they are cobbled together through what happens while you're busy making other plans. Their managers are aware that the environment is changeable and know they must continually readjust their vision, their strategy, and their organization. They do not follow a totally preconceived path, because its activities are developed and readjusted as it goes along. Marking is based on a process of apprenticeship, a series of experiences and accidents, trials and errors – and successes – each of which the business analyzes and draws lessons from for the future.

In most cases, territory markings that succeed and are admired for their audacity and imagination did not arise rationally; nor were they born as full-fledged ideas in the mind of a celebrated entrepreneur, to whom a magic formula suddenly appeared. The stories we hear after the fact gloss over the slow, often sinuous, journeys through which groups of individuals came together over many long years, overcoming obstacles, and seemingly dead ends. Ten to thirty years are often spent taking large and small steps, forward and backward and to the side. Marking is a pushing ahead, a way of going forward, and a never-ending construction site. Not only does the territory take time to put together, it never stops changing and can even erode. Only in textbooks is everything easy, linear, obvious, and finally, when economic success is found, so prettily rational, even folkloric.

EXECUTIVE SUMMARY

The Marking Enterprise discusses businesses that practice marking. They are models not only because of their economic performances, but also because of the mark they leave on society.

1. *Marking is a promise made as to how a company will interact with stakeholders.*
   - A wide number of stakeholders are addressed: the customer and the consumer, but also many other third parties who, in various roles, play decisive roles in building and securing economic exchange.
   - This moral contract relies on shared values that address broader stakes than mere spot consumption preferences. These societal wants include ethical values, social norms, cultural lifestyles, identity patterns, and so on.
   - Marking builds linkages with customers and society that go beyond a mere opportunistic transaction or mercantile approach. More than just satisfying an economic market, marking companies serve, even construct and govern, societal territories, sets of interdependent stakeholders.

2. *To achieve business success, marking companies embed themselves quite intensively in the dynamics of the societal fabric, and thereby fill social, political, cultural, or functional gaps.*
   - Two main types of marking exist: reactive and proactive.
   - Proactive marking defines approaches where companies create from scratch new paradigms. They act as change agents, they shape society in depth, playing a political role, in a civic sense, within the community.
   - Reactive marking defines a process in which a business exploits and conserves pre-existing social and economic spaces. It molds itself into a territory that already pre-exists.

- In both types of marking, the aim is for the company to become market leader, or more precisely, the center governing the territory it is embedded in.
- Reactive as well as proactive marking generates much added value.
- Territories are not abstract or symbolic entities, they are made of various roles and multiple functions that allow exchanges to occur, values to be addressed by the products, and products to reach the consumer.

3. *Marking companies manage differently.*
- They consider consumers to be intelligent, responsible adults, to be addressed by way of providing information.
- They free themselves from the tyranny of the fads and conventions that bog down trading-type businesses.
- The highly subjective and approximate concept of need gives way to the more powerful concept of awareness.
- They listen to society by listening for its weak signals. They bring back intuition, mistrusting strong signals of the conventionally agreed-upon, quantitative, measurable kind.
- To them, competitive benchmarking is an obstacle to innovation and marking.

4. *Marking companies do a deep job of marketing.*
- It is value-minded (value in use) rather than price-minded.
- The tangibility of the product is enhanced as opposed to its symbols.
- Its communications are more educational and reject marketing "glitter."
- Confrontation between manufacturing and selling is avoided.
- As marking is at the center of strategy, everyone works on marketing.

5. *Marking companies require organizational management of a special kind.*
- They are transverse and multidisciplinary.
- Inner members as well as outside stakeholders are driven by shared values, by a common mission.
- A sense of moral community binds the various parties.
- Sense making for action taking becomes a key competence.

NOTES

CHAPTER 1

1 See Chapters 5 and 6 for more details on the Club Med marking and territory approach.

2 "Need" originates in part from a bold and often erroneous assumption. Given a supplier with no direct acquaintance of the end-user (and vice-versa), for lack of proximity, the business substitutes for the face of the customer the face of a consumer. "Need" gives an assurance to the supplier or merchant, and to the customer as well, that everyone knows what he/she is talking about. Need becomes credible to the extent it can be expressed in numbers and is therefore measurable. It just has to be true – and therefore actionable, measurable and expressed in clear signals. The intuitive or qualitative then becomes unreliable, to be considered with caution.

3 The consumer-behavior experts categorize types of need. One now-classic distinction differentiates utilitarian needs from hedonistic needs. The hierarchy of needs articulated by Maslow (1943) extended into marketing, states, that consumers seek to satisfy their so-called symbolic needs (such as the need to be recognized as a specific individual and have a distinctive identity, the need to satisfy one's ego or the need for self-achievement) but only once their basic needs (to do with physiology and security) have been satisfied. This hierarchy of needs may lead management to play on, and with, symbolic needs before revising their understanding of basic needs.

English wavers between two words to describe needs. One is the word "need" itself, which refers to basic biological requirements. This is assumed to exist on its own, untouched by any wish to influence it by the business or its advertising. Then there is the word "want," resulting from the channeling of basic need toward a family of products or a specific brand through the twofold effect of dominant social models and persuasions by economic agents. Thus there is a need to drink, whereas the felt need to drink sweet carbonated drinks is a want (Solomon et al., 1999). Some analysts speak not of needs but of desires. A desire does not result from biological factors but from social pressures that buyers and consumers have internalized. Desires arise, persist or mutate because individuals are subject to the perceptions and judgments of others, hence of society (Bobcock 1993).

CHAPTER 2

1 In April 1997, the company was listed on the Paris Stock Exchange for 29.1 euros per share on a multiple of 44 times its 1996 net income. In July 2001, when the company was purchased by Mars, its share value had increased 5-fold, to 145 euros, based on a multiple of 35.

2 Masterfoods (brands such as Pedigree, Sheba, Whiskas, Canigou, Chappi), owned by Mars, a family company based in the United States, was the world leader in pet food. Its market share today is slightly above 19%. Third in line was Nestlé, with brands such as Friskies and Felix. In December 2000, Nestlé became No. 1 when it acquired No. 2, Ralston Purina (Cat Chow, Dog Chow, and Proplan brands). This acquisition placed Nestlé ahead of Mars and allowed the company to increase its pet food sales to 6.3 billion dollars and its market share to 22%. Two other players that specialized exclusively in premium nutritional food held approximately 5% of the world market each. Hill, a Colgate brand, focused on the veterinary sector, and Iams (Iams and Eukanuba brands) was bought out by Procter & Gamble in 1999. Retailer brands, such as Wal-Mart's Ol'Roy, were growing in importance, and would enter into direct competition with public brands.

3 A business school graduate, the 53-year-old Moroccan-born Lagarde, coming from a rural upbringing, had started his career in sales, marketing, and strategic planning. Later he became president of Thomson Électroménager, a European leader in washing machines, fridges, and ovens. He got in touch with Paribas because he was looking to acquire a business on his own. Instead, the bank asked him to head Guyomarc'h.

4 He would not budge when, in 1994, and in the span of a few months, the cost of palatability ingredients acquired to manufacture diets multiplied by ten.

5 Lagarde had teamed up with him at the head of various subsidiaries of Thomson Électroménager and Guyomarc'h over the previous 22 years. Both men shared the conviction that Royal Canin benefited from a presence in 50 countries, a strong brand well established among professionals, a unique know-how, and sincere passion for dogs.

6 Despite all these repressive policies, and the fact that prices were increased by 15 to 20% in only two years, none of the big retail banners were discouraged. They continued carrying the products. In 2001, 8% of Royal Canin's sales still originated from grocery stores in the three countries mentioned above. Worse, profit margins had increased. EBIT on grocery store sales were hovering around the 20% mark. The CEO nevertheless remained unhappy, to say the least. Grocery sales were still assessed as a major threat to a health nutrition culture and vision.

7 Henri Lagarde himself owned three cats and a dog. He used to say that his Siamese, who was 15 years old, did not have the same needs as his alley cat who was 8 years old or his Ragdoll, who was very young.

8 Unlike other breeds, Persian cats are only capable of scooping up kibble with the underside of their tongue. Having a high pH urinary, it is essential to prevent inducing urinary calculus.

9 For instance, even though they are both dogs, a Chihuahua and a Saint-Bernard have nothing in common. The latter's weight is 80 times that of the former, its growth period three times longer and its hair 40 times longer. The Chihuahua's digestive tract makes up 7% of its total weight, while that of the Saint-Bernard and other giant breeds is 2.7%. It is common sense that the fuel (food) poured into this giant machine cannot be the same as that which goes into a Chihuahua.

10 For instance a Persian cat with beauty in mind, a Ragdoll for a cat that will not chase birds, a Burmese for a friendly cat, a Siamese for a chatty cat.

11 The sales representative in charge of this client justified the occurrence by saying that Royal Canin's products were by no way at fault and that he had followed procedures to

the letter. Upon hearing of this incident, Lagarde immediately prevailed upon his employee to make the 340-mile trip the same day to apologize to the breeder. This was carried out, even though an examination showed that the product was not the cause of death.

12 Paribas had received many offers to buy Royal Canin. For instance, Nestlé had offered 100 million US dollars for it in 1993, and again in 1996 for 250 million dollars.

13 If Royal Canin growth levels remain at a comparable level for the next few years, the door is open for a valuation of more than 4 billion euros in 2010 (the multiple being calculated upon identical results).

CHAPTER 3

1 Born near Kingfisher, Oklahoma, Sam Walton was raised by his mother to have a passion to win, to be the best at whatever he was doing. His father taught him the value of working hard and being honest, values characteristic of the Bible Belt. Young Sam, appalled by the devastating effects of the Great Depression, promised himself that he would never be poor.

2 Legend has it that a Wal-Mart truck driver in Bentonville who joined the company in 1972 benefited from $707,000 in profit-sharing 20 years later.

3 In 1992, two big chains, Meijer and Fred Meyer, were already operating according to this model, although both covered small geographical areas.

4 An employee of the company for 23 years, Scott was nevertheless a relatively young man, in his early fifties. He would be likely to head the company for ten years or more. If Wal-Mart's overall growth rate is the same as it was under his predecessor's tenure – 17% annually – the company could reach a volume of sales exceeding $1 trillion before he retires.

5 Only 85 Neighborhood Markets had been opened as of January 2005.

CHAPTER 6

1 In fact, Club Med announced a minuscule profit for 2005, largely due to selling off properties. The repositioning's success still needs to be proven (Rivaud 2006).

2 Finally, beyond value judgments, did all this bad press hurt the giant's success? The answer is not easy. So far, sales have not suffered. However, some surveys indicate there has been a significant drop in shoppers' trust in Wal-Mart in recent years (McGinn 2005). But will that shaken confidence ever go as far as overcoming shoppers' attraction to Wal-Mart's undeniable low prices? Another intriguing signal is Wal-Mart's stock price, which dropped off more than 20% between early 2002 and November 2005. Two explanations given by financial analysts are the slowing down of same-store sales growth and the potential high cost of healthcare if Wal-Mart is ever forced to adjust its contribution upward. If this second explanation is true, it means that Wal-Mart is indirectly (through the erosion of its stock price) paying the price for not providing its employees with sufficient healthcare.

CHAPTER 7

1 Many of the observations and theoretical developments of economic sociology and the economics of conventions can be explained in terms of marking. A case in point is the transformation of customers into users, which marking translates into management terms. Marking also relates to the growing interest in the economics of quality, as information imbalances between supply and demand are seeing trust devices rapidly expanding into a world of alignments hinged on shared conventions.

CHAPTER 8

1 Push means that the company wants to convince retailers and intermediaries to "push" the product to buyers.

2 Pull means that the company wants to attract clients by "pre-selling" the product, generally through mass advertising.

CHAPTER 9

1 We will see later in this chapter that some prerequisites for successful marking may be less common and easy to manage.

CONCLUSION

1 The higher a company's Q ratio, the greater the market value of its non-tangible assets, and the greater its prospects of avoiding commoditization.

2 One of the most stimulating recent books on leadership ever to appear presents itself as a re-reading of great works of world literature such as Tolstoy's *War and Peace*, Cervantes' *Don Quixote* and Shakespeare's *Othello* (March and Weil 2005).

BIBLIOGRAPHY

ANGELMAR Reinhard and PINSON Christian, *Zantac (A)*, Fontainebleau, INSEAD, 1998.

BECKER Howard S., *Outsiders. Studies on the Sociology of Deviance*. New York, Free Press, 1973.

BECKER Howard S., *Art Worlds*. Berkeley, University of California Press, 1982.

BELL David E., Jeffrey M. FEINER and Iris, T. LI, *Wal-Mart Neighborhood Markets*, Harvard Business School, 2003.

BERGDAHL Michael, *What I Learned from Sam Walton*, Hoboken, John Wiley & Sons, 2004.

BERGER Peter L. and T. LUCKMANN, *The Social Construction of Reality: A Treatise in the Sociology of Knowledge*, Harmondsworth, Penguin, 1971.

BIRCHALL Jonathan, "Investors in attack of Wal-Mart," *Financial Times*, 2 June 2005.

BIRCHALL Jonathan, "Critics gun for Wal-Mart's Coughlin," *Financial Times*, 19 July 2005.

BIRCHALL Jonathan, "What Wal-Mart women really want," *Financial Times*, 10 October 2005.

BIRCHALL Jonathan, "Supermarket sweep: how the world's biggest chain is swapping tired for tidy," *Financial Times*, 10 November 2005.

BOBCOCK Robert, *Consumption*, London, Routledge, 1993.

BRADLEY Stephen P. and Sharon FOLEY, *Wal-Mart Stores, Inc.*, Harvard Business School, 26 September 1994.

BRIARD Clotilde, "Dyson se rêve en marque de high-tech," *Les Echos*, 18 April 2005.

BURT Ron, *Structural Holes. The Social Structure of Competition*, Harvard University Press, 1992.

CALLON Michel, MÉADEL Sophie and Vololona RABÉHARISOA, "The Economy of Qualities," *Economy and Society*, **31**(2), 2002.

CAMBON Paul, "Club Méditerranée: le Deuxième Souffle", *Label France*, Paris, Ministère des Affaires étrangères, 2001.

CHEVALIER Michel and Gérard MAZZALOVO, *Pro logo. Plaidoyer pour les marques*. Paris, Éditions d'Organisation, 2003.

CLARK Maureen, "Socially Responsible Business Brawl: Business Ethics Magazine Criticizes Cosmetic Maker Body Shop", *The Progressive*, March 1995.

COCHOY Frank, "Is the Modern Consumer a Buridan's Donkey? Product Packaging and Consumer Choice", Karin EKSTROEM and Helene BREMBECK (eds), *Elusive Consumption*, Oxford, Berg, 2004.

COLVIN Geoffrey, "Don't blame Wal-Mart," *Fortune*, 28 November 2005.

COTTA Alain, *Distribution, concentration et concurrence*. Paris, Institut du Commerce et de la Concurrence, June 1985.

CUNEO Alice Z., "Dyson hoovers up vacuum business," *Advertising Age*, 6 December 2004.

DAWAR Niraj, "What Are Brands Good For?", *MIT Sloan Management Review*, Autumn 2004.

DELOITTE, "2005 Global Powers of Retailing", *Stores*, January 2005.

DESJEUX Dominique, "L'ethnomarketing, une approche anthropologique de la consommation : entre fertilisation croisée et purification ethnique", *UTINAM*, no 21–22, Paris, L'Harmattan, 1997.

DUPUY François and Jean-Claude THOENIG, "The analysis of markets: From transaction to regulation." Gil PALMER and Stewart CLEGG (eds). *Constituting Management. Markets, Meanings, and Identities*. New York, Walter de Gruyter, 1996.

DUVALL Mel and Kim S. NASH, "Albertson's: a shot at the crown," *Baseline*, 5 February 2004.

DYSON James, *Against the Odds: an Autobiography*, New York, Texere, 2002.

DYSON James, "Combiner Technique et Esthétique," *Le Figaro*, 3 November 2005.

ENTINE Jon, "Shattered Image : Is The Body Shop too Good to be True ?", *Business Ethics*, September–October 2004.

EPSTEIN Edward J., *The Big Picture. Money and Power in Hollywood*. New York, Random House, 2005.

EVANS Stephen, "Wal-Mart flirt point arouse German market," BBC News, 16 November 2004.

FARSON Richard and Ralph KEYES, "The Failure-Tolerant Leader", *The Innovative Enterprise*, August 2002.

FENTON Evelyn M. and Andrew M. PETTIGREW, *The Innovating Organization*, London, Sage, 2000.

FESTINGER Léon, *A Theory of Cognitive Dissonance*, Stanford, Stanford University Press, 1957.

FLIGSTEIN Neil, *The Transformation of Corporate Control*, London, Harvard University Press, 1990.

FRAZIER Mya, "Wal-Mart eyes Tommy Hilfiger acquisition," *AdAge.com*, 27 September 2005.

GORMAN John, "Classic Case of Formula Forethought?", *Chicago Tribune*, 14 July 1985.

GOUILLART Francis and Frederick STURDIVANT, "Spend a day in the life of your customer", *Harvard Business Review*, January–February1994.

GRANOVETTER Mark, "Economic Action and Social Structures : The Problem of Embeddedness", *American Journal of Sociology*, **91**, November 1985.

GRAVI Philippe, "Les malheurs du Monde", *Le Nouvel Observateur*, 7–13 October 2004.

GRIMES Christopher and Lauren Foster, "Wal-Mart battles to bring a bargain to New Yorkers," *Financial Times*, 28 January 2005.

HAKANSSON Hakan (dir.), *International Marketing and Purchasing of Industrial Goods: An Interaction Approach*, IMP Project Group, John Wiley and Sons, 1982.

HART Christopher W.L., *Club Med (A)*, Boston, Harvard Business School, 1986.

HATCHUEL Armand, "Les marchés à prescripteurs. Crise de l'échange et genèse sociale", Annie JACOB et Hélène VÉRIN (dir.), *L'inscription sociale du marché*, Paris, L'Harmattan, 1995.

HERZBERG Frederick, *Work and the Nature of Man*, Cleveland, World, 1966.

HIRSCHMAN Albert, *Exit, Voice and Loyalty. Responses to Decline in Firms, Organizations and States*. Cambridge, Harvard University Press, 1970.

HOROVITZ Jacques and Michèle JURGENS-PANAK, *Total Customer Satisfaction*, Londres, Pitman Publishing, 1992.

INTERBRAND, Global Brand Scoreboard, 2003.

INTERBRAND, Hit Parade, 2004.

JOHNSON Jay L., "We're all associates," *Discount Merchandiser*, August 1993.

KAPFERER Jean-Nôel and Jean-Claude THOENIG, *La Marque. Moteur de la compétitivité des entreprises et de la croissance de l'économie*. Paris, McGraw-Hill, 1989.

KARPIK Lucien, *French Lawyers: A Study of Collective Action*. 1274–1994. Oxford, Oxford University Press, 1999.

KIM W. Chan and Renée MAUBORGNE, "Blue Ocean Strategy," *Harvard Business Review*, October 2004.

KIM W. Chan and Renée MAUBORGNE, "Blue Ocean Strategy: From Theory to Practice", *California Management Review*, **47**(3), 2005.

KLEIN Naomi, *No logo: Taking Aim at the Brand Bullies*, New York, Picador, 1999.

KOZA Mitchell and Jean-Claude THOENIG, "Organizational Theories of the Firm: A Special Issue", *Organization Studies*, **24**(8), 2003.

KUMAR Nirmalya, "The Power of Trust in Manufacturer-Retailer Relationships", *Harvard Business Review*, November–December 1996.

KUMAR MYLAVARAPU Vinaya, *Channel Confict at Apple*, ICFAI Center for Management Research, 2005.

LANDAU Martin, "Redundancy, Rationality, and the Problem of Duplication and Overlap", *Public Administration Review*, **4**, 1967.

LARRECHE Jean-Claude, Christopher LOVELOCK and Delphine PARMENTER, *First Direct: La Banque sans Agences*, Fontainebleau, INSEAD, 1997.

LASZLO Chris, *The Sustainable Company; How to Create Lasting Value Through Social and Environmental Performance*. Washington D.C., Island Press, 2003.

LAUFER Romain and Catherine PARADEISE, *Marketing Democracy*, New Brunswick, NJ, Transaction Publishers, 1990.

LOHR Steve, "Just googling: it is striking fear into companies," *The Ledger.com*, November 6, 2005.

MARCELO Ray, "Reliance Puts Rivals on Notice with Discount Phone Scheme", *Financial Times*, 2 September 2003.

MARCH James G. and Thierry WEIL, *On Leadership*. Oxford, Blackwell, 2005.

MARKETING, "Will quality make a difference at JS," 15 May 1997.

MASLOW Abraham, "A Theory of Human Motivation", *Psychological Review*, **50**, 1943.

McGINN Daniel, "Wal-Mart Hits the Wall," *Newsweek*, 14 November 2005.

MICHAUD Claude and Jean-Claude THOENIG, *Making Strategy and Organization Compatible*, Basingstoke, Palgrave Macmillan, 2003.

MINTZBERG Henry, *The Nature of Managerial Work*, London, Prentice Hall, 1973.

MORIN Pierre et Éric DELAVALLÉE, *Le manager à l'écoute du sociologue*, Paris, Éditions d'Organisation, 2000.

MUSSELIN Christine and Catherine PARADEISE, "Le concept de qualité : où en sommes-nous?", *Sociologie du Travail*, **44**(2), 2002.

NICOLAS Olivier, "Naf-Naf – Chevignon reprend l'offensive", *La Tribune*, 7 September 1998.

NORMANN Richard and Rafael RAMIREZ, "From Value Chain to Value Constellation : Designing Interactive Strategy", *Harvard Business Review*, July–August 1993.

PARRY Mark and Yoshinobu SATO, *Procter & Gamble: The Wal-Mart Partnership (A)*, Darden Business Publishing, University of Virginia, 1996.

PETERS Sophie, "Les hommes du marketing sous pression", *Les Échos*, 14 December 2004.

PFEFFER Jeffrey and Richard SALANCIK, *The External Control of Organizations*, New York, Harper and Row, 1978.

PINSON Christian and Vikas TIBREWALA, *United Colors of Benetton*, Fontainebleau, INSEAD-CEDEP, 1996.

PINSON Christian and Helen KIMBALL, *I've got a Swatch*, Fontainebleau, INSEAD-CEDEP, 1987.

PONS Frédéric, "Éric Fouquier, sociologue, explique le changement des modes de consommation", *Libération*, 25–26 December 2004.

POWELL Walter W., "Neither Market nor Hierarchy. Network Forms of Organization", *Research in Organizational Behavior*, **12**, 1990.

REED Robert, "Wal-Mart Suppliers are Feeling the Pinch," *International Herald Tribune*, 18 April 2006.

RETAIL NEWS LETTER, July–August 2005.

RIVAUD Francine, "Le Club Med prend le parti de l'embourgeoisement," *Challenges*, 5 January 2006.

RUDNITSKY Howard, "How Sam Walton does it," *Forbes*, 16 August 1982.

SELLERS Patricia, "Can Wal-Mart get back the magic?" *Fortune*, April 29, 1996.

SELZNICK Philip, *The Moral Commonwealth. Social Theory and the Promise of Community*, Berkeley, University of California Press, 1992.

SHILS Edward, *Center and Periphery*, Chicago, University of Chicago Press, 1975.

SLATER Robert, *The Wal-Mart Triumph: Inside the World no1 Company*, London, Penguin Books, 2004.

SOLOMON Michael, Gary BAMOSSY and Soeren ASKEGAARD, *Consumer Behavior: A European Perspective*, Prentice-Hall-Europe, 1999.

SOLOMON Michael, *Consumer Behavior. Buying, Having and Being*. New York, Prentice-Hall, 2003.

STRASSER Suzann, *Satisfaction Guaranteed. The Making of the American Mass Market*, New York, Pantheon, 1989.

TELANDER Rick, "Your Sneakers or Your Life", *Sports Illustrated*, 14 May 1990.

TESCO, Annual Review, 2005.

THÉVENOT Laurent, 'Organized Complexity: Conventions of Coordination and the Composition of Economic Arrangements', *European Journal of Social Theory*, 4(4), 2001.

THOENIG Jean-Claude, *Les performances économiques de l'industrie de produits de marque et de la distribution*, Paris, Institut de liaisons et d'études des industries de consommation (ILEC), 1990.

BIBLIOGRAPHY

THOENIG Jean-Claude, "How Far is a Sociology of Organizations Still Needed ?", *Organization Studies*, **19**(2), 1998.

THOENIG Jean-Claude and Charles WALDMAN, *Royal Canin*, Fontainebleau, INSEAD-CEDEP, 2003.

THOENIG Jean-Claude and Charles WALDMAN, *De l'entreprise marchande à l'entreprise marquante*, Paris, Editions d'Organisation, 2005.

TRUC Olivier, "Pour le Fondateur d'IKEA, c'est Kit ou Double", *Libération*, 24 August 2004.

VILLETTE Michel and Catherine VUILLERMOT, *Portrait de l'homme d'affaires en prédateur*, Paris, La Découverte, 2005.

WALDMAN Charles and Pascale BALZE, *Monoprix*, Fontainebleau, INSEAD, 1999.

WALDMAN Charles and Isabelle SOOD, *Tesco Plc*, Fontainebleau, INSEAD, 1999.

WALTON Sam, *Made in America: My Story*, New York, Doubleday, 1992.

WATCHDOG, "Body Shop Animal Testing Alleged a Sham?," www.animalpeoplenews.org, 1994.

WEICK Karl, *The Social Psychology of Organizing*, Reading, Addison-Wesley, 1979.

WEICK Karl, *Sensemaking in Organizations*, Thousand Oaks, Sage, 1995.

YOFFIE David B., *Apple Computer, 2005*, Harvard Business School, 2005.

ZALTMAN Gerald, *How Customers Think: Essential Insights into the Mind of the Market*, Boston, Harvard Business School, 2003.

INDEX OF NAMES

INDEX OF ENTERPRISES, BRANDS
AND INSTITUTIONS

INDEX OF CONTENT